TO EMBODY THE MARVELOUS

To Embody the Marvelous

The Making of Illusions in Early Modern Spain

Esther Fernández

VANDERBILT UNIVERSITY PRESS
Nashville, Tennessee

Copyright 2021 Vanderbilt University Press
All rights reserved
First printing 2021

Library of Congress Cataloging-in-Publication Data

Names: Fernández, Esther, 1975- author.
Title: To embody the marvelous : the making of illusions in early modern Spain / Esther Fernández.
Description: Nashville : Vanderbilt University Press, 2021. | Includes bibliographical references and index.
Identifiers: LCCN 2021005718 (print) | LCCN 2021005719 (ebook) | ISBN 9780826501806 (hardcover) | ISBN 9780826501790 (paperback) | ISBN 9780826501813 (epub) | ISBN 9780826501820 (pdf)
Subjects: LCSH: Puppet theater—Spain—History—16th century. | Puppet theater—Spain—History—17th century. | Illusion (Philosophy) | Wonder (Philosophy)
Classification: LCC PN1978.S7 F47 2021 (print) | LCC PN1978.S7 (ebook) | DDC 791.5/30946—dc23
LC record available at https://lccn.loc.gov/2021005718
LC ebook record available at https://lccn.loc.gov/2021005719

For Amelia, Ángel, and Chris

Die Dinge sind alle nicht so faßbar und sagbar, als man uns meistens glauben machen möchte; die meisten Ereignisse sind unsagbar, vollziehen sich in einem Raume, den nie ein Wort betreten hat, und unsagbarer als alle sind die Kunst-Werke, geheimnisvolle Existenzen, deren Leben neben dem unseren, das vergeht, dauert.

RAINER MARIA RILKE, *Briefe an einen jungen Dichter* (*Letters to a Young Poet*), 1903

CONTENTS

List of Illustrations   xi
Acknowledgments   xv

INTRODUCTION. Stages of Animation   1

1. Mechanics of Reductionism   10
2. Matters of God   29
3. Articulating Saintliness   56
4. Unruly Puppets   78
5. Technologies of Wonder   103
6. Trapdoors to *Desengaño*   127

CONCLUSION. When Statues Move   155

Notes   163
Bibliography   191
Index   217

ILLUSTRATIONS

ILLUSTRATION 1. Technical sketch of the *magrana*.   23

FOLLOWING PAGE 40

0.1 John Derian Company store shop window, East Village, New York.
1.1 Contemporary reproduction model of a *retablo mecánico*.
1.2 Animated nativity of *Belén de Nuestra Señora de los Reyes de Laguardia*, Álava (Spain).
1.3 The *Tarasca*, Alcázar de San Juan, Ciudad Real (Spain).
1.4 *Gigantes y cabezudos*, Alcázar de San Juan, Ciudad Real (Spain). Photograph by Jesús Caballero, courtesy of La Máquina Real.
1.5 Contemporary reproduction model of a *Tutilimundi*.
1.6 Contemporary reproduction model of a *Tutilimundi*.
1.7 Contemporary reproduction model of a *Tutilimundi*.
2.1 Articulations in elbows using metallic hinges. *Cristo de los Gascones*. Iglesia de los Santos Justo y Pastor, Segovia (Spain).
2.2 *La función del desenclavo* by "El mudo Neira" (1722).
2.3 Contemporary *Depositio* ceremony in Astorga, León (Spain).
2.4 Contemporary *Depositio* ceremony in Astorga, León (Spain).
2.5 Contemporary *Depositio* ceremony in Astorga, León (Spain).
2.6 Contemporary *Depositio* ceremony in Astorga, León (Spain).
2.7 Contemporary *Depositio* ceremony in Astorga, León (Spain).
2.8 Contemporary *Depositio* ceremony in Astorga, León (Spain).
2.9 Contemporary *Depositio* ceremony in Astorga, León (Spain).

XII *Illustrations*

FOLLOWING PAGE 80

2.10 Promotional poster for *Misterio del Cristo de los Gascones*.
2.11 Cristo de los Gascones in reclining position. *Iglesia de los Santos Justo y Pastor*, Segovia (Spain).
2.12 *Planctus Mariae* (Lament of Mary). *Misterio del Cristo de los Gascones*.
2.13 Christ interacting with one of the musicians. *Misterio del Cristo de los Gascones*.
2.14 Judas betraying Jesus. *Misterio del Cristo de los Gascones*.
2.15 Christ in transcendence. *Misterio del Cristo de los Gascones*.
3.1 Automaton figure of a monk, South Germany or Spain, ca. 1560.
3.2 Automaton figure of a monk, South Germany or Spain, ca. 1560.
3.3 Building process of the *retablo* for *El esclavo del demonio*.
3.4 Built-in stage (*retablo*) for *El esclavo del demonio*.
3.5 Puppets onstage during a performance of *El esclavo del demonio*.
3.6 Contemporary puppeteers manipulating stick puppets from beneath the *retablo* during a rehearsal of *El esclavo del demonio*.
3.7 Sculpted puppet body for *El esclavo del demonio*.
3.8 Sculpted puppet heads for *El esclavo del demonio*.
3.9 Puppet cast for *El esclavo del demonio*.
3.10 Angelio, devil figure in *El esclavo del demonio*.
3.11 Set for the house in *El esclavo del demonio*.
3.12 Set for the town in *El esclavo del demonio*.

FOLLOWING PAGE 120

3.13 Michael Landy, *Saint Jerome*, 2012.
4.1 Contemporary reproduction of Master Pedro's puppet show set.
4.2 Don Quixote interrupting the young interpreter.
4.3 Soloists in *El retablo de Maese Pedro*.
4.4 *El retablo de Maese Pedro*.
4.5 *El retablo de Maese Pedro*.
4.6 Opening scene of *El retablo de Maese Pedro*.

5.1   Don Quixote and Sancho flying on Clavileño.
5.2   Don Quixote and Sancho "fly" with the fireworks inside Clavileño.
5.3   The *panacousticon* (speaking-trumpet) in Athanasius Kircher's *Musurgia Universalis*.
5.4   A woodblock engraving from *The Honorable Historie of Frier Bacon, and Frier Bongay*.
5.5   Exitazo Tournée Roca (Big success Roca tour) promotional poster, 1900–1910.
5.6   *La dama de la fortuna*.
6.1   *La dama duende* (2000).
6.2   *La dama duende* (2017).
6.3   Caricature by Julio Cebrián.
6.4   *El galán fantasma* (1981).
6.5   Julia in the garden. *El galán fantasma* (2010).
6.6   Astolfo crossing the tunnel in *El galán fantasma* (2010).

ACKNOWLEDGMENTS

I CAN TRACE the origin of this book to the summer of 2009. I started thinking about it right after returning from a performance of Antonio Mira de Amescua's *El esclavo del demonio* (The devil's slave, 1612), directed by Jesús Caballero, at the Almagro International Classical Theatre Festival in Spain. What was unique about this production was that Caballero used an entire cast of puppets to stage a hagiographical drama. Before seeing Caballero's adaptation, when I thought about marionettes in relation to early modern Spanish culture, the only referent that came to mind was Miguel de Cervantes's iconic episodes of Master Pedro's puppet show in the second part of *Don Quijote de la Mancha* (2.25–2.26; *Don Quixote*, 1615). That year, after returning from my Almagro trip, my mind kept going back to the marionette production of *El esclavo*. The manipulation, the clothing, the set, and the special effects were exquisitely realistic and, simultaneously, magical in their miniaturized dimensions.

I contacted Caballero in the fall and asked him if I could visit his workshop to interview him about the process of designing and building the marionettes. After the semester ended, I went back to Spain and headed to Cuenca where the company is headquartered. I didn't know what to expect from that trip as it would be my very first time working with puppetry, and I was not familiar with Mira de Amescua's works from any prior research endeavors. At the same time, I could not suppress my curiosity to know more about the artistry involved in creating an entire *comedia de santos* (saint play) for the small stage.

Puppets are uncanny by nature, but I don't think I ever understood what an uncanny experience really felt like until I saw the severed wooden head of a devil smirking at me from Caballero's workbench. I remember the effort that it took for me to overcome such a disquieting emotion and resume my interview as if nothing had happened. The last thing I wanted was to raise the suspicions of my newly acquainted interviewee that the very sight of his marionettes troubled me. However, I could not remain nonplussed, and these beings upended not just my response to Caballero's artistry but also my research agenda to the point that I decided to put aside another project to step into the unknown field of early modern puppetry, as if an intellectual spell had been cast upon me.

My original idea for this new inquiry was to follow in the footsteps of John E. Varey's influential book *Historia de los títeres en España (Desde sus orígenes hasta mediados del siglo XVIII)* (1957) and broaden the section on early modernity. I spent several years researching different puppet traditions around the world, reading theoretical treatises on puppetry across history, finding references of marionettes in the literature of the period, interviewing puppeteers, and attending as many shows as I could. With three other friends, I even co-founded a puppet troupe that specializes in performing early modern Hispanic fiction for younger audiences.

Yet, as the reader will have noticed from the title of this book, my original plans to study marionette theater in the most traditional and historical sense did not come to fruition as expected. And, once again, another peculiar puppet encounter was to blame! I was living in New York at the time, and, on one of my walks in Lower Manhattan, I saw an intriguing *pupo* figure in the shop window of a vintage dealer's establishment in the East Village (see Figure 0.1). My friend found the *pupo* awkwardly amusing and suggested that I take a picture. Afterward, as I stared at the photograph of the displaced, motionless marionette, the same bewilderment that I felt when I contemplated that devil's head in Caballero's workshop was revived.

I then realized that what really fascinated me about these objects is what lay beneath their façade: their theoretical and material microhistories of animation and their survival over time. For this book, I ended up curating my own *Wunderkammer* (cabinet of curiosities) filled with eclectic artifacts, not just puppets but other kinds of *lively* objects that possess the potential for animation. Some are real; others can only be found in the pages of fiction writing. I wanted to create an object-based epistemology that reclaimed the artifacts' voices and, above all, revived their movements through time and history.

I found in early modernity the most suitable historical terrain to focus my exploration, as it is a period that strives to position itself between enchantment and disenchantment, illusion and reason. And here is where I began my journey through ideas that took me further than I had initially planned, going as far as to envision possible avenues to delve into what will be a much more ambitious future attempt to explore the history of animation in all of early modern Europe.

As happens on any voyage, even figuratively, one cannot undertake it safely without the support and trust of the many travel companions found along the way. I am especially grateful to my aunt Amelia Rodríguez de las Cuevas and to my uncle Ángel L. Rodríguez de las Cuevas: they are my life. Chris Garcés, my intellectual soulmate, has also illuminated many lines of this work with his erudite insights and unconditional care. I owe to my extended family, Adrienne L. Martín and Will Corral, Cristina Martínez-Carazo, and Marta Altisent, immense gratitude for helping shape me into the scholar I am. They were with me at the beginning of my career, and they never stopped nurturing me in so many ways. Mercedes Alcalá-Galán and Steven Hutchinson have also become part of this family, and this book is a tribute to my profound admiration for both. Isabel de Sena and Jesús Caballero have been the heart of this journey; without them, this project would not have been the same. My dear friend Miguel Ángel Balsa was the first person to see potential in this research and encourage me to further pursue it. He had just started to work on robots and dolls when he left us; hence, finishing this project fulfills an intellectual path that united both of us in our time at Cornell. His memory has never left me. This book is a tribute to him. My appreciation for Jonathan Wade, Jared White, and Jason Yancey is likewise infinite. Thanks to these steadfast companions, my passion for puppetry has now become a reality beyond the page. In no small way, this project has been possible thanks to these friends, whom I count as my brothers.

I am also indebted to very dear colleagues who have had my back over the last few years of intense writing and dealing with personal and professional extenuating circumstances: Bruce Burningham, María Chouza-Calo, Harley Erdman, Barbara Fuchs, Enrique García Santo-Tomás, Victoria L. Ketz, Erin Krusleski, Susan Paun de García, Andrés Pérez-Simón, David Rodríguez-Solás, Reina Ruiz, Molly Slattery, and Jonathan Thacker.

I am obliged to Zachary S. Gresham, my editor at Vanderbilt University Press, for trusting this project from the very beginning; Jeremy Rehwaldt for his incisive initial editing; and the anonymous reviewers for their generosity and knowledgeable comments that encouraged me to make the most of my ideas. I hope the book lives up to their standards.

Furthermore, I want to recognize the institutional support I have received from Rice University, in particular from the Dean's Office in the School of Humanities, the Department of Modern and Classical Literatures and Cultures, the Rice Humanities Research Center, the Office of Research, the National Humanities Center (NHC), Wiess College, and my very dear students, who are forever inspiring. The Centro de Documentación de las Artes Escénicas y la Música (CDAEM) has been a key institution in supporting my archival work through the years, especially Berta Muñoz Cáliz and Pedro Ocaña Triguero, who have now become very close friends.

Finally, I want to thank the puppeteers, artisans, church keepers, nuns, theater directors, curators, and photographers who populate the pages of this book and shared their expertise with me without ever asking anything in return. This project respectfully honors them, especially the Hermanas Agustinas in Medina del Campo, Jesús Alcántara, Adolfo Ayuso Roy, Eduardo Galán, Emilio Pedro Gómez, Javier Manrique González, Rafael Manrique Gutiérrez, Jesús Martínez Atienza, Antonio Sánchez del Barrio, and Anna Valls i Passola.

I view this book as a collective endeavor that gave me the opportunity to encounter exceptional people along the way, exchange creative ideas, and share conversations about small lively objects and things that happened to be larger-than-life for our cultural heritage.

COHEN HOUSE, RICE UNIVERSITY
May 9, 2020

Introduction.
Stages of Animation

> Art is all, and man can attain it all.
> ANDRÉS FERRER DE VALDECEBRO, *El templo de la Fama*, 1680

THE ARCHAEOLOGICAL MUSEUM of Seville is home to a bronze statuette of the Phoenician fertility goddess Astarté. Known to us as *Astarté de El Carambolo*, as she was found as part of the Treasure of El Carambolo (7th–6th centuries BCE),[1] the seated figurine draws attention for her many peculiarities, but perhaps nothing is more remarkable than what is absent: her left arm. In its place is a cavity that exposes the surreptitious nature of the otherwise stock-still statuette's fabrication, which reveals that, in advance of its loss, the left limb pivoted, thanks to a mechanism that allowed for ascending and descending articulation. The figurine found its way to the Iberian Peninsula over the centuries, and modern-day visitors now appreciate this relic as an artistic achievement of an ancient Mediterranean civilization that intersected with Peninsular culture. However, with its limb manipulated to "spontaneously" bless and greet its devoted subjects, contemporaneous perception most likely prized the statuette much less pedestrianly as, perhaps, divinity incarnate (Navarro Ortega 490). To wit, the sacred figurine's capacity for movement—and the believers' willing suspension of disbelief—transformed the artifact from a mere thing into a living goddess.

This Sevillian Astarté, the oldest animated sculpture extant in Spain, exemplifies a category of objects that can be animated for use in religious rites as well as secular theatrical contexts.[2] Further, while the mechanisms that make these statuettes move allow them to function as devotional and cultural agents in certain periods and performance practices, their animation points toward the realm of illusions, which is characterized as the fictional, the supernatural, and the irrational. Hence, these animated artifacts operate as material thresholds between the concrete reality they represent when they are inert and the eerie illusionism they call upon when they are in motion. Nevertheless, even if they remain concealed, there will be a moment that the mechanisms end up disclosing the objects' artificiality—either by human initiative or through the passage of time—which solidly grounds the objects in reality, but only after their mechanisms validate the artefacts' animation.

Because human beings are fond of using delusion, manipulation, and fantasy to rework the reality in which they live and the elements that constitute it, we find that each epoch has recourse to its own special effects (Orazi 27). In seventeenth-century Spain, illusion figuratively and literally helped people to effectively navigate social instability and the crisis of values that emerged with the onset of modernity.[3] The Protestant Reformation destabilized the unity of the Roman Catholic Church; science turned increasingly experimental, moving away from contemplation and betting on the study of the laws of nature; the forces of mercantilism opened international trade routes and networks that gave rise to Western capitalism; and nation-states emerged, supporting both strong monarchical governments and centralized bureaucracies.

Situated within these whirling forces of global vitality, animation came to be a powerfully representative emblem of the forthcoming zeitgeist of modernity. Objects with the potential to set in motion an artificial agency arose as promising metaphors for a new system of values, though not without a series of disenchanting turns. Herein, religion and superstition contrasted with humanity's increasing belief in the systematic knowledge that launched, during the sixteenth and seventeenth centuries, the Scientific Revolution, characterized as a "how-to revolution" that prioritized calculation and displaced cunning and esoteric practices (Eamon, *Science* 10–11).[4]

In response to these ideological clashes, *desengaño*, which translates into disappointment and lack of enthusiasm, turned out to be a pervasive sentiment during the baroque era in the Peninsula and, as Jesús Pérez Magallón puts it, "the foundation of a vital philosophy and an anthropology" (22). As such, the making of illusions became a complex but necessary task that operated in different levels of society, offering preparation for and relief from the anguish and the growing pains associated with epistemic shifts. As María M. Portuondo has stated so lucidly, early modern Spain "was a scenario where emotions and the cult of wonders and spectacle existed hand in hand with the dispassionate—if we believe this qualifier—observation of experiment" (269). On the one hand, animation mechanisms enhanced illusions visually and emotionally by evoking admiration and awe; on the other hand, the artificial nature of these artifacts questioned appearances, inspired doubt and suspicion of the veracity of the senses, and opened the door to skepticism and empirical thinking.[5]

I contend that the animated object is the ideal material and metaphorical mediator between imagination and reason. In early modernity, performance objects with the potential for motion became the agents of choice for creating a sense of awe while simultaneously imposing cognitive distance that inspired rational inquiry. It did not matter anymore that puppeteers handled their marionettes in full view of the public or that automata revealed their mechanisms as part of their aesthetic and functional skills.[6] On the contrary, these acts of disclosure marked the transition from the premodern to the modern by attempting to deemphasize preternatural beliefs while exploring the limits of the senses and reason.[7]

Such spectacular revelations expose the emergence of a modern re-enchantment based on acknowledging the artistic and technological mechanisms of wonder that foster doubt about creative forms of deception and practical industry (Kimmel 210). The theatrical power of the props and artifacts examined in this book generated a spiral of enchantment/disenchantment/re-enchantment that situates modernity as a period open to the appropriation of old values, genres, objects, etc. This leads to the reassessment of the marvelous through reason and emotional distancing, rather than rejecting it at face value.

Thus, this study establishes a theoretical framework of animation mainly within the context of sixteenth and seventeenth-century Spain, though their present instantiations are given careful consideration as well. Each of the chapters appraises animation in dialogue with a prop that represents a specific type of performativity, such as the *Cristos articulados* (jointed Christ figures), religious and profane puppets, automata, and animated stage sets. As disconnected as they might seem at first, these objects constitute a coherent gallery. They all deploy a rationalized sense of wonder and a new way of visualizing the spectacular via their mechanisms for motion. The jointed Christ, for instance, gives material form to the holy, while its animation illustrates the complex relationship between earth and heaven, faith and reason; the *admiratio* (surprise, wonderment) generated by the religious and profane marionette, in contrast, reevaluates the boundaries of fiction—sometimes, even the impossible—in art and entertainment. The self-operating automaton acknowledges the rise—not without anxiety—of science and technology in the modern world. And, the theatrical trapdoor serves as a strategic man-made spatial and theatrical perforation between the ordinary and the artificial extraordinary that breaches social order.

Furthermore, each of these artifacts and scenarios has made its way into the present, which suggests that the most basic mechanisms for animation have not lost their power to engage us. Animation suggests that there is always something unknown and mysterious behind appearances. No matter how advanced science and technology become, the suspension of disbelief persists as a temporary reality when confronted by animated objects. In each of the case studies I consider, I have traced the objects' lives beyond early modernity into the present to evaluate precisely what remains of their original meaning and functionality while uncovering the reasons for their continuity and never-ending fascination.

In what follows, I introduce each of the artifacts that has informed this investigation to show how the interplay of the factual and metaphoric meanings of animation becomes a cultural agent in close dialogue with the broader narratives of modernity in religious theatrical experiences, social entertainment, fiction writing, and performance practices.

In the first chapter, "Mechanics of Reductionism," I escort the reader along the lines of inquiry that contextualize the book's overall content. I look at early modernity as a transformative period where amazement (via animation) is articulated by means of ideological and material innovation. Specifically, I outline the depth and breadth of the *mechanistic metaphor* (i.e., the comparison of the universe, nature, and the human body to an elaborate machine) developed by natural philosophers and show how it illustrates modern thought. This metaphor is associated with the Scientific Revolution, the cultural rationalization of religiosity (to a certain extent), and, ultimately, disenchantment. Its material symbolism distills the power of change through the accuracy of mechanical principles and scientific knowledge. Within this material approach to modernity—viewed as an era that *sets in motion* new ideas—I present an overview of performance objects with the potential for artificial agency to delve deeper into the implications of animation in the religious and secular theatrical contexts where these artifacts were originally contextualized.

In the second chapter, "Matters of God," I address Christian wonder in religious rites through the visual and symbolic imagery of the *Cristo articulado*. Beginning in the thirteenth century, but most notably from the fifteenth century on, churches across the Iberian Peninsula staged the *Depositio-Elevatio* (Burial and Resurrection) ceremony during Holy Week using these puppet-like figures to convey both the human and holy nature of Christ in an accessible manner. My analysis traces the origins and development of these wood carvings in Western culture. I claim that, within the context of the Easter liturgy, the subtle animation of these sacred props created an estrangement effect that engaged the faithful in approaching the Resurrection with a sense of critical piety and reluctance toward conventional wonder. Tracing the continuity of these ceremonies into the twentieth and twenty-first centuries, I examine the production of *Misterio del Cristo de los Gascones* (Mystery of the Christ of the Gascons, 2007). I consider this play to be a milestone in Spanish performance history for its revisionist take on the life of Christ and of faith in a broader sense. Director Ana Zamora smooths the edges between the religious and the secular using a life-sized jointed Christ as her protagonist to explore the ways in which the human-divine duality still can be negotiated in the present, precisely, through the very power of animation.

Chapter 3, "Articulating Saintliness," continues the examination of pious props, but this time in actual theatrical contexts outside the church. During the seventeenth century, Spain witnessed the widespread popularity of a new type of theater company, the *máquina real* (royal machine). These companies were unique in the way they staged hagiographic plays in the *corrales de comedia* (Spanish playhouses) using only puppets. Within the obsessive culture of saints that saturated Spanish society at the time, marionettes came to embody an approachable, playful form of saintliness. This chapter addresses aspects of overlapping ontological development between puppets and saints as liminal presences that move with ease between the sacred and profane. I argue that hagiographies performed by marionettes were more effective than those staged with live actors. Similar to the reflexive experience activated by the *Cristo articulado* in the faithful, the máquina real turned religiosity into machinery in miniature that piqued curiosity about its artificiality while simultaneously distancing its viewers from falling into passive, contemplative awe. To conclude, I illustrate how contemporary stage director Jesús Caballero and conceptual British artist Michael Landy, both inspired by a similar interactive and experiential approach toward hagiographies, have reinvigorated an animated culture of saints through technological and artistic innovation in light of posthumanism and its redefinition of the human.

While the second and third chapters focus on the artificial animacy of the religious figure as devotional and didactic visual aids in the approach to Christian awe, Chapter 4, "Unruly Puppets," transitions to the secular and fictional milieu of entertainment in the hands of *Don Quijote de la Mancha* (*Don Quixote*, 1605–1615). In a novel driven by themes of enchantment and disenchantment, Cervantes (1547–1616) exemplifies a visionary artistic failure in Master Pedro's puppet show (2.25–2.26). The novelist uses marionettes to warn his protagonist and his audiences against the power of appearances and to encourage, instead, a new way of looking, beyond the aesthetics of *admiratio*, through knowledge. Cervantes devises a cautionary puppet tale based on the meaning of desengaño—a deceiving world of illusions and the inexorable disappointment that humans face at the onset of modernity. It is no coincidence that after World War I, during another highly dehumanizing era, Spanish composer Manuel de Falla (1876–1946) found inspiration in this peculiar puppet show for his opera *El retablo de Maese Pedro* (Master Pedro's puppet show, 1923). Foregrounding the marionettes by placing them at the very center of his operatic work, Falla conceived an anti-opera just as Cervantes envisioned his experimental performance within the first modern novel—or anti-novel—heavily marked by social and artistic non-conformity.

Besides puppets, animated props remain abundant throughout the second part of *Don Quijote*, especially as objects of duplicity maneuvered by schemers who seek to control the protagonists. Clavileño the flying wooden horse (2.40–2.41) and the enchanted head owned by Don Antonio Moreno (2.42) stand out as the two most sophisticated artifacts in the novel in terms of the simulated experiences they recreate: an interstellar space flight and the quest for absolute knowledge, respectively. Thus, in Chapter 5, "Technologies of Wonder," I maintain that in both of these material performances, the supernatural is disclosed as the byproduct of technologies related to theater and entertainment that took root in the seventeenth century. For the novelist, Clavileño and the oracular head become artifacts of secular magic and modern re-enchantment as forerunners of futuristic imagination in the world of show business, science, and technology.

Chapter 6, "Thresholds of *Desengaño*," rounds out my overview of early modern animated performances by examining the theater of Pedro Calderón de la Barca (1600–1681), the playwright who best embodies the baroque ethos by masterfully molding the notion of desengaño for the stage. *La dama duende* (*The Phantom Lady*, 1629) and *El galán fantasma* (The phantom lover, 1637) are considered sister *comedias* (plays) because of the spectral illusionism they deploy. The protagonists in both plays use secret trapdoors to perforate their everyday lives and step into a fantastic world of their own making to cope with confinement and social oppression. Just as Cervantes did with Clavileño and the enchanted head, Calderón de la Barca deconstructs the irrational belief in superstition and presents the paranormal fully attuned to creativity, innovation, and even social dissent. Nonetheless, many contemporary directors have not fully grasped the subtleties at work in this very particular crafting of spatial illusions, which are inextricably tied to the social anxieties of the time. As a consequence, these daring portals that provide a path to the properly modern have shifted over the years into gratuitous tunnels of entertainment. This malleability of animation proves once again how its persistence depends upon its fragility as well as the constant reworking of its meanings.

In my concluding remarks, "When Statues Move," I reflect on the meaning of the animated statue in relation to the taming of the marvelous, a process to which I return in every chapter. I consciously have not devoted a full analysis to this artifact because, unlike all the other objects considered, it belongs exclusively to the realm of the fantastic. The jointless presence of the moving statue is reserved for purely supernatural scenarios mainly found in mythological and magic plays and fantastic narratives. Nonetheless, when we analyze how these figures coped with their agency, they happened to be fully subjected to their creator's control. Even the actors who personified them on stage had to rigorously self-discipline their bodies to realistically recreate a sense of controlled life into the inert matter, another allegorical step toward modernity within theatrical culture and beyond.

While all of the chapters engage with artificial animacy and the crafting of enchantment in the early modern period, few studies to date have approached wonder by taking materiality and performativity as their primary foci. This scholarly oversight represents, in my opinion, a serious gap in the broader fields of early modern cultural studies, art history, and theater and performance, especially considering that the baroque arose from the confluence of illusion and an overabundance of a spectacular language of visualization in the midst of a rapidly globalizing world.

Early modernity was a period of vigorous transformation that affected all aspects of life where the commitment to futurity shaped contemporary realities and currents of thought. For Mari-Tere Álvarez, futurity refers, indeed, to a vision of a future that is not fixed (9). Here, again, transformation pushes against apparent boundaries so that we may look beyond and, ultimately, overcome them through knowledge and reason. The theatrical nature of early modern literature and the arts responded to the influx of change and novel ideas by exhibiting a meaningful dynamism in their form and content while becoming critically engaged with the public. Consequently, the micro-histories and social lives of each of the artifacts discussed in this book open up unconventional paths for us to understand the nascence of modernity through an original vantage point, where animation stands up as a principle open to change, experimentation, adaptability, and radical creativity.

1. Mechanics of Reductionism

> The baroque artists know well that hallucination does not feign presence, but that presence is hallucinatory.
> GILLES DELEUZE, *The Fold: Leibniz and the Baroque*, 1988

THE SIXTEENTH AND seventeenth centuries in Europe were marked by political and social change, scientific and technological innovation, and an expansionist vision of the future (Villaseñor Black and Álvarez 1).[1] For Rodríguez de la Flor, this was an era of constant movement that fed into the climate of misperception and uncertainty: "All is change, all instability, the *perpetuum mobile* and ephemeral pulsation in the vision that baroque culture projects of a world that is itself turbulent and transformed by profoundly serious events that push it off the rails and roads along which it used to flow in a past that suddenly seems mythically distant" (*Pasiones* 13). The turn toward transformation opened new paths to understanding the world and its illusions, where epistemic anxieties driven by skepticism also came into play (Portuondo 252).[2]

Contemporary intellectuals such as historian Ambrosio de Morales (1513–1591) and writer Cristóbal Suárez de Figueroa (1571–ca.1644) relied on the rhetoric of the miracle to explain the science and engineering concealed behind the craft of artistic illusion-making, but this framing was evocative rather than equivalent (Kimmel 210). Indeed, machines and other animated artifacts became conceptual and didactic metaphors illustrating an automated approach to the workings of the modern world. Therefore, it is not surprising that natural philosophers and scientists such as Thomas Hobbes, René Descartes, John Wilkins, Robert Boyle, and Isaac Newton started using mechanical theories that hinted at alternative paths to consider religion, human nature, politics, and science in the new and emerging social order.[3] Within this rhetorical background, theology emerged as the queen of the sciences (Walsham 523); God as the great engineer; and the world, the state, and the human body as machine-like operations.

Among the mechanistic metaphors, the automaton and the mechanical clock were especially well suited for conveying the idea of animation as the outcome of hidden technologies. As Minsoo Kang explains, this type of artificial animacy reconceptualizes the meaning of the miraculous:

> There was no question now of any kind of otherworldly agency in its [the automaton's] function, but they took up the automaton precisely for its ability to arouse a powerful sense of awe. And once deprived of its magic, it became a source of the *good kind of wonder* that inspired a decorous desire for the discovery and understanding of the worldly order. This allowed thinkers to use the device as a conceptual and didactic object with which to illustrate the wonders of the world-machine, the state-machine, and the body-machine. (115; my emphasis)

Analogous imagery continued throughout the Enlightenment, as leading European intellectuals drew upon comparable mechanistic metaphors to discuss the shifting associations between technology, subjectivity, and commercial networks (Wetmore 37). In a broader cultural sense, automata no longer belonged exclusively in the domain of courtly entertainment but were exhibited in public spectacles where they captivated viewers because of their ability to transgress traditional automated limitations (44).

In accordance with machine-driven metaphors illustrating the entry of Western Europe into modernity, people had no choice but to become masters of appearances and pretension to navigate the deceptive world in which they lived, as Cervantes and Baltasar Gracián (1601–1658) intuited in the two greatest Spanish novels about desengaño, *Don Quijote* and *El criticón* (The critic, 1657), respectively. The idealistic, sincere, free hero and man of feelings exemplified by the figure of Don Quixote became an outcast in the new baroque epoch. To survive with dignity, man was now forced to be strategically cautious and driven by rational will, just as Gracián characterizes the cerebral and judicious Critilo in contrast with the other protagonist, Andrenio, the impulsive, natural man. Humanity is forced to become *uomo astratto, homo artificialis*—a "human mechanism" similar to a motionless stone statue, capable of restraining its passions under its cold and impenetrable façade (Rodríguez de la Flor, *Pasiones* 124–25). This conception parallels Hobbes's characterization of early modern people as being devoid of autonomy and at the mercy of a world conceived of as a machine.

Socio-Political Ticking

The allegorical potential of the mechanistic metaphor extended to the field of political philosophy. The mechanical clock represented the functioning of the modern state. In the fourteenth and fifteenth centuries, these clocks symbolized temperance as well as prudent and timely governance (Bradbury and Collette 362). Throughout early modernity, the image of the clock evolved to illustrate centralized power and authority. Indeed, not only the clock but also fly systems and other sophisticated automated artifacts were used as persuasive propagandistic and doctrinaire instruments of absolute monarchies to legitimize their power in a visual, celebrative way (Merino Peral 25).

The rise of absolutism in Europe was primarily driven by the crises and religious wars of the 1500s and 1600s. Local autonomy and political rights were relegated to secondary status in favor of peace and safety in those countries eroded by ongoing religious conflict. For Hobbes, the European wars of religion justified the turn toward natural philosophy because these conflicts made it impossible to rely on or to believe in the absolute truth of anything except the science of mathematics. In his *Leviathan* (1651), the British philosopher constructs an account of how the state as an "artificial person" could exert absolute authority. He argues that the state is much like an automaton, created from a contract between every person, all of whom agree that they will lay down their individual rights to create an artificial being to preserve themselves from a nasty, brutish, and short life, to borrow from Hobbes. Thus, the state becomes an all-powerful and entirely artificial "person," capable of owning property, collecting taxes, and monopolizing the legitimate use of violence. This, however, is only possible when the state is animated by a sovereign—a real person or body of people—acting on its behalf.

In Spain, the mechanistic metaphor applied to political philosophy symbolized absolutism in a particular way. After the death of King Philip II in 1598, absolute monarchy entered a period of decline. In addition to the domestic and foreign policy challenges, absolutism was losing its strength because of the rise of the *valido*, the right-hand adviser or favorite of the king. As validos, the Duke of Lerma (1553–1625) under Philip III and the Count-Duke of Olivares (1587–1645) under Philip IV would become notorious political figures throughout the seventeenth century. In this sense, the mechanical clock was the perfect device for evoking a concealed mutual dependence between the monarch and his advisers: while the king symbolized the hand of the clock that gave the time by ruling, his validos were the mechanisms determining his actions. The mechanical principles of the clock, in its different variants, were broadened to visualize other political and economic matters in Spain at the time. The hourglass clock illustrated the expiration of political life while the sundial alluded to the subordination of politics to religion.[4]

Modern rationalism was also developed to be a practical methodology in science and technology, two areas strongly influenced by new conceptions of entertainment and theatricality. For natural philosophers, man could question nature, discover its secrets, and improve upon it, if only through artificial means (Eamon, "From Secrets" 322; see also Reula Baquero 88). Machine-driven toys, *lusus scientiae* (jokes of knowledge), and stagecraft technologies designed by artists, scientists, and engineers were leisure-based machines that encouraged curiosity and inspired admiration among viewers rather than superstition or irrational fear. Written by Italian and Spanish painters and architects, stagecraft manuals such as *Practica di fabricar scene e machine ne' teatri* (Manual for constructing theatrical scenes and machines, 1638) by Nicola Sabbatini (1574–1654) and *El museo pictórico, y escala óptica* (The pictorial museum and optical scale, 1797) by Acisclo Antonio Palomino de Castro y Velasco (1655–1726) became a genre of technical books that remained in vogue well into the eighteenth century (Paun de García 20).

The Scientific Revolution disqualified animist ideas by elucidating the agency of inanimate objects as part of mechanical and rational processes (Mayr 55). As Richard Viladesau has noted, the Scientific Revolution separated modernity from previous periods in Europe (4), and this certainly was the case in Spain. Although earlier scholarship promoted the idea that seventeenth-century Spain did not fully experience scientific growth, this assertion has been challenged and overcome. Scientific development indeed took place in the Iberian Peninsula, but it happened in isolation from the rest of Europe.[5] Some advances in science and technology became useful in warfare during a period obsessed with territorial expansion. For historian Michael Roberts, technical and strategic innovations were important for the so-called military revolution that took place in the seventeenth century. Firearms acquired a greater degree of effectiveness and accuracy, and martial skills gave way to the efficient scientific creativity of the engineer on the battlefield (Samson 20–21). Calderón de la Barca was among the writers who explored military innovation in various plays such as *El sitio de Bredá* (The siege of Bredá, 1625) and *El galán fantasma*, for example.[6]

During the Counter-Reformation, artistic animation played a key role in devotional art and, as a result, it influenced religious practices and brought back a judicious re-enchantment by the end of the Protestant Reformation in the mid-1600s. The twenty-fifth session of the Council of Trent (1541–1563), convened by Pope Pius IV in 1563, legitimized the dogmatic and worshipful power of images. Religiosity, then, began to acquire a living texture in its celebration of the materiality and theatricality of the ineffable. Priests turned into masters of histrionics by wrapping their personae and sermons in highly sophisticated spectacles with the aid of props. Sacred sculptures, some refurbished from the late medieval period, acquired a new agency through animated features to "rekindle devotion or protest neglect," in Caroline Walker Bynum's words ("Violent Images" 22).

Although the Reformation introduced serious objections regarding religious imagery and mechanical devotional objects, these artifacts proliferated in Catholic settings (Riskin, "Machines" 29). Apart from the figures with pragmatic purposes, such as those with clock mechanisms for time keeping, we find a wide range of mechanical beings, such as Christs, virgins, devils, angels, animals, and even animated three-dimensional biblical scenes of heaven, paradise, or the nativity, in temples and cathedrals. This mixed aesthetic of a moving religiosity engaged the faithful in imaginative, reflexive contemplation rather invasive delusion. This type of meditation, theorized by the Jesuit Luis de Puente (1554–1624), entails first imagining the concept on which one will then meditate (Aparicio Maydeu, "La comedia" 45). As I demonstrate in the second and third chapters, technology permeated sacred animated objects as a way to encourage the faithful to visualize the concept and then to look beyond the artificiality of illusions, exercising an interactive piety vis-à-vis the mysteries of faith.[7]

Up to this point, we have explored the ways in which the rationality behind mechanical animation helps to explain a new world order that impacted religious, socio-economic, political, and scientific values. In the sections that follow, we move away from figurative interpretations of animation to focus on artificial agency from artistic and theatrical perspectives in religious and social contexts of leisure. Processes of animation forged their way into a highly visual culture to dialogue with performance practices and entertainment, two fields that will inform this book's historical literary and theoretical inquiry.

In early modern Spain, theater was a mirror of society as well as an imaginative and ideological medium to evaluate and experiment with alternative realities. Coupled with the trend toward observation and reflection was the production of a more thoughtful type of entertainment in which the creation of illusions was regarded as a meticulous artistic process in itself, at both a material and conceptual level. Theatrical practices outside the playhouse found substitute stages in churches, private residences, royal palaces, and streets. Individuals from all ranks played with their identities, assuming new roles to either fit into society or resist it. William Egginton asserts: "The public theater of the sixteenth and seventeenth centuries contributed to the theatricalization of everyday life because it created an epistemological situation in which each and every person could not only watch, identify with, and desire an imaginary reality on the stage, but could also become a microcosm of this stage, playing roles and developing characters for the appreciation of an internalized audience; and, of course, there would always be something to conceal" ("An Epistemology" 404–5). The many modes of representation and ways of making and living theater expanded considerably, diversifying the social and cultural significance of theatricality at the time.

On the one hand, in the technical sense of the word, animation is an intrinsic part of the spectacular as it generates artificial wonder. On the other hand, the idea of endowing inert matter with life implies the setting off of mechanical and intellectual processes concealed behind an artistic façade. As Basil Jones explains in relation to puppetry, "Our inquiry has to come to grips with this work of the puppet and its manipulator, where meaning is generated more by *process than by content*, more by movement than by words. It is the *process which reveals the workings* of the play's thoughts" (67; my emphasis).[8] The focal role that animation gives to the process rather than to the end result illustrates how the animated artifact is a generator of novel meanings for well-worn tropes, ideas, and practices, which is a fundamental line of research throughout this study.

Pious Technologies

Animated sculptures in ceremonial contexts have had a long and extensive history originating with ancient civilizations, as we saw with the goddess Astarté. Consider, for example, the numerous inventions attributed to Greek mathematician and engineer Heron of Alexandria

(10–86 CE), which have established him as a pioneer in the art of special effects and a predecessor of modern robotics. His best-known invention was the *aeolipile* (with variants *aeolipyle* or *eolipile*), a forerunner of the steam engine. Heron also devised entire mechanical sets for tragedies where figurines moved automatically.

This fascination with artifacts that reproduce basic movements to evoke artificial *anima*, or life, continued to develop over different epochs and across different cultures. With the advent of quantitative science and new humanistic propensities in early modernity, the principles of animation were likewise applied to visual and performing arts for popular entertainment and educational purposes. Indeed, most of the objects examined in the chapters that follow do not belong to traditional theatrical settings per se, as their purpose goes beyond leisure. Some are even exhibited in spaces explicitly built according to the artifacts' needs to exert their dogmatic purposes more effectively. These vibrant things were made to possess a "passive agency" (Gell, *Art and Agency* 129) that the manipulator could activate to fit a specific purpose at a precise moment.[9]

Discussing performance objects in relation to animation calls for a brief digression to review the differences and relations between object, thing, and prop according to thing theory, even though these terms end up being interchangeable most of the time. The object refers to a thing that is "relatively stable in form" (Hodder 7). An object also has the capacity to "manifest, respond to, or transmit meaning that originates in humans" (Bernstein 69–70). A thing invites people to confront it on its own terms while implying a psychological investment on the part of the person in relation to the thing. In Robin Bernstein's words: "An object becomes a thing when it invites a person to dance" (69–70). Lastly, a prop is an object triggered by an actor that goes on a journey on stage over the course of a play.[10] While these definitions are slightly different, they underline two main ideas that will emerge in the chapters that follow: first, the object, the thing, and the prop depend closely on those who manipulate them, recalling, in some instances, the aforementioned principle of passive agency; second, they can also be perceived as having their own life, as "spontaneous subjects, equivalent to the figure of the actor" (Sofer 9; see also Veltruský 88).[11] As Bil Baird states: "When the puppet performs before an audience, he begins to create a kind of life. I say before an audience, because only in the imagination of an audience does a puppet begin to exist" (15).[12]

It is not a coincidence that during the Middle Ages and increasingly in the thirteenth to fifteenth centuries, the Catholic Church began using articulated figures with characteristics similar to those of the puppet in liturgical ceremonies and public festivities to help the faithful better grasp, in a concrete and a metaphoric way, the essence of Christian wonder.[13] One of the most emblematic articulated religious figures from Spain that exemplifies this concept is the Christ of Burgos (14th c.), housed to this day in the Burgos Cathedral. In his *Voyage en Espagne* (Wanderings in Spain, 1843), French poet Théophile Gautier (1811–1872) provided testimony about the unsettling feeling he experienced when contemplating the latent animacy of the crucifix, which the author refers to as a "fantôme crucifié" (crucified ghost):

> It is not formed of colored stone or wood, but actually consists of a human skin (at least, so they say), stuffed in the most artistic manner. The hair is real hair; the eyes are furnished with eyelashes, the crown of thorns is really composed of thorns, and, in a word, not one detail is omitted. Nothing can be more lugubrious, or more disagreeable to behold than this crucified phantom, with its ghastly life-like look and its death-like stillness. The skin, of a brownish, rusty tinge, is streaked with long lines of blood, which are so well imitated that you might almost think they were actually trickling down. It requires no very great effort of the imagination to believe the legend which affirms that this miraculous figure bleeds every Friday. (41)[14]

To enhance this visual hyperrealism, the sculpture has movable arms and head and conceals a receptacle for "blood" connected to one of its wounds to recreate the effect of bleeding, as Gautier implies in his description. This emphasis on the bloody aesthetic of the Crucifixion, disseminated by Franciscan and Dominican theology since the late Middle Ages, resulted in the so-called *Crucifixus Dolorosus* (plague cross).¹⁵ Rather than being an invitation to idolatry, this intense sensuous experience triggers an "interactive fascination, not fall on your knees awe" (Bennett 5). Therefore, artifice permeates the essence of the sacred and brings it to life in what theologian Rudolf Otto has dubbed the *numinous*—that which, similar to the *uncanny*, fascinates and terrifies at the same time.

In exemplary literature, the nuanced sensationalism of the jointed Christ sculpture moves into the realm of miracles without leading readers to explore the critical process of illusion-making. In chapter 19 of the anonymous work *Castigos e documentos del rey don Sancho IV* (The book of punishments of King Sancho IV, 1292), a crucified Christ unfastens his body from the cross and, with the nail that had bound his right hand, transfixes the face of a nun who is about to escape the convent with her lover.¹⁶ Immediately thereafter, the figure returns to the cross, but his right arm remains forever loose as a sign of the aforementioned miracle. Likewise, in the eighteenth-century magic play *El mágico de Salerno, Pedro Vayalarde* (The magician from Salerno, Pedro Vayalarde, 1715–1720) by Juan Salvo y Vela (?–1720), a crucified Christ bows his head in a sign of forgiveness. In the same way, in the octosyllabic poem by José Zorrilla (1817–1893), "A buen juez, mejor testigo" (A good judge, best witness, 1838), based on the legend of the Christ of la Vega, a Christ figure frees his right hand from the cross to recall an unkept promise of marriage. All of these cautionary tales seem to accept the animation of the sacred sculpture as part of their narratives to illustrate a moral lesson without spurring further inquiry into their miraculous agency. Animation of sacred props is simply taken for granted as part of the popular religiosity prevailing during the late Middle Ages.¹⁷

Going back to the artistic iterations, as in the case of animated Christ figures, articulated Virgins were also built to move, often to receive the body of Christ in their arms after the Descent.¹⁸ Others were meant to inspire an extravagant theatricality, such as the no-longer-extant Virgin Our Lady of Solitude sculpted by Gaspar del Águila (n.d.) for a private commission in 1578. This figure had two detachable heads, one dejected and another joyous, which could be affixed depending on the occasion (Sánchez López 142).¹⁹ In literature, there are also multiple examples in which a statue of the Virgin Mary comes to life to perform a miracle. "La abadesa preñada" (The pregnant abbess) from *Milagros de Nuestra Señora* (The miracles of Our Lady, ca.1260) by Gonzalo de Berceo (ca. 1195–1264), the "Cantiga IV" of the *Cantigas de Santa María* (Songs of Holy Mary, ca. 1270–1290) by King Alfonso X the Wise (1221–1284), and "Margarita la tornera" (Margarita the gatekeeper, 1837), also by Zorrilla, illustrate this phenomenon. Once again, exemplary literature appropriates miraculous animation for didactic purposes without inquiring into the meaning of Christian awe. It would seem that the tridimensional quality of the animated figure in religious contexts could heighten its conceptual complexity through a sensorial experience. The faithful could, then, come to terms with the divine by witnessing firsthand a *moving wonder* and, in some cases, with the necessary critical distance induced by watching the celebrant orchestrating it.

In addition to the animated sculptures of Christ and the Virgin, there were other religious figures that used theatrical animation in very specific ways and for different devotional purposes. In southern Germany, the *Palmesel* (Palm Sunday donkey) refers to the procession that celebrates the entrance of Christ into Jerusalem on Palm Sunday, represented by a Christ figure riding a wheeled donkey. In Spain, in the so-called *procesión de la borriquilla* (procession of the donkey), the animal has no wheels: instead it is carried as a *paso* (processional float) on the shoulders of the *costaleros* (bearers). In this instance, motion does not come from the mechanisms of the sculpture as in the German case but from the physical effort of the costaleros. Thomas M. Landy explains:

> The costaleros are physically obscured from the onlookers, but onlookers are very much aware of what it takes to carry the heavy pasos. People cheer on the costaleros at various points, and *the costaleros keep the pasos rocking modestly but rhythmically from side to side, providing an element of movement and power that a carriage supported on wheels could never match.* When costaleros cycle out for a rest break, they mill about visibly among the penitents, still wearing their costals—the distinctive cloth head and neck gear that protects their heads and necks when they carry the paso. At least as much as any group

in the procession, they symbolize an ideal Christian life for onlookers: they bear the burden of making it meaningful and carrying it on, and signal that at least in Seville, the Christian life is regarded not just as an individual challenge, but as an effort that requires a whole group working together. (n.p.; original emphasis)

As with the crucified Christ or the sorrowful Virgin, the *borriquilla* enhances the same "unconventional intimacy with human actors and spectators of the liturgical theater in which it takes part" (Harris, "Inanimate Performers" 196). Because this sculpture is incorporated into a processional context, it makes Jesus's triumphant entrance into Jerusalem a hyperreal experience in which the real and the fictional are joined together—not seamlessly, though—through the artificial moving Christ. Religious animation deploys, once again, an *immersive distancing* toward piety and devotion.

Another religious statue endowed with a unique sense of animation in the Iberian tradition is the so-called *Santiago del espaldarazo* (14th c.), a figure of the apostle Saint James kept to this day in the Monastery of the Huelgas Reales in Burgos. According to legend, the statue granted knighthood to noblemen by bestowing upon them a ceremonious *perzcotada* (blow on the shoulder) with a sword, which moved up and down thanks to the statue's jointed right arm.[20] This sculpture was conceived as an instrument of divine power without any kind of worldly intercession, just as Tirso de Molina (1579–1648) envisioned the iconic Stone Guest in his attributed play *El burlador de Sevilla* (The trickster of Seville, ca. 1612–1625). Because human justice is tainted, the artificial hands of these non-humans act as impartial, legitimate judges.

In addition to their inherent and distinctive divine agency, all of the figures considered so far operate in isolation and articulate concepts holistically rather than with precise stories that follow a causal plot. Longer and more structured religious narratives used clusters of figurines working in unison on miniaturized stages to bring a complete story line to life. Among this type of animated fictions, the *retablo mecánico* (mechanical theater) is a crucial artifact for displaying religiosity for the laity. From the fourteenth century onward, wandering artists carried wooden boxed sets with figurines from the Bible similar to those in an altarpiece but endowed with slight mechanical movements (see Figure 1.1). This portable micro-theater encouraged a communal experience that was closer to edifying entertainment than a devotional encounter. As the retablo mecánico became more popular, it developed into a puppet show devoid of its original religious thematic.[21]

The animated manger or nativity was a tradition closely related to the retablo mecánico but specifically focused on the nativity scene and set inside the church. Scholars have attributed its origins to Saint Francis of Assisi (ca. 1181–1226), based on the nativity scene he staged for the Mass he offered on Christmas Eve in 1223 in Greccio, Italy. This tradition took root in Catholic countries, mainly among the Franciscan, Dominican, and Jesuit orders. During the Counter-Reformation, it was used as a didactic tool for visually enhancing the Christmas celebration. The popularity of the animated manger reached its peak in Spain during the baroque era as religiosity acquired a greater degree of artifice thanks to new technologies at the service of church interests. Currently, two animated mangers are extant in the Iberian Peninsula: the nativity of Nuestra Señora de los Reyes de Laguardia (see Figure 1.2) in Álava, dating to 1749, and the nativity of Tirisiti in Alcoy (Alicante) from the middle of the nineteenth century. In both cases, the figurines move along rails powered by springs and hinges manipulated below the set.[22]

The *Misteri d'Elx* (Mistery play of Elche, ca. 13th c.) is another religious animated tradition still extant in the Peninsula that is now part of the UNESCO Masterpieces of the Oral and Intangible Heritage of Humanity.[23] The celebration takes place yearly on August 14 and 15 inside the Basilica of Santa María de Elche (Alicante) to commemorate the Virgin of the Assumption. This short play is performed in old Valencian and Latin, and its religious awe heavily depends on two aerial devices known as the *magrana* (or *mangrana*) and the *araceli* that descend from the dome of the church. The magrana, translated as pomegranate, has a spherical shape reminiscent of a celestial orb (see Illustration 1).[24] When it drops down, it opens up like golden leaves, exuding a divine light and releasing a youth who embodies the angel who announces Mary's death. Later, the araceli, a platform representing

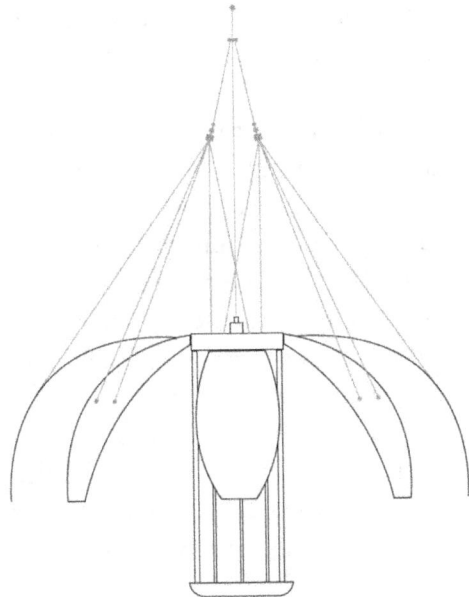

ILLUSTRATION 1. Technical sketch of the *magrana*. Sketch by Jesús Caballero and Jaime López, courtesy of La Máquina Real.

a choir of angels, descends to escort the Virgin's soul to heaven. The Holy Trinity slides down, later on, on the same platform just before the final apotheosis. In all these interludes, the Virgin is the only artificial being—a statue—while all the other characters are played by live actors. The power of animation consequently falls into the surrounding scenery that conveys a totalizing display of Christian wonder around the hieratic figure of the Virgin.[25]

The mechanical altarpiece, the animated nativity, and the Misteri d'Elx paved the way, to a certain extent, for the máquina real, the epitome of religious animation in popular culture in seventeenth-century Spain. These professional companies specialized in staging hagiographical plays in playhouses using an entire cast of marionettes. The shows they staged were in high demand, especially during Lent, when actors were temporarily banned from performing on the stage and no other theatrical entertainment was available. Puppets, then, and the special effects that characterized these miniaturized productions gave shape and form to saintliness in a unique and interactive manner (as noted further in Chapter 3).

Reviewing the development of religious animation from the jointed Christ figure to the máquina real, there seems to be an evolution toward longer, more spectacular narratives in which the intercession of animation develops over time into a requisite means to enhance devotion through a religiosity that was gradually more dependent on artifice. A fitting conclusion to the analysis of the religious performance objects with simulated agency in early modern Spanish culture comes with the ritual monster known as the *Tarasca*, which may be the perfect bridge between Christian and pagan forms of animated entertainment.

According to the legend, this dragon-like creature of Celtic origins lived in the French town of Tarascon, where it held the entire population in fear. Saint Martha single-handedly defeated the dragon and presented it to the people in the name of the Savior. The first record we have of a Tarasca is from Seville in 1282, after the Christian reconquest of the city, and the myth remains alive and well to this day (Gilmore 368).

During the seventeenth century, the Tarasca evolved into a more elaborate attraction and became part of the Corpus Christi procession, assuming the shape of a papier-mâché mechanical beast with an elongated neck carrying a figurine of a woman, who symbolized vice and temptation (see Figure 1.3). In Toledo, for example, the Tarasca carried a tiny blond statuette of Anne Boleyn that represented Henry VIII's sexual depravity and Boleyn's assumed role as a catalyst for the Protestant Reformation (Gilmore 368). In addition to the female figurine, the Tarasca was usually accompanied by the *gigantones* (giants), forerunners of the *gigantes y cabezudos* (giants and big-heads; see Figure 1.4).[26] As the pagan aspects of the Tarasca became more prominent in the eighteenth century, King Charles III banned it by royal decree in 1780.

The Lives of Shadows

In a context further removed from religiosity, other forms of animation also played important parts in the development and negotiation of new ideas that needed an extra visual aid to fully come to life. Shadow theater, for example, is one of the oldest and more critical forms of puppetry known in the Peninsula. It goes beyond mere entertainment, as it was thought to transgress social mores and educate audiences in cultures that prohibited representations with figures but allowed silhouettes to perform. It is precisely their allegorical and ethereal essence that turned these cutout figures into socially daring attractions.

Arabic shadow shows, or *khayāl al-ẓill*, made their way to the Iberian Peninsula during the Caliphate of Cordoba (929–1031), a time of rich social and cultural exchange between the Arabic and Mediterranean worlds. In Spanish-Arabic literature, the first testimony of shadow puppetry can be found in the *Kitāb al-akhlāq wa Siyar* (The book of morals and behavior, n.d.) written by Spanish Muslim scholar Ibn Hazm (994–1064). In this work, the narrator alludes to the practice of shadow plays in Al-Andalus and describes them as magic lanterns: "The closest thing I have seen resembling this world, are shadow images, these are figures mounted on a wooden wheel that is made to revolve rapidly, so that one group of figures disappears as another appears" (qtd. and trans. by Monroe 99). James T. Monroe also mentions the Spanish-Arab poet Ibn Šuhayd of Cordoba (992–1035) and his *Risālaṯ al-tawābiʿ wa al-zawābiʿ* (The treatise of familiar spirits and demons, 1025–1027) as another reference that underlines the presence of shadow theater between the tenth and eleventh centuries in the Peninsula. In this treatise, Ibn Šuhayd refers to a specific type of puppet representing the Jew. This character was, no doubt, a ridiculed stock figure that would have originated from the complex relations between the Arabic and Jewish communities when the latter became involved in the civil wars of the Taifa Kingdoms, following the collapse of the Caliphate of Cordoba.

Although shadow puppetry would accompany recitals of classical works of Arabic poetry as an added feature that brought the texts to life, there were also scripts specifically written for these types of marionettes. This is the case in the plays by the famous ophthalmologist and poet from Mosul, Muḥammad Ibn Dāniyāl (ca. 1238/1250–1310/1311). His humorous yet critical texts for shadows gained widespread fame in Egypt and most likely reached the Iberian Peninsula, as three of his plays are found in the manuscript 469 in the library of the Escorial.[27]

Ibn Dāniyāl's trilogy—comprising *Tayf al-khayal* (The shadow spirit), *ʿAjib wa-Gharib* (The amazing preacher and the stranger), and *Al-Mutayyam waʾl-yutayyim* (The love-stricken one and the lost one who inspires passion)—is considered the oldest collection of shadow plays that we know of in the Islamic world. Among the three plays, *Tayf al-khayal* reveals an intrinsic connection with one of the major works of Peninsular literature, the *Celestina* or *Comedia de Calisto y Melibea* (Play of Calisto and Melibea, 1499), attributed to Francisco de Rojas (ca.1473–1541). Ibn Dāniyāl's play features Umm Rashid, a marriage broker who shares specific traits with Celestina, the iconic protagonist of the *Comedia*. In addition to the character of the procuress, Ibn Dāniyāl and Rojas depict a world of promiscuous nobility framed within social satire with an ultimate moralizing intention in their works.[28]

Shadow theater gradually became a more multifaceted artistic endeavor that used scientific advances to develop new forms of animated illusionism. Jesuit priest and scholar Athanasius Kircher (1602–1680) invented the magic lantern, a type of visual spectacle through reflections and refractions of light and shadow. In his *Ars magna lucis et umbrae* (The magnetic art of light and shadow, 1646), Kircher describes the magic lantern as a type of "representative magic" (Kircher 360). Inspired by the effects of Kircher's artifact, Mexican poet and playwright Sor Juana Inés de la Cruz (1651–1695) refers to human existence as a shadow play because of the contrast between light and darkness in her poem "Primero sueño" (First dream, 1692). Just as other animated entertainments, the magic lantern transformed itself into a concept beyond its materiality, but it did not stop evolving technically into more sophisticated forms of illusionism.

Dutch physicist Christiaan Huygens (1629–1695) contributed to the design of a second prototype of the magic lantern in 1659. The artistry of its visual effects was used to create grandiose theatrical courtly settings in Italy and Spain. During the eighteenth century, the magic lantern settled in Spain as a popular form of entertainment, especially with sounds added to the projected images. Most of these itinerant shows were orchestrated by a sole artist and staged in public spaces. By modifying some of the principles of the magic lantern, Belgian physicist Étienne-Gaspard Robert (1763–1837), better known as Robertson, devised the phantasmagoria in the 1780s. His invention was equipped with a special lantern (phantoscope) mounted on wheels to be moved closer or farther away from a screen. Glass slides were painted with figures that changed shape with the movement of the phantoscope, giving the impression of ghostly apparitions.

Comparable to the magic lantern, the *tutilimundi* (also known as *cosmorama*, *mundinovi*, and *mundonovo*) was another optical attraction inspired by the principles of cutout puppetry. It was unique in that it was enhanced by a system of lenses that required sophisticated manufacture, set-up, and manipulation (see Figures 1.5, 1.6, and 1.7). As with most optical diversions, the tutilimundi was an itinerant show that entertained while it educated its audiences, as evidenced by the fact that it was allowed in Spanish convents throughout the seventeenth century (Sánchez 88).

Such a steady development of optical illusions greatly affected the meaning and aesthetic of baroque stagecraft and the theatrical experience as a whole. During the 1650s, the science of engineering became synonymous with dramatic expertise. Playwrights made sure to exhibit their artistic and technical imagination in the scenery for their most spectacular plays (Kimmel 218). In certain cases, special effects were expressly designed to show off a specific company's technological means. In art and entertainment, the tension between the display of illusions and its revelation pervaded, opening up a path for scientific knowledge in the theater of wonder that developed in early modernity.

However, we mustn't forget that a sense of crisis and disenchantment in Spain coursed through the seventeenth century and influenced the ideas that propped up material performances and the visual arts. While artists experimented with optical illusionism, anamorphosis, distorted images, and excessive ornamentation to display technological innovation, they simultaneously gave concrete form to disillusionment, confusion, and other concepts that were impossible to see except through faith or belief (e.g., holiness or saintliness). People found an escapist path for coping with their everyday reality and a preexistentialist void in this baroque visual saturation. Paintings imbued with a sense of movement (perceptible in both the subjects and their clothing), sculptures with movable parts, puppets, animated shadows, automatons, and mechanized stages evoked deceptive reality beyond their appearances. It is no coincidence that the seventeenth century was the age when reason sought to tame wonder through scientific advances. Lorraine Daston and Katherine Park note: "In the High Middle Ages wonder existed apart from curiosity; in the sixteenth and seventeenth centuries, wonder and curiosity interlocked" (15). Animation infused objects with life and, at the same time, invited viewers to rationalize their artificial agency by exposing the artistic techniques and mechanistic principles involved in the process.

At this theoretical crossroads, modernity beckons, and questions emerge at the nexus between animation and theatricality: What forces brought animated objects to participate in religious ceremonial practices and secular performances in early modernity? What is animation or artificial life being used to hide on an existential level? How are agency and the power of things deployed in these theatrical contexts? In which ways do animated props interact with the larger narratives of modernity? Why have these lively props survived to this day? What have they kept intact or lost along the way from their original meaning and function? Why do they continue to fascinate us in an era of revolutionary changes related to the functions and aesthetics of animation? The following chapters address these queries by focusing on a gallery of animated props whose mechanisms of agency are put to test as they engage with notions of religiosity, art, entertainment, science, and social norms.

2. Matters of God

> When does the god come into being? The image is cast, hammered, or sculptured: it is not yet a god. It is soldered, put together, and erected; it is still not a god. It is adorned, consecrated, prayed to—and now, finally, it is god once man has willed it so and dedicated it.
>
> MARCUS MINUCIUS FELIX, *Octavius*, 22.5

THIS EXCERPT FROM the *Octavius*, a philosophical dialogue written in defense of the Christian faith by apologist Marcus Minucius Felix (fl. 200–240 CE), resounds with the fascination that religious rites, which give material form to the divine, still inspire today. Humanoid performance objects have been used over the centuries in religious contexts and catechistic efforts to evoke spirituality and the holy. The puppet stands out as a singular prop for its capacity to embody incorporeal entities such as gods, demons, saints, and the spirits of the dead (Gross, "The Madness" 43). The marionette's metaphorical ability to conflate the animate and the inanimate makes it the "proper stand-in for the invisible" (Johnson 86) and the agent of choice to mediate what Michael Malkin has coined the "plausible impossible"—that is, "the unreal and remote made real and immediate" (6–7). Besides, in the language of puppetry, certain words such as *marionette* or *retablo* originate from precise religious contexts. In particular, the term *marionette* comes from the name given to the small statuettes of the Virgin Mary that were used in the telling of biblical stories in medieval France. Additionally, the word *retablo* is derived from the Latin expression *retro tabula* (behind the altar). In Spain, *retablo* refers to an altarpiece—recall the analysis from Chapter 1 on the refurbishing of figurines for animated nativity scenes.

Accordingly, we may infer that in ritualistic contexts, the animated figure compels the faithful to negotiate a series of polarities—the real and the illusory; the visible and the invisible; the natural and the supernatural; the human and the holy—through critical engagement, imagination, and playfulness. The animated religious figure problematizes the duality it mediates while inviting the faithful to participate in an interactive experience to complete its meaning. This process, attuned to modern sensibilities and an active gaze, anticipates the ability to see and think beyond appearances and to look for new ways to conceive of the world's seemingly limitless possibilities. Further, through a quasi-dialectical engagement with the devotee, the *holy puppet*, with its uncanny élan, generates new modes of self-knowledge (*phronesis*). These new petit narratives put into question the binaries, hierarchies, and master narratives upon which early modernity was so firmly anchored.

After the thirteenth and fourteenth centuries, the quest for illusory naturalism in religious imagery in Europe led to the crafting of a gallery of animated statues representing Christ, the Virgin, and the Christ Child as well as the apostles, angels, and devils. The religious experience was increasingly "literalized into encounter with objects" (Bynum, *Dissimilar* 29). Furthermore, these *religious action-figures* could perform a wide array of motions, from the most basic movements to sophisticated actions such as talking, bleeding, weeping, or even flying.[1] In the Iberian Peninsula, beginning in the seventh century, some religious communities started exploring the expressive and ritualistic functions of artificial animated beings in the privacy of their congregations as a way to forge deeper connections with biblical narratives and hagiographies (Swift 33). These performance objects were vehicles for venturing into incarnational theology through a regulated sensual experience and a play-relation with the divine (Moshenka 44). Consequently, the holy prop gradually became legitimized as a powerful pedagogical tool in liturgical and para-liturgical ceremonies open to the broader Christian community.

Originating in the tenth century, life-size processional wooden sculptures were paraded during Holy Week festivities in Spain. The *pasos* (processional floats) carried by bearers displayed scenes of the Passion and episodes from the Gospels, which increasingly adhered to a more realistic aesthetic. The *procesión de la borriquilla* (examined in Chapter 1) was one of these immersive scenarios. The figures in a procession acquired an off-putting strangeness, particularly because viewers had to critically reconcile the non-human qualities of the sculptures—soullessness and voicelessness—with their human aura as they moved in the same space and time as those who contemplated them.[2] Quoting Susan Verdi Webster:

> The spatial and temporal status of the sculptures in procession significantly enhance their mimetic effects, and their unique kinesthetic character allows them dramatic entrance into the realm of human experience. They are able to move both physically (through articulated limbs) and spatially (through the streets of the city). Furthermore, the incorporation of sculpture within a processional context acts to change a most fundamental aspect: the sense of time. No longer static, eternal images of altars and *retablos*, their temporal state is extended so that they merge with the spectators' own experience of space and time. (167)

The competing impulses of placing these statues between their objectness and their humanness generated an emotional disquiet among the community of faithful and stimulated an active meditation to conciliate the twofold nature of the figure.

This reflective process was especially delicate with regard to the *Depositio Sepulchri* (descent from the cross and burial), one of the most perplexing mysteries of faith and a pillar of Christian doctrine. In the 1200s, the *Cristo articulado* (jointed Christ figure) started to be used in Western Europe to represent the unity of Jesus's divine and human essence. Priests manipulated these figures in full view of their congregations, and their subtle animation edifyingly illustrated Christ's transition from human to deity. Such practices went beyond mere spectacle to provide a mental space for celebrants to meditate and articulate the meaning of Christian wonder.

This chapter traces the genealogy of representations of Christ as they gradually come to be three-dimensional and partially animated. I then delve into the function of the jointed Christ figure in Spanish Depositio rites up to the 1700s. Through the mediation of these articulated props, religious awe became empirical. Ironically, most of these ceremonies ended up being banned during the Enlightenment because of their supposedly extravagant theatricality and did not reemerge until the twentieth century in local religious festivities, devoid, however, of their original conceptual subtleties. Yet, with the aim of evaluating the transhistorical performativity of the jointed Christ, I focus the last part of the chapter on analyzing the only contemporary production that I know of that features a *Cristo articulado* in the starring role, the *Misterio del Cristo de los Gascones* (Mystery of the Christ of the Gascons, 2007), written and directed by Ana Zamora. Touring globally since its premiere, *Misterio* is a unique *reanimation* of a medieval mystery for twenty-first-century audiences. Driven by historical rigor and daring creativity, the jointed Christ recuperates in a secular context its original theological nuances—in liturgical and devotional contexts—in this staging vis-à-vis the concept of holiness at a time when the human and the divine demand constant redefinition.[3]

Beyond the Altar

The representation of Christ has endured fierce controversy over the entire arc of Catholicism's artistic and material history. It is generally accepted that Christian art was conceived of as aniconic rather than representational, based on the second of the Ten Commandments: "Thou shalt not make unto thee any graven image" (Exodus 20:2 and Deuteronomy 5:6). Nonetheless, to make the holy accessible, it needed a tangible presence. Religion evolved to become a combination of internal beliefs, ritual practices, and material devotional culture (Ivanic 334). Predictably, the consumption of images fell into abuse, which resulted in the reforms of the First Iconoclasm (726–787), promulgated by Emperor

Leo III, which in turn triggered a wider iconoclastic struggle between Eastern and Western traditions that lasted over one and a half centuries.

In the West, it was not until the thirteenth century that Saint Thomas Aquinas (1225–1274) and Saint Bonaventure (1221–1274) established arguments in favor of the cult of images inside the temple, which were crucial for future debates on the topic (Freedberg 198). Aquinas's and Bonaventure's teachings deliberated on some of the inconclusive *sententiae* found in the *Libri quattuor sententiarum* (The four books of sentences, ca. 1150) by scholastic theologian Peter Lombard (1096–1160).[4] Both apologists agreed that by having images inside the church, the act of preaching would be more effective. Visual representations helped to instruct a typically illiterate laity on holy matters. Images transmitted emotions and ensured their persistence in the memory of the faithful. Despite these irrefutable reasonings, the controversy surrounding images remained alive in Europe out of the fear that fixed pictorial representations would inadequately oversimplify theological notions and encourage idolatry.

Matter ever seeks form in human desire, and so do religious concepts, yet sought-after visual expression all too often risks reification (Huizinga 173). The Protestant Reformation called the cult of images into question, and reformer John Calvin (1509–1564) symbolically reduced man's disposition to a "perpetual factory of idols" (1:108). Material representations of the divine were not reinstated until the Council of Trent. Its last, twenty-fifth session, *De invocatione, veneration, reliquiis, santorum, et sacris imaginibus* (On the invocation, veneration, and relics of saints, and on sacred images, 1563), specifies how images should be used and interpreted:

> Bishops shall carefully teach this, that, by means of the histories of the mysteries of our Redemption, portrayed by paintings or other representations, the people are instructed, and confirmed in (the habit of) remembering, and continually revolving in mind the articles of faith; as also that great profit is derived from all sacred images, not only because the people are thereby admonished of the benefits and gifts bestowed upon them by Christ, but also because the miracles which God has performed by means of the saints, and their salutary

examples, are set before the eyes of the faithful; that so they may give God thanks for those things; may order their own lives and manners in imitation of the saints; and may be excited to adore and love God, and to cultivate piety. (235)

Various treatises followed this decree, including Federico Borromeo's *Della pittura sacra* (On sacred painting, 1624), Giovanni Andrea Gilio's *Dialogo degli errori de' pittori* (Dialogue on the errors and abuses of painters, 1564), Joannes Molanus's *De picturis et imaginibus sacris* (Treatise on sacred images, 1570), Carlo Borromeo's *Instructiones fabricae et supellectilis ecclesiasticae* (Instructions for church building, 1577), and Gabriele Paleotti's *Discorso intorno alle immagini sacre e profane* (Discourse on sacred and profane images, 1582). Expanding on the basis of Trent's twenty-fifth session, these discourses focused on how to prevent lasciviousness in devotional representations, especially once *meditatio humanitatis Christi* (meditation on Christ's humanity) became legitimized as a practice.

To comprehend fully how the church eventually approved of images as *lively objects* of edification, it is important to keep in mind the theatricality of the Mass, an allegorical interpretation of the rite initiated by Carolingian theologian Amalarius of Metz (ca. 775–850). In his *Liber officialis* or *De ecclesiastico officio* (On the liturgy, 1101–1115), Amalarius approaches the liturgy in terms of sacred drama and the celebrants' vivid performance, which even overshadow the significance of the sermons' words.[5] John Wesley Harris explains:

> [Amalarius] did not, of course, propose to make a play out of the Mass, but he showed how every detail of the service could be interpreted as an image of one of the events of Jesus's last days and be presented by the officiating clergy with appropriate signs of sorrow, guilt, anguish or joy. . . . Understanding the actual words of the service was less important if the congregation could be presented with a vivid re-enactment of the key events of Jesus's life, on which their faith was based—one image was worth a thousand words. (23–24)

Amalarius's theatrical understanding of the liturgy granted it a central place in the history of Western drama (Hardison 40). For the theologian, the Mass follows a logical narrative divided into three parts in which Christ is the sole protagonist: 1) Christ's arrival on Earth, his life before the Passion, and his teachings align with the portion of the liturgy from the Introit to the Gospel reading; 2) the Passion and the Holy Burial correspond to the liturgical elements from the Offertory to the *Pater Noster*; and, 3) the Resurrection and Ascension of Christ are represented at the denouement of the liturgy. This intelligible plotline was accentuated by the spatial changes inside churches at the time, as the altar was pushed back to increase the distance between the priest and the congregation—and, in so doing, demarcating a fourth wall (J. W. Harris 71).

Amalarius's followers and leading theologians widely disseminated his ideas. Among them were Honorius Augustodunensis, Hugh of St. Victor, Sicardus of Cremona, Innocent III, John Beleth, Durandus of Mende, and, most importantly, Thomas Aquinas.[6] At the beginning of the sixteenth century, however, Amalarius also found influential opponents. Claude de Vert (1645–1708) was among those who feared that a *playful* understanding of the Mass would promote paganism and idolatry. In his treatise *Explication simple, littérale et historique des cérémonies de l'Église pour l'instruction des nouveaux convertis* (Dogmatic, literal, and historical explanation of the ceremonies of the church for the new converts, 1706), he proposes a purely historical and literal understanding of the liturgy.

In Spain, Amalarius's dramatic interpretation was well received, and Castilian poet Gonzalo de Berceo established a correspondence between his poem, "Del Sacrificio de la misa" (On the sacrifice of the mass, ca. 1236–1246), and Amalarius's ideas. Gonzalo de Berceo's poem is, indeed, the first work in a vernacular language that explains each part of the liturgy in purely theatrical terms.[7] The text resembles a stage director's notebook wherein the poet systematically elucidates the symbolism of each of the celebrants' representative actions, their gestures, their voice inflections, their vestments, and even the orchestrated participation of the congregation. Following a similar reading of the Mass, churches in the Peninsula implemented ritual variations adapted to meet the specific needs of each of their communities. Preachers embodied this melodramatic religiosity in their oratory practices with the aid of visual props such as crucifixes, skulls, and bones, as well as special effects (e.g., incense and candlelight) that heightened the theatrical atmosphere of these revamped liturgical celebrations.

Toward the Holy Puppet

The longing for a sensorial encounter with the sacred, especially with a Christ in human form, continued to develop from the late Middle Ages onward through creative avenues that enhanced a certain fictionality and playfulness. Baby Jesus dolls, for example, allowed nuns to reenact evangelical scenes and "open up the way to God" within limits acceptable to their confessors (Klapisch-Zuber 311, 327). Some meditation handbooks at the time encouraged these interactions, and, as historical records have revealed, some of the sisters even had visions of these dolls coming alive (Moshenska 47).[8] From a more theologically grounded perspective, Saint Anselm of Canterbury (ca.1033–1109) and Saint Bernard of Clairvaux (1090–1153) were the first Christian thinkers to write about the Passion of Christ while stressing his human nature, a perception that Holy Week celebrations carry on and materialize with their theatrical floats.

On Good Friday during the Passion, Christ is unnailed from the cross and placed in an urn as a sign of his burial (*Depositio Sepulchri*). That same day, the three Marys visit Jesus's tomb (*Visitatio Sepulchri*). On Easter Sunday, before matins, the crucified body of Christ disappears from the sepulcher to rise again, glorified, at God's right hand at the main altar (*Elevatio Crucis*). Throughout this highly spectacular sequence of events, Christ's tangible presence becomes essential in providing an edifying experience of the mystery of salvation. The jointed Christ figure is the ultimate prop to infuse these ceremonial scenes with a realistic dramatism. But, before delving into the exact mechanisms of such holy puppets, I want to point out other symbolic objects that were also representative of the body of Christ in the hands of the celebrants, which, somehow, help us understand the development toward the visual and ideological impact of the *Cristo articulado*.

The Host, the cross, or a combination of both sacred props were used as material synecdoches in the liturgy and in other devotional practices in accordance with the doctrine of concomitance, which grew to be a way of thinking about the indivisible presence of Christ.[9] Bynum explains:

> Often thought to have developed as a rationalization for withdrawing the chalice from the laity, the doctrine was in fact older than this practice. Formulated in the eucharistic disputes of the eleventh century as a defense against literalist claims that Christ, really present in the consecrated host, was broken and digested, the doctrine meant not only that Christ's blood was fully present in the consecrated wafer but also that the Christ present in the sacrifice of the mass was the Christ of the resurrection, "invisible, impassible, indivisible." (*Christian Materiality* 22)

Celebrants created micro mise-en-scènes around these props to enhance their vivid humanity from the pulpit. Dominican historian Alberto Castellani (ca. 1459–1552) records in his *Liber sacerdotalis* (Priests' handbook, 1523) how priests would display the Host using a bier or a canopy (K. Young 129–30). Similarly, in the rites in which the cross was exhibited, the priest swathed it in a linen shroud and subsequently took it to the sepulcher. For theater historian Karl Young, the cross was better suited than the Host to represent the dead and the burial of Christ. Yet, during the raising, when both props were presented together, the scene gained enormous visual effectiveness (132).

The Depositio-Elevatio commemorated at the Abbey Church of Durham in the sixteenth century displayed the cross in quite a spectacular way. According to an anonymous compilation from 1593, a painted Virgin opened as a diptych containing an image of Christ from which a crucifix could be detached. The multiple folds of such an articulated display of religious wonder follow the craft of sixteenth-century prayer beads and miniature altarpieces that fit in the palm of one's hand and, when opened, reveal complex biblical scenes carved with extreme precision and artistry. Young cites the original text that describes the Durham ceremony, which I transcribe below, as it illustrates a unique *mise en abyme* of the lively presence of the cross that lures the faithful to participate in both a literal and symbolic search for spiritual depth:

> Over a certain altar in the "south alley of the lantern" was a merveylous lyvelye and bewtifull Immage of the picture of our ladie, socalled the Lady of Boultone, whiche picture was maide to open with gymmers from her breaste downdward. And within the said Immage was wrowghte and pictured the Immage of our Saviour, merveylouse fynlie gilted, houldinge vppe his handes, and holding betwixt his handes a fair and large Crucifix of Christ, all of gold, the whiche Crucifix was to be taiken fourthe euery Good Fridaie, and eueryman did crepe vnto it that was in that churche as that daye. And ther after ytwas houng vpe againe within the said Immage. (139)

Similarly, the *Regularis Concordia* (ca. 970), a foundational document of the English Monastic Reform, compiled by Æthelwold, Bishop of Winchester (ca. 909–984), illustrates another highly creative manipulation of the cross. In this case, the cross is endowed with a voice, an act of ventriloquism that fully turns it into a puppet.[10] Debra Hilborn explains: "The cross is made to sing Christ's words, and the congregation is able to hear him from the cross, beginning the conflation of Christ with the cross that will play out even more forcefully in the *Depositio Crucis*" (170).[11] Such a particular sound effect has a literary precedent in "The Dream of the Rood" (anonymous, 10th c.), one of the oldest Christian poems in Anglo-Saxon literature, wherein the narrator, during a dream-vision, talks with the cross on which Jesus was crucified. In its speech, the cross alternates between the pronouns *me* and *us* as evidence of its identification with the body of Christ during the Crucifixion.

Even though all of the stagings described up to this point share in a meticulous handling of the sacred props by the celebrants, their *synecdochal objectiveness* could not do proper justice to the holistic corporeal magnificence and spiritual challenge of Christ's death and resurrection. We could, therefore, argue that the *Cristo articulado*, conceptually more complex than the Host or the cross and visually more engaging, mediates a deeper relationship of the devotee with God.

Piety and play overlap with the jointed Christ figures in an organic manner, almost as if they were made to complement each other. We find that the jointed Christ has a dual artistic and spiritual functionality.

For most of the year, the humanized wood carving remains on display in the church either crucified behind the altar or reclining in a glass urn until Good Friday when the Depositio ceremony begins. The figure has basic articulation systems in the arms that move the limbs up and down, and, in some cases, it may have artificial joints in the neck, the pelvis, and the knees. Movement can be implemented in several ways. Ruth Fernández González has identified up to seven possible articulation systems:

1. metal hinges
2. "articulación de galleta" (pin joint)[12]
3. "articulación de galleta metálica" (metal pin joint)
4. metal kneecaps
5. "sistema de fosa y bola" (pit and ball system)
6. internal rubber system
7. "bisagras axilares" (axillary hinges; 28–56).

During the Depositio and the Elevatio, the presence of Christ's body—and its subsequent absence—corresponds to the physical martyrdom of Crucifixion and the miracle of the Resurrection. Such representations when mediated by the jointed figure provide a comprehensive visual rhetoric and an analytical link between the humanity and the holiness of the redeemer. On the one hand, most of these wood carvings openly exhibited their artificial joints. This aesthetic feature made them "both like and unlike living bodies" (Moshenska 74). On the other hand, during the Descent reenactment, the articulated Christ required a visible operator, whose participation as part of the scene contributed to the estrangement effect. Thus, while contemplating the movable crucifix, the devout had to willingly suspend their disbelief as they were reminded at all times of the artificial nature of the figure through its visible jointedness and the priest's manipulation.[13]

From the twelfth century on, devotion came to be directed toward a more human God, but, ironic as it might seem, the exaltation of the anthropomorphism that emanates from these figures highlighted Christ's holiness (Rublack 37). Antonio Iturbe Sáiz has rightly observed:

"It was not merely a question of worshipping a holy Christ, but rather of finding a way for Christ himself to become the actual embodiment of a sacred representation" (689). The wood carvings' lack of *anima* preserved the essence of the holy in its purest form, just as classicist Jean-Pierre Vernant states: "In the context of religious thought, every form of figuration must introduce an inevitable tension: the idea is to establish real contact with the world beyond, to actualize it, to make it present, and thereby to participate intimately in the divine, yet by the same move, it must also emphasize what is inaccessible and mysterious in divinity, its alien quality, its otherness" (153).[14] The jointed Christ figure moves, according to Vernant, insofar as it invokes the human and the holy by appealing to the faithful because of its approachability without compromising its ability to inspire reverence. For these reasons, art historian Kamil Kopania, theater scholars Juan J. Barreiro and Marcela Guijosa, and literary critic Joe Moshenska, among others, have drawn strong parallels between the jointed Christ figure and the puppet. Such correlation implies a perception of devotion both as a communal rite and an intimate imaginative experience.

Handling the Descent

During the Depositio rite, two deacons embodying the roles of Joseph of Arimathea and Nicodemus act as puppeteers as they remove the nails from the cross of the crucified Christ. At this precise moment, the jointed arms of the figure drop down from inertia. Lowering the arms could be considered a very basic theatrical artifice, but its visual impact elevates the humanity of the wood carving while heightening the expectations of the lay faithful by foreshadowing the resurrection of the Redeemer. Plato (ca. 428–347 BCE) and Aristotle (384–322 BCE) saw the puppet as a "pure line of movement," in Chiara Cappelletto's words (327), and the dropping of the arms in this precise instance comes to illustrate motion at its barest.

Accordingly, religious objects in late medieval times were considered "vibrantly active stuff" (Bynum, "Notes" 12), capable of manifesting divine agency. The articulated Christs persisted in this context as *lively*

FIGURE 0.1. John Derian Company store shop window, East Village, New York, 2015. Photograph by and courtesy of Esther Fernández.

FIGURE I.1. Contemporary reproduction model of a *retablo mecánico*. Photograph by Jesús Caballero, courtesy of La Máquina Real.

FIGURE 1.2. Animated nativity of *Belén de Nuestra Señora de los Reyes de Laguardia*, Álava (Spain). Photograph by and courtesy of Jesús Martínez Atienza.

FIGURE 1.3. The *Tarasca*, Alcázar de San Juan, Ciudad Real (Spain), 2019. Photograph by Jesús Caballero, courtesy of La Máquina Real.

FIGURE 1.4. *Gigantes y cabezudos*, Alcázar de San Juan, Ciudad Real (Spain), 2019. Photograph by Jesús Caballero, courtesy of La Máquina Real.

FIGURES 1.5-1.6. Contemporary reproduction model of a *Tutilimundi*. Photograph by Jesús Caballero, courtesy of La Máquina Real.

FIGURE 1.7. Contemporary reproduction model of a *Tutilimundi*. Photograph by Jesús Caballero, courtesy of La Máquina Real.

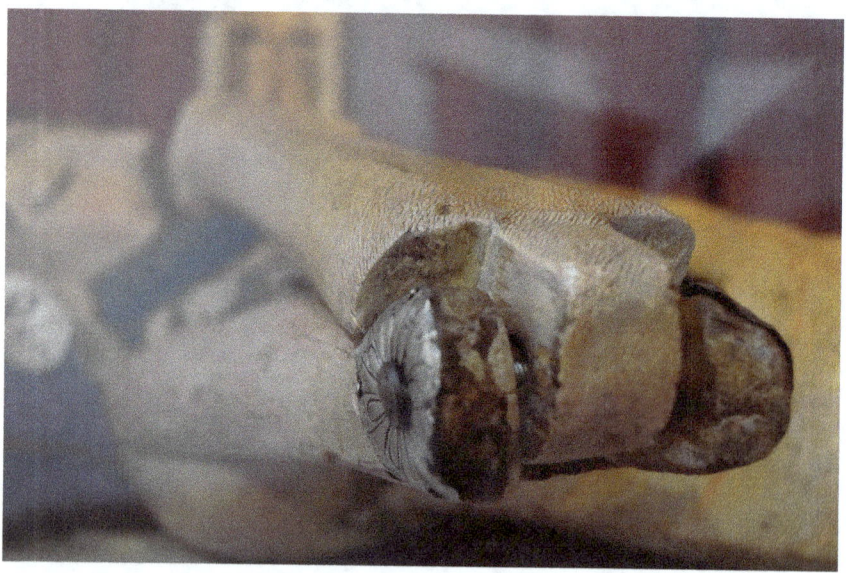

FIGURE 2.1. Articulations in elbows using metallic hinges. *Cristo de los Gascones*. Iglesia de los Santos Justo y Pastor, Segovia (Spain). Photograph by and courtesy of Javier Manrique González.

FIGURE 2.2. *La función del desenclavo* by "El mudo Neira" (1722). Oil on canvas. 194 × 194 cm / 76 × 76 in. Monasterio of Santa María Magdalena, Medina del Campo (Spain). Photograph by and courtesy of Antonio Sánchez del Barrio (Fundación Museo de las Ferias, Medina del Campo).

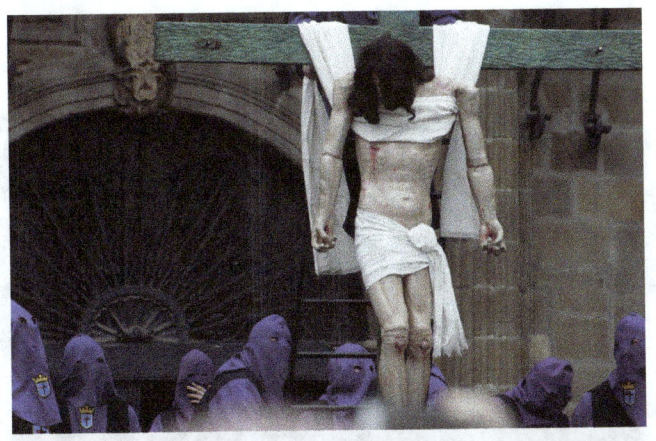

FIGURES 2.3–2.8 Contemporary *Depositio* ceremony in Astorga, León (Spain). Photographs by and courtesy of Emilio Pedro Gómez.

FIGURE 2.9 Contemporary *Depositio* ceremony in Astorga, León (Spain). Photograph by and courtesy of Emilio Pedro Gómez.

matter because of the devotional, creative, and even critical engagement they promoted among the faithful. Peter Dent has argued: "Viewers approached images of the crucified Christ with an expectation of dialogue operating at various levels. Even approaching such objects with the focused attention of the art historian rather than the devotee, the changing intensity of the formal address allows us to hear elements of this dialogue on our journey around and through the sculpture" (80). Even though the Descent implied a very basic gesture, its expressivity within the ritualistic context where it happens was ample enough to invite the congregants to interpret its significance, paralleling the puppet's unique ability to conflate "materiality and imagination" (Cohen, "Puppetry" 123).

Although Jesus died on the cross, the minimal action of the figure dropping its arms is what makes it come alive, prefiguring the miracle of the Resurrection. William Egginton argues that doctrinal truths "are best expressed in simple, stylized forms, because more complex forms ... will tend to obscure symbolic meaning behind the allure of the forms themselves, encouraging the spectator to ask 'what happens next?' as opposed to the proper pedagogical question, '*what does it mean?*'" (*How the World Became a Stage* 50–51; my emphasis). Therefore, the bare staging of the Descent exemplifies Egginton's idea, and it may even be the reason why the Depositio rite never developed into a dramatic dialogue, unlike the Visitatio and the Elevatio, as the actual scene takes place on a purely spiritual and imaginative level and does not require a direct exchange of words to enhance its meaning for the devotee.[15]

The oldest known account in Europe of a Depositio ceremony featuring a jointed Christ is the Ordo, held at the convent of Benedictine nuns at Barking, Essex, in 1370. During this rite, the Christ figure was detached from the cross and lowered by two clerics who then washed the painted wounds on the wood carving before placing it in the Holy Sepulcher (K. Young 166).[16] Such an act of tending emphasized the theatricality of the ceremony as a whole; this was also the case in the Depositio described by the Ordo of Prüfening Abbey (ca. 1489) in Bavaria, where the laity were invited to participate and take part in the rite (Fernández González 8).

Although written accounts of these ceremonies are scarce, there is a considerable number of jointed Christ sculptures from the thirteenth to the fifteenth centuries that have survived throughout Europe.[17] Kopania has catalogued sixty-four jointed Christs from this period in Italy; nineteen in Germany; sixteen in Spain; twelve in Austria; three in Switzerland; two each in Portugal, the Czech Republic, Poland, and France; and one in Norway (38–43). Most of these sculptures conform to a general set of aesthetic norms, but they also can be categorized according to the mechanisms by which they are built, namely 1) sculptures with articulated arms and elbows (see Figure 2.1); 2) figures with movable heads and tongues; and 3) those with a wider range of motions in their heads, tongues, arms, and legs (Kopania 240).[18]

Among the sixteen extant statues on the Iberian Peninsula, the five dating from the 1200s are in Segovia, Aguilar de Campóo, Liria, Lugo, and Toro; the five from the fourteenth century are located in Burgos, Orense, Palma de Mallorca, Tui, and Villalcampo; and the six from the fifteenth century are in Arrabal de Portillo, Castillo de Lebrija, Esguevillas de Esgueva, Fisterra, Palencia, and Vilabade. While these wood carvings are numerous in Spain, historical records alluding to local Depositio ceremonies are much scarcer, and most of the ones we know of trace the rite to the end of the seventeenth century. The "Hordenanzas y constituciones de la Santa Cofradía de la Virgen de la Soledad" (Ordinances and constitutions of the holy confraternity of the Virgin of Solitude, 1672), for example, alludes to a Depositio that took place in the Church of San Martiño de Moaña in Pontevedra (Galicia), where the figure was placed in a real sepulcher that would be displayed later in the burial procession.[19]

Uniquely, another historical record that sheds light on the performative aspects of these ceremonies is the floorplan from 1691 for the *Devallament de la creu* (Descent from the Cross) at the Cathedral of Santa María de Palma in Majorca. This Depositio required the use of various simultaneous stages, similar to *tableaux vivants* (living pictures), which transformed the whole church into an all-encompassing stage. Francesc Massip Bonnet has researched the particulars of this specific ceremony as he details in the following:

> The choir of the cathedral community who, as was usually the case in the Iberian and Italian peninsulas, was placed at the center of the nave . . ., from whose eastern door a passageway leads to the stage that is situated above the stairs to the presbytery and in front of the high altar. A platform represents Mount Calvary where there is a Crucifix with a jointed Christ figure on the verge of descending that will shortly be lowered. Another passageway intersects the first and leads to two other platforms: to the right is Pilate's Court, to the left a group of singers who provide voice accompaniment for the presentation. In the longitudinal passageway Saint Peter mourns, his voice seemingly emanating from the choir; in the transverse passageway, on the left, the Marias and Saint John mourn, and on the right side, Joseph of Arimathea and Nicodemus, together with the singers, approach Pilate to request permission to bury the body of Jesus. (64)

The spectacular nature of these rites led conservative religious authorities to issue edicts of prohibition in the eighteenth century that gradually made the Depositio disappear altogether.

In the absence of other historical sources, these legal documents provide us with a valuable record for elucidating what was considered particularly threatening in the staging of these ceremonies. Fray Diego Martín y Rodríguez (1720–1789), the bishop of Coria, wrote an illuminating edict regarding the Depositio that took place in his diocese in the province of Cáceres throughout the 1700s. I have transcribed an excerpt that I consider illuminating, as it places heavy emphasis upon the theatrical nature of the rite, indicated by the carefully chosen parlance for its description:

> Some engage in licentious stares, others in idle talk, others raise their harsh voices and still others shed sighs and real tears, like raindrops in a storm, then pass through the soil of the heart without dampening or fertilizing it, and as they are mechanically pulled from the eyes by the *power of artifice* and *Externalities*, so are hard hammer blows to pull the nails from the Dead Body of the Lord from the

fly system (as it should be called). Which is used in some villages for *raising and lowering with a rope the hands of the image* of Our Lady of Solitude to dry the eyes and Receive the crown and the nails from the assistant priests and *other inventions* that are disrespectful of the seriousness with which this tender event should be celebrated. (qtd. in Domínguez Moreno 151; my emphasis)[20]

Apart from their predictable dose of moral criticism, Martín y Rodríguez's words shed light on a full-fledged performance around the jointed Christ figure. Thus, beyond such graphic written accounts, the most valuable testimony available for understanding the role of the *Cristo articulado* in Spanish Depositio rites is the painting *La función del desenclavo* (The act of the descent from the cross, 1722) by a local artist known as "El mudo Neira" (Neira the Mute), whose true identity remains unknown (see Figure 2.2).

Western iconography has a long tradition of depicting the Descent. Although there are slight variations in how Christ is lowered and the figures involved in the setting, all paintings of the Depositio portray Christ as a naturalistic human figure.[21] *La función* is unique insofar as it is the only representation we know of that features an articulated wood carving with visible joints as the protagonist of the scene. As the word *función* (act, staging, performance) in the title indicates, the painting focuses exclusively on the performative aspects of the ceremony that took place in the no longer extant Augustinian convent of Nuestra Señora de Gracia in Medina del Campo (Valladolid).[22] The canvas portrays a preacher delivering the "Sermon of the Descent" and two clerics on ladders in the act of removing the nails from the crucifix at the precise moment when the figure's right arm drops.[23] Unlike other famous iterations of the Descent by Rogier van der Weyden (*Descent of Christ from the Cross*, ca. 1435) or Peter Paul Rubens (*The Descent from the Cross*, 1612–1614), which portray the characters in the scene engaged in a groundswell of motions and emotions, *La función* converges all of its action on the unnailed arm of Christ and on the Virgin, also depicted as a mechanical figure. For Antonio Sánchez del Barrio, this canvas should be understood as a photographic testimony of these ceremonies (21), even though it ironically belongs to the eighteenth century, a period when such rites began to fall into disuse in the Peninsula.

Later, in the nineteenth century, many local Depositio ceremonies would disappear altogether. Allegations that animated sculptures abused the credulity of the faithful and moved them to mockery rather than to devotion was the primary cause for their prohibition and neglect. Nonetheless, when we look closely at the dynamics of these rituals, these judgements seem to misunderstand the point of the animated figures' contributions to Christian faith, since the interaction they triggered in the faithful was one of reflective devotion rather than delusional piety.

We will have to wait until the twentieth century for these rites to be revived as an essential component of regional Holy Week commemorations in Spain.[24] The Depositio ceremonies still have an enormous sentimental and traditional value for the local communities that have reclaimed them today. Nevertheless, the complex representational and spiritual roles they once played when they first came into use have been reoriented toward upholding folkloric traditions that blend religious beliefs with popular culture and festive celebrations (see Figures 2.3 to 2.9).[25]

The Jointed Christ Figure Reimagined

We may argue that, for better or worse, the jointed Christ recovered its original ceremonial complexity on the contemporary stage, particularly in the way it articulates the earthly and the heavenly. Ana Zamora, one of the most prominent Spanish directors, has embarked on the herculean task of rethinking and adapting the Depositio-Elevatio rite for modern-day theater audiences.[26] Her *Misterio del Cristo de los Gascones* has become the signature production of her company, Nao D'amores. Since the play's premiere in 2007, it has not stopped touring, receiving prestigious awards and wide critical acclaim in Spain and abroad (see Figure 2.10). The success of her unique production marks a milestone in the history of Spanish theater and performance precisely because of the way the director connects the humanness and emotional expressivity of the life and Passion of Christ to the heterogeneous twenty-first-century viewer who is disconnected from the theological historical baggage of these rites.

Zamora embraces the theatrical event in the same terms that Marvin Carlson has described it, as a global sociocultural artistic gathering, "whose meanings and interpretations are not to be sought exclusively in the text being performed but in the experience of the audience assembled to share in the creation of the total event" (20). As Zamora has mentioned in various interviews, her artistic mission with *Misterio* is "to make theater for the present day, to move contemporary audiences with texts from centuries ago" (qtd. in García Garzón 25). While this creative aspiration could be the goal for almost any other theater company dedicated to the staging of classical theater, with Nao D'amores, it is a much more complex and daring endeavor, as most of its repertoire expressly belongs to the pre-baroque era, and the majority of the plays tend to be unknown to the general public.[27]

Zamora's *Misterio* rescues the tradition of mystery plays deeply rooted in Catholicism and puts it to the test on the contemporary stage. Her production, whose title and theme might seem exclusivist at face value for their explicit religiosity, turns out to be universally inclusive, thanks to the way she conceives of her protagonist. On this, the director notes:

> Christ continues to be a figure that can be analyzed and reinterpreted from different points of view. We have reviewed the philological and anthropological aspects ... but also the modern referents, from Bill Viola's installations to the story Pasolini tells in his film, *The Gospel According to Matthew*. They are all different ways of viewing the figure of Christ. The vision of Nao D'amores unites them all and maintains a relation with the quest for a very human Christ, a puppet of destiny with regards to the material and the spiritual, a classical hero who discovers, like any other person, that in the end he will die. (qtd. in Macho)

As we have explored in previous sections, the jointed Christ artistically and spiritually bridges the human and the holy nature of Jesus by creating a devotional and theatrical space conducive to active and imaginative meditation for the faithful.

Zamora takes advantage of the nuanced expressiveness of the articulated wood carving to maintain the ceremonial essence of the Christ figure. Through meticulous manipulation, she highlights its most dramatic and human side without diverging into either demystification or irreverence. To achieve this subtle equilibrium between the human playfulness and magnificent rituality that runs through the play, the director makes sure that in every aspect of the production—from the dramaturgy to the actual performance—the audience can find something with which to relate, while, at the same time, sensing an elusive and reverential distance.

Zamora opted to premiere the play at the Romanesque Church of Los Santos Justo y Pastor in Segovia where the historical jointed Christ figure is currently housed. After performing before local audiences as an homage to her hometown, she deliberately chose the Abadía Theater for the commercial opening in Madrid. This iconic urban venue was previously the Church of La Sagrada Familia, closed to worship in 1977 and desacralized in 1990 to be converted into a commercial theater that, nevertheless, retained the original building's structure.[28] Such space and stage generate an intimate bond among the audience members, similar to what would be expected from a ceremonial experience.

Always driven by personal experience in her creative processes, the director found in her native Segovia the protagonist for *Misterio*: the oldest extant Romanesque jointed Christ figure in Spain, known as the Cristo de los Gascones (Christ of the Gascons; see Figure 2.11).[29] Like most Cristos articulados, this figure's legendary origins have been passed down by generations of locals, a process that has furthered its holy and fabled nature. In a peculiar book dedicated to the history of the streets of Segovia, Mariano Romero relays the following folktale: "It seems that on the Franco-Spanish border, two villages disputed the ownership of the Holy Christ figure, and they decided to carry the image on a mare, allowing the animal to walk freely along the road, whereupon the horse arrived at the doorway of this church where it dropped the Christ figure and then fell down dead, the common belief being that it was, somewhere, buried in the entranceway" (Sáez y Romero 164).

In addition, Garci Ruiz de Castro points to an isolated annotation from the *Comentario sobre la primera y segunda población de Segovia* (Comments on the first and second populations of Segovia, 1551) that refers to the role that the Christ played during sixteenth-century Holy Week festivities: "In this city [Segovia] there is a street named Cal de Gascos. This street was populated by Gascons and that is how it earned its name. They were *obliged* to perform the Passion of Our Lord *every year*" (qtd. in Ruiz de Castro 7; my emphasis).[30]

Based on this sole reference, the director recreates an entire plot inspired by the life of Jesus and some of the episodes from the Passion. The dramatic script is a collage of literary excerpts drawn from Spanish lyrical and dramatic religious works dating from the fifteenth century. Among these sources are *Lamentaciones fechas para la Semana Santa* (Lamentations for Holy Week, ca. 1476) and *Representación del nacimiento de Nuestro Señor* (Representation of the birth of our Lord, ca. 1476), both written by Gómez Manrique; Alonso del Campo's *Auto de la Pasión* (Passion play, 1486–1499); Diego de San Pedro's *Pasión trobada* (The Passion sung by troubadours, ca. 1480) and *Las siete angustias de Nuestra Señora* (The seven lamentations of Our Lady, 1481); and Fray Íñigo de Mendoza's *Coplas de Vita Christi* (Verses on the Life of Christ, ca. 1483) and *Varias obras religiosas* (Various religious plays, 15th c.).

The circular storyline opens with Mary grieving over the death of her son and then shifts to a flashback of Jesus's life that begins with his birth and ends with his resurrection. The *Planctus Mariae* (Lament of Mary) functions as the lyrical and dramatic motif that runs as a litany through the entire story—"Oh, what a sorrow, what a sorrow, / for my son and my Lord! / Oh, what a sorrow."[31] These words link the different scenes while stimulating the audience's participation. Mary acts as a Brechtian narrator who interrupts the plot to denounce the injustices suffered by her son. This technique, however, should not be interpreted as an anachronistic theatrical *tour de force*; rather, it is a defining feature of medieval mystery plays that inspired Bertolt Brecht (1898–1956) to develop his concept of epic theater in the early twenty-century (Elliott

142–43).[32] The continuous and simultaneous references to her *son* and her *Lord* remind the audiences at all times of the twofold nature of Christ while establishing a critical distance vis-à-vis the dramatic narrative (see Figure 2.12).

The set follows the same circularity of the narrative and reproduces a cosmic sphere on the ground as a symbol of holiness.[33] Lighted candles encircle the stage, each 'illuminating' a different scene in the life of Jesus, similar to a *via crucis* but broadened to include other episodes from his human existence before the Passion, as illustrated in the following outline of the play's dramaturgy:

ACT 1   Scene 1.1. Presentation
        Scene 1.2. Arrival of Christ to the Church
        Scene 1.3. Lament of the Virgin
        Scene 1.4. Birth

ACT 2   Scene 2.1. Baptism. First Anguish
        Scene 2.2. Beginning of the Journey: Christ as Teacher. Second Anguish
        Scene 2.3. Temptations: Mary Magdalene. Third Anguish
        Scene 2.4. Public Life and Entry into Jerusalem. Fourth Anguish
        Scene 2.5. Last Supper. Fifth Anguish
        Scene 2.6. Kiss of Judas. Sixth Anguish
        Scene 2.7. Denial of Peter. Seventh Anguish

ACT 3   Scene 3.1. Way to Calvary
        Scene 3.2. Crucifixion, Descent, and Lamentation

Scene 3.3 Resurrection
Scene 3.4. Ascension
Scene 3.5. Epilogue

These scenes are strung together through the literal and symbolic circular bond that absorbs and intensifies the Christ-puppet's sacred presence and essence.

Likewise for the repetition of the *Planctus Mariae* and the encompassing scenography, the music, which is curated by Alicia Lázaro, the company's musical director, operates as another unifying force in the overall production. Liturgical scores from Renaissance songbooks such as the *Pasionario toledano* (The Toledo Passion songbook), *Cancionero de Segovia* (The Segovia songbook), and *Cancionero de Palacio* (The Palacio songbook) run through the scenes as organic extensions of the plot. While the score is performed by live musicians, these artists also have ancillary acting parts in the play. Their twofold role intuitively weaves the ritualistic and revered musical aura of the mystery into the narrative fabric (see Figure 2.13).

But, the puppet-Christ is the *pièce de résistance* of the overall production and Zamora's primary artistic avenue to approach religiosity without falling into dogmatism. To this end, the director explains: "Faced with a kind of theater that is not regulated by rigid realist paradigms, nor concerned with anachronisms, we chose puppet theater as an option that combines all the possible improbabilities" ("Una travesía" 15). Specifically, Zamora features a life-size replica of the Cristo de los Gascones with a wider range of hinging mechanisms than those used in the original thirteenth-century wood carving. On the one hand, the improved articulation system allows for broader expressivity and range of motion for the marionette onstage, which engenders a deeply human vision, particularly in the most iconic moments of Jesus's life, e.g., entry into Jerusalem, the Last Supper, the Kiss of Judas, and Peter's Denial (see Figure 2.14). In some of these scenes, the puppet-Christ appears as a hero in an all-too-human drama in which there is still room for subtle humor. At other times, in moments of greater theological solemnity, the marionette preserves a more traditional hieratic presence of the Christ figure.

Following Rudolph Arnheim's theories on perception and visual art, this lively jointed Christ radiates an omnipresence that fills the stage with its human and holy essence at all times: "The sculpture exceeds the limits of its material body. The surrounding space, rather than allowing itself to be passively displaced by the figure, adopts an active role; it invades the body and takes power over the surfaces that form the shape of the concave units" (270). The director experienced firsthand the puppet's compelling in-betweenness in her home, as Nuria Barrios describes in a delightful anecdote:

> Ana Zamora has not forgotten the first night she contemplated the Cristo de los Gascones laid out on the spare bed in her Madrid house. It had his feet gently bent to conform to the twin bed. Certainly, that afternoon Ana and her company, Nao D'amores, had rehearsed *Misterio del Cristo de los Gascones*, a theatrical jewel whose main character is Christ. It is also certain that the guest, and actor, was just a replica of the Romanesque woodcarving that is venerated in the Church of San Justo in Segovia. Thus, it was not a miracle, but the copy was so exact and the night was so dark that Ana felt a mixture of awe and laughter. (Barrios)

The manipulation of the puppet's gaze throughout the performance contributes to this well-conjugated duality. The way in which it opens and closes its eyes over the course of the play reinforces its liminal nature, moving between a joyful human spontaneity when it dances, plays instruments, jokes, or wows the public and a hieratic presence when it closes its eyes as a sign of meditation and transcendence (see Figure 2.15).[34]

The all-pervading tension between the Christ protagonist's human and holy presence onstage is further explored in the way the actor-puppeteers handle the figure. They all move in full view of the audience using techniques inspired by traditional Japanese Bunraku. The veil that covers the actor's face is similar to the hood used by *kurokos*, the puppet manipulators in Bunraku and even, I claim, shares certain features with the headpiece worn by penitents of Franciscan brotherhoods during

Holy Week processions in Spain. By concealing their human features, the bearers of sacred images embrace a theomorphic presence to stress the anthropomorphism of the figure they manipulate (Webster 165).

Zamora presents an analogous objective. Her *Misterio* inspires modern-day spectators to explore the multiple articulations between the human and the holy, thus revitalizing the collective experiential nature of medieval mysteries. Like the Depositio rite, whose lack of an established dialogue allowed the faithful to interact imaginatively with the jointed wood carving, this contemporary neo-mystery motivates audiences to engage critically and spiritually with the play to find their own message based on their own personal beliefs and horizon of expectations. And, according to Zamora, many have succeeded: "The truth is, I've seen atheists get more excited than believers. The spectator discovers a work that does not provide answers to universal questions but does stir up all that we have failed to resolve, and it causes us to reflect in a more ritualistic than Christian way" (qtd. in Macho).

I had the opportunity to experience firsthand a poignant and unique episode that illustrates this profound personal involvement of the audience at one of the performances of the *Misterio* at the annual International Golden Age Drama Festival at the Chamizal in El Paso, Texas, in 2013. During the post-production question-and-answer session with the director and the actors, a local woman stood up in the five-hundred-seat auditorium and avowed that even though she could not understand all the dialogue in old Spanish, she deeply empathized with the Virgin's expressions of pain as she mourned the death of her son. The woman further explained that she could identify with the same grief many mothers in Mexico's Ciudad Juárez have experienced upon losing their own sons and daughters during the period of rampant violence the city was then experiencing because of drug cartels. If in the past the animated wood carvings stirred imaginative devotion toward an understanding of Christ's sacrifices and holiness, on the contemporary stage these props appear to connect with our own humanity, as puppets, in general, "measure the size of the souls" (Gross, "Love" 82).

Errol King's review of the same 2013 performance of *Misterio* at the Chamizal similarly stresses the overwhelming effect that Zamora's protagonist had on the audience. He explains:

> In a session at the Association for Hispanic Classical Theater (AHCT) Symposium the day after the performance, one Golden Age Scholar exclaimed that the public had viewed a play that, following conventional wisdom, should not have connected with its audience, but [it] did. In more than twenty-five years as an employee at the Chamizal National Memorial, one park ranger indicated that he had never seen so many audience members remain in their seats for a question-and-answer session with a theater troupe. (172)

Such testimonies reveal how the jointed Christ on the modern stage has retained its original function as an artistic and conceptual link between the personal experiences and social realities of a present-day global audience and the figure's innate sacredness. While most spectators nowadays do not look to strengthen their religious faith inside a commercial theater auditorium, they are open to engaging with questions loaded with theological and philosophical implications—sin and punishment, life and death, sacrifice and immortality, and so on—especially when presented through an eclectic, innovative performance that highlights the mixed company of human and nonhuman actors.

Could the *Misterio* be the "Holy Theatre" that Peter Brook aspired to in *The Empty Space* (1968), as an almost unattainable experience? Could Zamora have successfully staged a ritualistic experience capable of filling the soul of the contemporary theatergoer, no matter their religious or cultural background? In the twenty-first century, traditional religious imagery still retains certain characteristics of its original devotional purpose, but it also has become a mass phenomenon that reaches far beyond religious celebrations and devotional practices. One example in Spain is the artistic trend that presents the body of Christ devoid of all spirituality, favoring instead its physical beauty in a kind of pseudo-morbid fetishization (Fernández Paradas 325–26). Zamora, for her part, endows Christological imagery with innovative nuances to reimagine an inclusive figure that moves with ease in secular theatrical contexts but without falling into easy desacralization at any point during the performance. The director expands the function of the articulated Christ sculptures and projects this neo-mystery beyond its original performative and devotional parameters. In addition, her artistic finesse in handling the holy puppet resides in the way she conceals the seams of time beneath a rigorous creativity, allowing the figure to operate its own original solemnity on modern-day spectators. Therefore, Christiane Klapisch-Zuber's argument regarding early modern women playing with baby Jesus dolls and breaking the divide between reality and figuration can be applied aptly to Zamora's Christ protagonist: "When we play, there is always an image involved, and if the game is played to the limit it is the image that ends up manipulating us" (329).

In *Travels in Hyperreality* (1986), Umberto Eco states that materiality and materialism in Western culture mediate our modern conception of God with a number of values tied to capitalism and a rampant egocentricity. Eco notes:

> If you follow the Sunday morning religious programs on TV you come to understand that God can be experienced only as nature, flesh, energy, tangible image. And since no preacher dares show us God in the form of a bearded dummy, or as a Disneyland robot, God can only be found in the form of natural force, joy, healing, youth, health, economic increment (which, let Max Weber teach us, is at once the essence of the Protestant ethic and of the spirit of capitalism). (53)

Although Eco argues that a so-called bearded dummy cannot invoke transcendence in the modern era, Zamora seems to have succeeded in creating a prototype that moves audiences to reconsider the divine through rationalized religiosity and an inclusive aesthetic. Jointed Christ figures can be much more complex dummies, particularly if they are endowed with motion that entices us into interacting with them. Nowadays, articulated religious statuary and sacred puppetry may not fully preserve their original devotional functions and their hieratic physicality, but some contemporary re-appropriations help us reconsider the relationship between the human and the holy.

On the cover of his recent book, *Iconoclasm as a Child's Play* (2019), Moshenska features a 1972 Mattel action figure—actually, a lumberjack—named Josh McBig, who belongs to artists Shelley and Pamela Jackson's hypertext project *The Doll Games* (1970–1976).[35] The Jacksons' theatrical performances (or micro-installations, as I see them) bring new artistic and intellectual use to worn out, broken, apparently trivial vintage dolls. McBig's exaggerated masculine appearance, displaced sacrificial aura—as he is thoroughly displayed in a crucified position—and dramatic brokenness turn him into a ludicrous, suffering modern Christ figure (Moshenska 66).[36] But, McBig's material and symbolic disjointedness is what provides another way to approach the sacred, through the experience of the mundane. Although the *Cristos articulados* are far from falling into McBig's comic pathos, their playfulness and vulnerability have had a definitive impact in their animated performance histories. Devotees over time were able to self-identify and question their relationship to the world at large with, by, and through these animated Christ figures because of their approachable human auras, which swathed their holiness—not the other way around.

3. Articulating Saintliness

> I persist in believing that the appearance of Saint Michael, of Celestial voices, of miraculous flowerings of lilies and roses, and the transfiguration of a martyr are more appropriate to our small stage than to conventional theaters where the personality of the actor, too real and too familiar, destroys all impression of the supernatural.
>
> MAURICE BOUCHOR, *Mystères païens*, ca. 1920

AS DEMONSTRATED IN the previous chapters, puppet-like figures had an established and visible presence in religious rites and exemplary literature in the Peninsula well before early modernity. However, it was during the sixteenth and seventeenth centuries that marionettes began to appear more prominently in works of fiction that emphasized their dramatic and metaphorical attributes. Among the most iconic iterations of puppetry in fiction writing are chapters 25 and 26 of *Don Quijote*, Part 2 (1615), featuring Master Pedro's puppet show, whose suggestive dénouement has become one of the most representative episodes of the novel. Here, the knight is beguiled by the marionettes' magic and attacks them as if they are real people. As a writer, Cervantes seemed most intrigued by the inner workings of puppetry and performance objects, as he noted in some of his works. While in his *Novelas ejemplares* (Exemplary novels, 1613), he does not withhold his criticism of the puppeteer lifestyle, it is in *Don Quijote*—as we shall see in Chapters

4 and 5—where he focuses on the object's potential agency as a generator of experimental performances that advance the artistic, technological, and conceptual ideas of modernity.

Apart from Cervantes's oeuvre, other early modern literary works include specific references to puppetry, such as Francisco López de Úbeda's novel *La pícara Justina* (The rogue Justina, 1605); Bernal Díaz del Castillo's chronicle *La historia verdadera de la conquista de la Nueva España* (The true history of the conquest of New Spain, 1632); Vicente Suárez de Deza y Ávila's *Saynete de los títeres* (Farce of the puppets, 1663); and Juan Ruiz de Alarcón's play *Mudarse por mejorarse* (Moving to better one's status, 1617–1618), considered the first reference in Spanish literature to a puppet show professionally staged in a playhouse (Varey, *Historia* 118).[1] Thus, we will partially set aside fictional contexts in this chapter to focus on expanding the historical scope of religious artificial animation initiated in Chapter 1.

Puppetry and other forms of artificial agency in entertainment contexts achieved a high degree of technical and aesthetic sophistication in certain parts of Europe during the sixteenth and seventeenth centuries. Some artists even put themselves at risk with the Inquisition for their cutting-edge creations. This was the case for Federigo Commandino (1509–1575) and Giovanni Torriani (1500–1585), known in Spain as Juanelo Turriano, both of whom were accused of being necromancers for perfecting their animated artifacts, which bear a resemblance more to the automaton than to the marionette (Boehn 60). Most of the professional puppeteers who traveled through Europe were of Italian origin and, like Commandino and Turriano, some even acquired international fame for their shows. Marionettes with strings, wires, bars, or rods were gradually perfected over time to the point that plays and theater venues were created to meet the specific technical needs of these miniaturized wooden actors.

Beginning in 1580, Naples and Venice develop into specialized artistic centers of puppet theater, and their popularity soon spread to other European cities (McCormick, Cipollo, and Napoli 9–10). The construction of a theater for Italian marionettes in London in 1573 predates the establishment of the first theater for actors in that city by three years, and, as Susan Young notes, Elizabethan dramatist Thomas Dekker (c. 1572–1632) claims to have attended a marionette production of Shakespeare's *Julius Caesar* (1599) before it premiered that same year at the Globe performed by actors. Beginning in 1629, a version of *Hamlet* (c.1599–1601) for puppet theater toured several countries in Europe and received significant international acclaim (9). After these pioneering Shakespearean shows with marionettes, other renditions of the Bard's plays staged with puppets continued to premiere around the world, becoming its own genre.[2] Much of its appeal should be attributed to Shakespeare's conceptualization of wonder, which finds an effective and accessible medium for all audiences in the marionette theater (Garber 40). Nevertheless, the most conservative sectors of society became alarmed by the popularity of these shows that, in their judgement, deluded the spectator without following any moral or spiritual agenda (Boehn 61). As with the jointed Christ figure, animation and delusion, once again, go hand in hand for those moralists who judge artificial agency from a one-sided perspective without considering its conceptual nuances.

In early modern Spain, theater venues that specialized exclusively in plays for marionettes did not catch on in the same way as they did in other parts of Europe. Puppetry and its artistic derivatives were, instead, integrated as an added layer of visual theatricality in a variety of performance practices. Court theater and mythological plays often included optical illusions and extravagant props that gave the impression of being animated. An example was the staging of the *Comedia de Merlín* (Comedy of Merlin), performed in 1629 at the Jardín de los Naranjos (Orange Tree Courtyard) at the Alcázar Palace in Seville.[3] The magical nature of the play called for a series of zoomorphic props such as "a bare dragon painted in silver and gold ... with wire wings," "a large dragonhead eating a woman," "a hollow lion completely covered in fur with claws and head," and "a large fish filled with rice" (Pérez Sánchez 64).[4] Although none of these artificial beasts were fully animated per se, their hyperreal appearance was achieved through carefully chosen materials that made them look alive.

Beyond these auxiliary roles in courtly entertainment and with the exception of the máquina real, puppet theater in Spain was more of an itinerant attraction easily adaptable to any context and preserving its affinity with popular culture. The wandering puppeteer, immortalized in Cervantes's Master Pedro, may have been a professional alternative for conmen who were hard-pressed to creatively survive the economic precariousness of the period. Some puppeteers were associated with gangs of performers and swindlers who were active across Europe until well into the eighteenth century. Barbara Maria Stafford explains:

> Beginning in the seventeenth century an exotic *mélange* of English, French, Spanish, Italian, German and Dutch artists—augmented by the odd Turk, Chinaman and Gypsy—crisscrossed the continent. Jacques Lacombe's *Dictionnaire encyclopédique des amusements* (Encyclopedic dictionary of amusements, 1792) evoked this ambiguous cast of *banquistes* who lived at the expense, and on the edges of, the public they duped. He vividly seized from the perspective of the often-burned eighteenth-century consumer, the dangerously ill-defined and unincorporable outsider character of these cheats. (88–89)

In two of his *Novelas ejemplares*, "El licenciado Vidriera" (The glass graduate) and "El coloquio de los perros" (Dialogue of the dogs), Cervantes develops a vision of puppeteers similar to the one Stafford describes, inherently tied to these traveling artists' picaresque way of life.

In Spain, we will have to wait to the first half of the seventeenth century for puppets to be appropriated for the commercial stage by the *máquina real*. This type of professional company, as I anticipated in the previous chapter, specialized in the staging of *comedias de santos* (hagiographical plays) in the *corrales* (Spanish playhouses), mainly during Lent when other theatrical entertainments were prohibited. The expression *máquina real* appears for the first time in a 1632 contract signed by Miguel Lobregat, owner and director of one of these companies, and actress Beatriz Pereira (Cornejo Vega, "Primeros tiempos" 19).[5] However, the precise origin of the terminology remains uncertain. Francisco Cornejo Vega has come the closest in providing a possible explanation based on the various definitions of the noun *máquina* (machine) and the adjective *real* (royal) found in both Sebastián de Cobarrubias's

Tesoro de la lengua castellana o española (Treasury of Castilian or Spanish language, 1611) and the *Diccionario de autoridades* (Dictionary of authorities, 1726–1739).

As the word *máquina* alluded to complex machinery or an assemblage of pieces systematically organized in a theatrical context at the time, it could refer to the orderly configuration that these companies required to synchronize the fly system, the special effects, and the puppet manipulation in each of their performances. Cervantes seems to be aware of the minuteness behind the theatrical enterprise in general, as he defines it as a "gran máquina" (great machine) in the prologue to his *Ocho comedias y ocho entremeses nuevos nunca representados* (Eight plays and eight new interludes, never performed, 1615).[6]

For the adjective *real*, Cornejo Vega suggests three hypotheses that offer an all-encompassing, viable explanation. The first implication refers to the royal permission that these companies were required to have in order to perform. A second meaning is suggestive of the courtly residences where such puppet shows were in high demand. And, the third hypothesis arises in relation to the new stage designed around 1640 by Italian engineer and scenographer Cosimo Lotti (1571–1643) for the Royal Coliseum of el Buen Retiro in Madrid. The new architectural configuration with a proscenium arch, side wings, and a backdrop could have inspired the design for the máquina real's stage that followed a similar arrangement, only on a smaller scale ("Apuntes" 18–20).

These companies' use of marionettes to perform dramatic hagiographies in early modernity is exceptional not only in Spain but also in the history of Western theater. The máquina real transformed itself into an artistic laboratory of animated saints that presented its audiences with an accessible, yet defamiliarized, approach to the notion of saintliness. In a way, the wooden protagonists follow a religious edifying mission similar to that of the jointed Christ. Insofar as puppets are not realistic, they activate a more critical and creative response toward devotion in the spectator. If the *Cristos articulados* brought the faithful closer to understanding the human and the divine nature of Christ (thanks to their subtle animation), the máquina real gave an animated presence to the invisible and larger-than-life concept of sanctity and displayed a multi-sensory experience around it. Simon Ditchfield has argued that the cult of saints in early modernity was a "synaesthetic experience" that required "a *language* that was visual as well as textual, symbolic and spiritual as well as concrete and literal" (554; my emphasis). If we follow Ditchfield's premise, the máquina real would emerge as the ultimate medium to transmit this holistic experience around sanctity, thanks to the all-encompassing *language of puppetry*.

Just as Zamora recovered the artistic and conceptual function of the jointed Christ figure for the twenty-first-century stage, in 2002, independent scholar and puppeteer Jesús Caballero and his research team began retracing the operation of a máquina real based on available, though scarce, historical documentation. Through a labor of artistic archeology, Caballero succeeded in recuperating this all-but-lost Spanish religious and theatrical tradition. But, what is more important for the purpose of this book is that Caballero's recovery project has also salvaged a fundamental, but forgotten, connection between puppets, animation, and saints at the onset of modernity.

A similar line of inquiry, although from a very different aesthetic, was revisited by British conceptual artist Michael Landy in his exhibition *Saints Alive* (2013). With a series of interactive and kinetic sculptures of saints performing their respective martyrdoms, Landy explores and reaffirms some of the principles intuited by the máquina real four hundred years ago. He and Caballero have revived—each in his own way and with very disparate intentions—an animated culture of saints in the midst of our posthumanist era that contemplates new, wondrous forms of the human through the arts and technological innovations.

Wooden Saints

From the sixteenth century onward, religious theater found a niche in secular society. Private residences, religious processions, Jesuit colleges, and playhouses became stages to display a theology in movement that was at the heart of Spain's early modern popular culture. Moreover, the *comedias de santos*, promoted by the Council of Trent and the Compañía de Jesús (Society of Jesus; Aparicio Maydeu, "La comedia" 22), came to occupy a central role during the Counter-Reformation. These plays were instruments for endorsing Catholic doctrine and bringing the public closer to the experience of Christian wonder during a period that came to be known as the "century of saints" (Morrison 10).

This appellation refers to the Church's desire to determine and regulate holiness through beatification and canonization. Local religious communities wanted to prove that their saints deserved honors while enhancing their communal identity and collective memory (K. Thomas 30).[7] Between the 1400s and 1500s, only two saints were canonized in Spain; however, in the 1600s, twenty-three individuals were beatified, and twenty canonized (García Cárcel 34). In addition, the devotional literature as well as the biblical and hagiographic culture that emerged in the fifteenth century spread through convents and monasteries, undoubtedly contributing to the increasing number of mystics and ascetics (Cantarino 13). Moreover, people's willingness to engage with divine intervention and religious awe in their everyday lives also helped to normalize the increasingly popular cult of saints.

Since theater was already an intrinsic part of Spanish culture, it was predictable that it furthered this trend by regularly staging hagiographies. Saint plays soon became one of the most effective ways to transmit piety through the arts (Bastianutti 713). That said, performing saintliness onstage had to conform to a very specific set of requirements and doctrinal issues particularly when hagiographies were staged in the playhouses, which were highly profane spaces by definition. In such settings, the religious essence of the *comedia de santos* had to be carefully controlled and contained while retaining accessibility for all types of spectators so that they could understand the story and empathize with the protagonists to ultimately be moved by example.

Whereas the 1563 decree issued from the twenty-fifth session of the Council of Trent addressed the indoctrinating efficacy of religious performances, some ecclesiastical authorities continued to express serious doubts regarding the irreverent reception of dramatic hagiographies if actors embodied saints. Even if there were cases in which performers moved audiences to worship, artists, in general, were known for leading libidinous private lives, and the saintly qualities of the characters they portrayed ran the risk of being tainted by association.⁸

Substituting puppets for actors could safely eliminate many of the moralists' apprehensions, as long as the puppets did not represent obscenities (McCormick, Cipollo, and Napoli 12).⁹ As pointed out by Oscar Wilde (1854–1900) two centuries later, marionettes lack personality and private lives ("Puppets and Actors"). Consequently, in their condition as inanimate objects, devoid of a soul and consequently free from all sin, they channel a virtuous spirituality in a way that seems safer and more transparent than the fallible, utterly human actor. This is not to say that puppets completely replaced actors in hagiographic dramas; on the contrary, traditional productions were still carried out successfully, but the *máquina real* offered an alternative way to perform saintliness that was unique to Spanish culture of the period. John E. Varey states: "Insofar as most of the entertainment I have discussed thus far arrived from abroad, one might wonder what the Spanish invented. And the answer is: the performance of complete *comedias* by marionettes—especially the *comedias de santos*—a preference of Madrid residents during Lent and a very appropriate form of entertainment for the country and century of Calderón" (*Historia* 244).

Puppets provided an aesthetic sugarcoating for complex theological teachings, making these plays seem more approachable for the populace. Perhaps the only theological problem the *máquina real* may have encountered was merging the saints' supremacy of free will with the concept of manipulation implied in the marionette's intrinsic nature. Nonetheless, as Dale Shuger aptly notes, the association between the puppet and the notion of manipulation appears to be absent from the early modern Spanish imaginary (24). Indeed, when the puppet metaphor was invoked to criticize Catholic morals, the target of its condemnation was idolatry and not the dynamics of control and subjugation (Shuger 16).¹⁰

The increasing popularity of the *máquina real* was due, in part, to the fact that marionettes were allowed to perform during Lent, when other theatrical performances with live actors were officially banned from the stage. Although the *máquina real* did not exist in seventeenth-century England, in 1623 puppeteer William Sands used a wagon and a collapsible stage to tour *The Chaos of the World*, a puppet show based on several episodes from the Old and New Testaments. While other plays that dealt with Catholic themes were prohibited at the time, Sands managed to keep his show running by arguing that puppet performances were different from regular stage plays (Butterworth 136)—using the same arguments that allowed the máquina real to perform during Lent.

Additionally, in contrast to regular Spanish acting companies, which required a constant renewal of their stage productions, the máquina real developed its own stable repertoire of 'greatest hits' based on a series of plays that could be easily adapted to the language of puppetry and the taste of contemporary audiences. Among the most frequently performed titles by the máquina real were Juan López de Úbeda's *Comedia de san Alejo* (Play of Saint Alexius, 1579); Antonio Mira de Amescua's *El esclavo del demonio* (The devil's slave, 1612); Luis Vélez de Guevara, Antonio Coello, and Francisco de Rojas Zorrilla's *La Baltasara* (The Baltasara, 1634); Manuel de León and Diego Calleja's *Las dos estrellas de Francia* (The two stars of France, 1662); Fernando de Zárate y Castronovo's *San Antonio Abad* (Saint Anthony Abbot, 1668); and Juan Pérez de Montalbán's *La gitana de Menfis, Santa María Egipciaca* (The gypsy of Menphis, Saint Mary of Egypt, 1621–1625).

It should not come as a surprise that all of these plays share a common denominator in their plots: the perilous lives of their protagonists before their rise to saintliness. In this respect, we may recall a useful distinction between two kinds of hagiographies: those that develop the saintly life of the main character, and those that focus, instead, on the tortuous road to sanctity. While the first type implies a contemplative plot, difficult to adapt to the performance requirements of puppet theater, the second, filled with adventure, easily sustains dramatic interest while keeping the marionette alive on stage at all times. As noted, the successful staging of the life of a saint entailed, above all, dramatic interest, which depended on how much the protagonist had to struggle with the three foremost temptations: the world, the devil, and the flesh (Garasa 6). Playwrights were conscious of the anticlimactic elements of the hagiographic genre, and they did not hesitate to alter their storylines to make them more appealing for the small stage. This explains why the *comedia de santos* usually includes apocryphal scenes that are also timely in their social significance, which strengthens the bond with the spectators.

Despite the action-driven plots in all hagiographic dramas, the saintliness of the protagonist had to emerge sooner or later, and it was in these exact instances when the marionette would deploy its most subtle complexity, at the conceptual and performative level, far surpassing that of actors. Puppets and saints share points of overlapping ontological development that allow them to dialogue naturally on stage. Like the saint, the marionette is an *object* of veneration, wonder, and terror that occupies a liminal space between reality and imagination (Cohen, "Puppetry" 123) and, I will add, between familiarity and strangeness. Puppets are, therefore, unique props for engaging with new alternative languages and realms such as the cult of saints.

Insofar as saintliness is an abstract and interior quality, materializing the spiritual grace or *olor de santidad* (aroma of saintliness) on stage was an exceedingly delicate matter. Nonetheless, the marionette, functioning as the "proper stand-in for the invisible" (Johnson 86), has the capacity to "stimulate spectators and performers to fill in details in their imaginations and project expressive qualities upon the objects in motion, thus alluding to divine grace by their mere presence" (Cohen, "Puppetry" 124). In this sense, what was natural and innate for the puppet seemed much more artificial and challenging to recreate for a professional actor.[11] Christian wonder always ran the risk of appearing false or even grotesque when performed by humans. No matter how cutting-edge the special effects surrounding such scenes were, the actor's embodiment of the supernatural always seemed superficially deceitful.

A similar concern was shared centuries later by the French Symbolists. The difference was that for the nineteenth-century poets and playwrights, the corruption of human acting was purely artistic instead of a moral distortion of holiness. In his *Mystères bibliques et chrétiens* (Christian and biblical mysteries, 1920), poet Maurice Bouchor (1855–1929) declares: "Not because of religious scruples but rather reasons of convenience, taste and aesthetics, I find the representation of religious characters such as Jesus Christ or the Holy Virgin by actors to be extremely disagreeable" (12). The puppet, however, coexists much more effortlessly than the performer with the otherworldly because it embodies the nexus between reality and wonder (Malkin 6–7).

Within this liminal/plausible zone, the marionette could tolerate high doses of pain and violence as a vital part of its dramatic essence.[12] The puppet's extraordinary ability for self-destruction and subsequent reconstruction duplicates the saint's victimhood and martyrdom since, like marionettes, saints are predestined to endure the most extreme tortures but forget them once they become "blessed in death." Bynum explains: "The saints do not appear to feel their torture. Although to modern tastes there is something almost pornographic about the slashings and penetrations of the slim, smooth, beautiful—and highly objectified—bodies of Agatha and Sebastian (and I do not discount the complexity of medieval responses as well), medieval theory was clear: the saints were blessed in death by the anesthesia of glory" ("Violent Images" 15). Ironically, while this tendency toward the "brokenness" of the puppet evokes the deepest essence of saintliness, it simultaneously becomes a powerful instrument for iconoclastic practices scattered across Europe during the Reformation. Sacred figurines were distributed among children to play with and inevitably destroy. This desacralization of the religious figure as a shattered toy came to epitomize the smashing of material representations of the holy (Moshenska x).

The marionette's malleability allowed it to become the dramatic agent par excellence for representing "supernatural verosímil" (plausible supernatural; Risco 17). But the puppet was not alone in such a suggestive undertaking. Religious automata offered a similar artistic medium for negotiating Christian wonder in early modernity. Elizabeth King has brilliantly researched the genealogy of a supposedly Spanish automaton from the sixteenth century that represents a Franciscan monk that walks, lifts the cross and rosary, and silently prays. This automaton currently resides at the Smithsonian in Washington, DC. Measuring fifteen inches in height, the monk is made of wood and iron (see Figures 3.1 and 3.2). Its mechanisms activate by a key-wound spring.[13] According to King, it could have been modeled on Franciscan brother Diego de Alcalá (1400–1463), canonized in 1588 as the first Counter-Reformation saint.

The legend surrounding this artifact goes back to King Philip II, who purportedly commissioned it from Turriano after his son and heir Don Carlos recovered from a near-fatal fall in 1562. Diego de Alcalá is credited with magically appearing to Don Carlos during his convalescence and miraculously healing him. The king wanted to honor the friar by recreating him in effigy to "model an act of the spirit" (Elizabeth King, "Clockwork Prayer" 1) that would endure the vagaries of time. As with the dramatic hagiographies performed by the puppets of a máquina real, this automated praying monk enhanced his power of sanctity through artificial animation and mechanical repetition. Its aural *duende* (or magic spirit), as King refers to it, finds a correlation in the uncanny of a máquina real show (1).

As Keith Thomas claims in *Religion and the Decline of Magic* (1971), salvation could be attained by consecutive and repetitive prayers; hence devotion, in certain instances, could develop into an automatized practice. Belgian mystic Elizabeth Spalbeek (1246–1304) embodied this idea by performing scenes of the Passion on a daily basis for over ten years through a choreography of repetitive gestures that resembled those of a sacred (human) automaton.[14] The affinity of puppets—and automata—with saints leads us, then, to consider the ways in which artificial animation, in its different degrees of sophistication, dialogues with the concept of saintliness in artistic and scientific registers.[15] For Fernando Rodríguez de la Flor, saintliness is "a linguistic fact; it reaches its full dimension through acts of language; it coagulates in texts, but those texts are certainly found encrypted inside spectacular machines" ("La santidad" 265). This line of inquiry could justify the origin and persistence of the máquina real in Spain's performance history during the 1600s. These companies reconceptualized dramatic hagiographies by enhancing the material culture of saints and fostering a new way to look at the intricacies of saintliness through the inner workings of animation.

The Archeology of the *Máquina Real*

Some of the most important peninsular puppet-theater traditions, such as the Portuguese *Os Bonecos de Santo Aleixo* (Saint Aleixo Puppets) in Évora from the mid-nineteenth century and the Spanish *Los títeres de la tía Norica* (Aunt Norica's Puppets, c. 1790) from Cádiz have had the good fortune of surviving over time thanks to the transmission of the puppeteer craft and the ongoing restoration of the original marionettes from one generation to the next.[16] Unlike these local traditions, the máquina real faded into oblivion at the end of the seventeenth century and has been absent from most of the world's theater histories and popular-culture recollections. Only over the last decade have Jesús Caballero and his research team of scholars, actors, artists, and musicians started a multidisciplinary collaborative project to rehabilitate this unique Iberian legacy.

This artist collective—appropriately named La Máquina Real and based in Cuenca—has been in operation since 2002 as an art laboratory that tests performance history through rigorous interpretation, material reconstruction, and performance.[17] In 2009, Caballero premiered one of the most popular plays in the repertoire of the máquina real, *El esclavo del demonio* by Mira de Amescua (ca. 1577–1644). This is also the only *comedia* for which we have some additional historical information about its staging by a máquina real due to an ill-fated performance where a false fire alarm was announced at the Corral del Coliseo (Coliseum Playhouse) in Seville in 1692.[18] The goal for this inaugural production was to recreate an archeological performance by a máquina real. A year later, in 2010, the company premiered *Lo fingido verdadero* (Seeing is believing, ca. 1608) by Lope de Vega (1562–1635), another hagiographical drama, this time inspired by the life of Saint Genesius, the patron saint of actors and victims of torture. For this second production, invited director Claudio Hochman developed an experimental mise-en-scène, stripping the máquina real stage of all ornamentation and fully exposing the bare structure of the retablo and the human effort behind the making of religious wonder.[19] In what remains of this chapter, I turn my attention, though, to the archeological artistic recovery of the máquina real through the analysis of *El esclavo*. I explore the ways in which the dramatic saintliness, theorized in the first part of the chapter, is put into practice and tested for twenty-first century audiences.

Mira de Amecua's *El esclavo* is inspired by the Portuguese Faustian legend of Saint Giles (Gil) of Santarém (1185–1265), a venerated hermit who sold his soul to the devil out of lust. The playwright probably took inspiration from Fernando del Castillo's *La primera parte de la historia general de Santo Domingo y de su Orden de Predicadores* (The first part of the general history of Saint Domingo and his Order of Priests, 1584) or Alonso de Villegas's *Adición a la tercera parte de Flos Sanctorum* (Addition to the third part of *Flos Sanctorum*, 1588; Castañeda 32). As in most saint plays, *El esclavo* does not fall short of the apocryphal banditry scenes that bring the plot closer to the audience's sensibilities so that they can easily identify with flashes of social reality.

Because the máquina real used only puppets to represent all of the characters, the stage of a regular commercial playhouse had to be modified to accommodate the marionette's relatively small size. To do so, the máquina real had to customize a wooden structure, known as a *retablo*, proportionally adapted to the puppets' measurements and technical needs. Calling these ephemeral stages *retablos* stressed the religiosity of the overall performance and evoked similarities with the so-called *monumento*, an adjustable altarpiece with a painted frame and small arch that resembles a sepulcher, which was temporarily assembled for Holy Week celebrations (Cea Gutiérrez 46–47). Since retablos were too heavy to carry from one place to another, they had to be custom-made and assembled on the spot to fit on the main stage of the playhouse where the company was performing (Cornejo Vega, "Primeros tiempos" 23).

If we compare the dimensions of the retablo built by Cristóbal Franco for a máquina real performance at the Corral del Príncipe (Príncipe Playhouse) in Madrid in 1772 (25 feet long by 11 feet wide) to the regular measurements of a traditional stage for actors (27 feet long by 15.7 feet wide), we note that the puppet stage is made to perfectly fit inside the main stage (see Figures 3.3 and 3.4). This coupling of stages was intended to serve the marionettes' needs while highlighting their presence, but it also could be interpreted as a way to confine the hagiographic fiction and demarcate a moral distancing from the rest of the playhouse.

The embedded stages reminded the spectators to acknowledge the double dose of fiction—the hagiography and the puppet performance—they were simultaneously watching. Egginton theorizes a similar spatial distancing in early modern theatrical contexts in the following terms: "The constitution of a frame separating realities that are nevertheless susceptible to interpenetration and mise en abîme, *precisely because the spaces that comprise them are mimetically related*, is an essential characteristic of theatricality and therefore a technique most typical of the period defined by its ascendance, the Baroque" (*How* 79; original emphasis). The máquina real applies this strategy of baroque perspectivism to enhance an interactive and critical approach to saintliness while envisioning the development of modern theater. In this regard, it is revealing to compare the distancing effect created by the retablo of a máquina real with the immersive experience of the medieval ceremonies that were held inside a church, designed to fully absorb the sacred essence of their holy surroundings without allowing any spatial and critical perspectivism.

Although there is sufficient historical data about the dimensions of the retablo to create a faithful reconstruction, there are fewer records about the type of puppets used by a máquina real. The only direct mention that we know of is by the anonymous chronicler who witnessed the ill-fated performance of *El esclavo* in Seville in 1692. In his account, the narrator refers to the puppets of a máquina real as: "twisted figures, in the style of puppets, performed several *comedias* with such proficiency and imagination, and the figures were so neatly dressed, endowing them with movement with wires that were so life-like and with such perfect voices and actions that it was a thing deserving of tremendous admiration" (BCC ms. 84-7-19, ff. 244r-247v; qtd. in Cornejo Vega, "Apuntes" 28).[20] In the absence of more concrete details about the original marionettes, Caballero deduced their measurements and articulation mechanisms by taking the dimensions and the structural design of the stage as a starting point. Caballero worked from the hypothesis that the marionettes must have been between three and four feet tall and manipulated by strings or rods from above or mounted on fixed pedestals when operated from the pit beneath the retablo (see Figures 3.5 and 3.6).

For the sculpting of the puppets, Caballero largely mirrored the procedures of seventeenth-century Spanish religious statuary (see Figures

3.7 and 3.8). Each of the figure's limbs were carved individually and assembled with hinges, a technique referred to by Mitchell A. Wilder and Edgar Breitenback as the "technology of the saints" (24–25). This accurate expression comes to demonstrate once again how animation and religiosity fit organically within each other in artistic contexts to heighten the overall devotional experience.[21] Caballero also drew on seventeenth-century artisanal methods to paint the puppets: applying several coats of plaster, sanding them, painting the details (in tempera, acrylic, or oil paint), and varnishing the figures. The physical appearance of the marionettes of a máquina real was no doubt drawn from baroque religious iconography, which at the time functioned as the referent par excellence for all hagiographic drama.

Indeed, one of the peculiarities of these plays is the stage direction *como se pinta* (as it is painted) that is repeated next to the most iconic scenes of a particular saint's life. This reference to the pictorial representation implies that the set and the characters' gestures should closely follow the iconographic tradition of that specific hagiographic episode. Ignacio Arellano explains: "The pictorial model and the codified iconography of saints are very important when configuring these scenes: the phrase '*como se pinta*' appears frequently and, although it is not explicitly stated, the importance of the model in numerous cases is obvious" (*Convención* 244; my emphasis). Audiences at the time were familiar with religious imagery and would immediately recognize the most representative scenes of a saint's life, whether portrayed using puppets or actors.

For each of the characters in *El esclavo*, Caballero made various replicas, each dressed and characterized following the demands of the different scenes. Don Gil, for example, transforms from a hermit to a bandit, then finally to a penitent. Lisarda, the leading female character, evolves from a lady to an outlaw, only to appear later on as a disfigured slave. And, the devil, Angelio, a stock character in most religious plays, appears first as a false suitor and subsequently makes his much-awaited entrance as the traditional demonic figure with red face and horns (see Figures 3.9 and 3.10). Since there was not time to make meticulous changes to the puppets during the performances, each marionette had multiple versions in all its different characterizations and attires.

Although the marionettes' visual opulence was undeniable, the puppeteers concealed behind the scenes also put on extraordinary performances with their own bodies, reminiscent of an acrobatics show. For Susan Young, "the motion of a marionette under the control of a skilled operator has a magical quality and because the impulse must be transmitted through the length of the strings, it seems to become less a part of the human activity of the operator and more an expression of a life force of the marionette itself" (23).[22] The puppeteers of a máquina real, as any other puppet manipulators, had to have the dexterity and strength to hold awkward poses for extended periods of time while manipulating the marionettes in a restricted space. Such physical demands explain why in a 1654 account book for a máquina real, four of the five employees were also experts in acrobatics (Cornejo Vega, "Un siglo" 23).[23]

Miniaturized sets and special effects also stress the religious wonder created by the marionettes and their skillful operators within these animated hagiographies. We know that the most common backdrops used by a máquina real were a forest, a garden, a living room, and a church (Varey, *Historia* 291). These settings were painted on canvases and hung as background curtains, a technique that is still being used in most traditional puppet shows today (see Figures 3.11 and 3.12).[24] A bullfighting arena was also a common and very popular setting, as most plays concluded with the reenactment of a bullfight by marionettes as a festive affirmation of Spanish popular culture. Moreover, in the case of the *comedia de santos*, the symbolic meaning of the bullfight contributed to the sacrificial economy of a saint's life and alluded to the sacrifice required for humans to transcend their sheer animality.

The supernatural element that saturated some of the scenes was further enhanced by visual and sound effects. In *El esclavo*, most of the otherworldly elements are displayed in the third act, when Don Gil and Lisarda are closest to repentance and are about to enter the realm of Christian wonder. The following stage directions exemplify a series of *coups de théâtre* involving death (in the form of a skeleton), the devil, and the angels:

1. Enter Don Gil, embracing a *skeleton* covered with a shawl. (97)
2. He *uncovers* her [Lisarda], and the *skeleton falls through a trap door* in the stage. (98)
3. Angelio steps onto a *revolving stage machine*, which *takes him out of sight*, replacing him with the figure of a *devil*. Skyrockets and guns are fired. (99)
4. The vision of the *devil* disappears. Trumpets sound. An *angel* and the *devil* fight, *suspended above the stage on machines*; then they vanish. (99)
5. Enter *an angel or two* in triumph, to the sound of music, with a sheet of paper. (100)
6. Music plays. A curtain is drawn, *revealing Lisarda's corpse* kneeling in the garden next to a crucifix and a skull. (107; my emphasis)[25]

The dramatic effects and visual qualities developed in these stage directions are heightened by a codified system of audiovisual effects, which transforms the small stage into a meticulous apotheosis of wonder.

While pyrotechnics demarcate the paranormal atmosphere, music mainly defines the protagonists' spiritual changes.[26] There were two basic musical devices in dramatic hagiographies that were used to express the holy: the hornpipes accompanied celestial apparitions, and liturgical scores introduced religious ceremonies deployed on stage (Arellano, *Convención* 258). The máquina real possibly adhered to this established musical code. For Caballero's production, composer Guillermo Bautista wrote several pieces for baroque guitar, dulcian, recorder, cornet, viola da gamba, bass, and the string-bass; some of them specifically emphasized the protagonists' moral failings. Considering the skillfully manipulated marionettes, the custom-made stage, and these intricate special effects, the máquina real succeeded in materializing wonder in all of its magnificence, though condensed on a miniaturized scale with nonhuman actors.

As I mentioned in this chapter's introduction, the artistic mission of the máquina real was to create an alternative way to approach hagiographies that promoted a more active piety than those afforded by other artistic devotional iterations. When religious awe was permeated via the language of puppetry, the marvelous was open for reevaluation from various perspectives. On the one hand, audiences did not feel intimidated by these heavily theologically driven plays and so approached them with greater confidence. On the other hand, spectators had to draw on a more analytical awareness to interpret a performance far removed from realist referents. Moreover, viewers' curiosity about the concealed mechanisms of the máquina real came into play, opening another avenue for establishing a critical distance from the slice of religious fiction they were contemplating.

If we add to that the artificiality of the marionette and the multiple frames of the puppet stage, the máquina real turns into a totalizing, defamiliarizing kinetic spectacle.[27] Audiences had to reconcile Christian wonder with the artificial constructs that uphold these performances. From this process, devotion turns into an active practice. In her analysis of the máquina real, Shuger supports this idea, stating: "It is impossible to pinpoint a specific moment when modes of seeing changed or to know the precise contours of any audience's journey along the continuum of spectatorial distance. At the very least, though, we know that by the time that the máquina real became part of the theatrical repertoire, a regular theatergoer had seen more than a few plays that admonished him or her to perceive a distinction between the objects of representation and the things represented" (16). More so than traditional theater, these shows implied a major commitment to the suspension of disbelief from the very beginning. The language of puppetry bled into the Catholic orthodoxy and the religious awe that these hagiographic plays convey while simultaneously stressing their theological complexity. Thus, we should not be surprised to learn that the máquina real disappeared toward the end of the seventeenth century, which coincides with the time when the *comedia de santos* began to blend with magic plays while entering the secular realm of the supernatural.

Modern Object-Centric Sainthood

The máquina real came to occupy a central role in early modern popular culture by generating an animated theology that invited audiences to fully engage with its meaning, as was expected from a "land of theologians," as literary critic Marcelino Menéndez y Pelayo (1856–1912) referred to seventeenth-century Spain (408). Nonetheless, a long-standing prejudiced view of puppetry as lowbrow art and children's entertainment, together with the gradual loss of knowledge in hagiographical matters, uprooted this performance tradition from the history of Spanish theater and even from the cult of saints.

In Central European countries, where socialist governments once prohibited the staging of nativity plays, the public is reclaiming them now (Hledíková 220). By contrast, in Spain, throughout the twentieth and twenty-first centuries, audiences tend to relegate any religious-themed productions, from nativity plays to medieval mysteries or *comedias de santos*, as historical curiosities worthy to be viewed at a museistic distance. Caballero and his team took a serious gamble—just as Zamora did with her *Misterio*—by resurrecting the global nature of the puppet in its purest form without reconfiguring it according to post-traditional puppet theater values. The máquina real recovery project not only salvages a national cultural heritage that slipped through the cracks of Western performance history but also attests to the significance of the fruitful dialogue between saintliness, playfulness, and the arts that still pervades in modern-day societies and is waiting to be critically and experientially re-activated.

Michael Landy, a renowned British conceptual artist, has also tested new ways of interaction between contemporary audiences and the culture of saints in secular settings (see Figure 3.13). Invited as the National Gallery's eighth Associate Artist, during his residency Landy created an exhibit, titled *Saints Alive* (2013), that explored the portrayal of saints in Christian iconography in an interactive manner. While Caballero reconstructs a whole tradition from the ground up, restoring these saintly miniatures back onto their original seventeenth-century stage as faithfully as possible, Landy brings saints to life by literally breaking them down (Penny 7), as ironic as that may sound.[28] This act of artistic destruction perfectly complements Caballero's endeavor from a more conceptual postmodern vantage. As with Caballero, Landy is trying to visualize the inner workings of saintliness by recuperating the saints' forgotten narratives and by looking behind the appearances of their lives, which artistic iterations have crystallized in a series of artificial poses without questioning them. In the exhibition catalog, Collin Wiggins notes the artist's search for the "grim and shocking in reality" (34) hidden in these saint tales.

To discover and understand that reality, Landy engages in a process of destruction, reassessment, and reconstruction. Nicholas B. Penny, director of the National Gallery at the time, described Landy's creative process as follows: "Michael began by cutting things out; these cuttings combined and multiplied and grew, eventually into three dimensions; and then they began to move" (7). His series of kinetic sculptures (e.g., Saint Apollonia, Saint Jerome, Saint Francis of Assisi, Saint Catherine, and Saint Thomas) were all inspired by paintings housed at the National Gallery and were made from recycled mechanical pieces, scrap materials, and objects found in flea markets or on eBay.[29] Like Fray Gil of Santarem and other sinner-saint protagonists featured by the máquina real, Landy's animated figures confront worldly temptations, and their stories graphically exemplify the processes of physical self-destruction. By pushing pedals and pressing buttons, visitors can bring the interactive mechanical sculptures to life to experience firsthand scenes of martyrdom in these now-forgotten hagiographies.[30] In this sense, Landy contributes to the genealogy of twentieth and twentieth-first century artistic experiments that blur the line between creation and destruction, which, in the context of religious figurative art, reevaluates the iconoclast polemic.[31]

All of the saintly marionettes and artifacts examined throughout this chapter, with their revised and newly acquired performative and cultural functions, forge a vital link between the life histories of religious marionettes and the uses to which they have been put in various Iberian and European transhistorical contexts. While religious puppetry today does not retain its original function as a popular devotional entertainment, this religious loss has to be weighed against the artistic and academic gains that emerge from novel manipulations and explorations of these holy actors. Caballero's and Landy's initiatives prove that the culture of saints is still very much *alive*, but it seeks to be questioned, tested, and transformed—that is, *reanimated*—by contemporary artists and audiences just as it was meant to be experienced in the early modern world with the máquina real.

4. Unruly Puppets

> The horse of Don Gaiferos in his headlong gallop leaves a vacuum behind him, into which a current of hallucinating air rushes, sweeping along with it everything that is not firmly fixed on the ground. There the soul of Don Quixote, light as thistledown, snatched up in the illusory vortex, goes whirling like a dry leaf; and in its pursuit everything ingenuous and sorrowing still left in the world will go forevermore.
>
> JOSÉ ORTEGA Y GASSET, *Meditations on Quixote*, 1914

IN THE TWO preceding chapters, I explored how religious animated figures—the *Cristo articulado* and the máquina real puppets—create a conceptual intimacy with divinity and saintliness, respectively, by articulating the sublime through their visible jointed materiality. Even though these two props were conceived as agents of illusion, the artists behind these creations intentionally left some breaches exposed to entice those who engage with the devotional objects to look beyond appearance and come to terms with the making of spiritual illusions. In the specific case of the *Cristo articulado* and the saintly puppet, their joints and strings hinted at their artificiality and induced a more reflective, critical devotion.

In this chapter and the one that follows, I continue my investigation of the man-made animation of theatrical props, but I turn my attention from religious practices to historically informed fictional entertainment contexts. I focus on Cervantes's *Don Quijote* because it is a novel that foregrounds the object's artificial agency in a variety of episodes from very different perspectives. Nevertheless, in order to explore this line of thought, instead of focusing on the *making* of illusions as I have done in Chapters 2 and 3, I adhere to Cervantes's experimental approach to assess their *unmaking*. Thus, in the case studies that follow, I read the deconstruction of fictional illusions as a meticulous artistic process that forces readers and the novel's protagonists to detach from appearances and engage with rational observation, which is a binding rite of passage into modernity at the empirical cost of experiencing desengaño.

During the seventeenth century, the turmoil that affected southern and central Europe found its way to Habsburg Spain, which experienced its own crisis that originated with King Philip II and reached its peak in 1640 under the rule of Philip IV. National and foreign challenges destabilized the country's political and social structures, severely affecting its military power, demographic growth, and economic wealth. To a certain extent, literature and the arts helped the country navigate these unsettling times by providing escapist routes to avoid reality and by experimenting with new ways of thinking and seeing. Writers, in particular, saw in the puppet and the automaton a promising metaphor for the anxieties that came with the uncertainty of the period. In an increasingly mechanistic era in which scientific inquiry permeated social and cultural expressions, the puppet and the automaton opened the "disconcerting possibility of the agency of things" (Bell, "Playing with the Eternal Uncanny" 49).

Cervantes was conversant with the innovative intellectual and scientific horizons that were emerging at the time. In one respect, he used *Don Quijote* as a vehicle for testing the concepts of enchantment and disenchantment in multiple scenarios where the *making of illusions* revealed the failures of perception, recognition of which would ultimately lead to new understandings and ontological discoveries.[1] The novelist purposefully played with the puppet and the automaton in his masterpiece by placing them in a variety of theatrical settings and making them into the leading agents to break through appearances. Such *acts of dismantling* grow into creative processes, very much aligned with the contemporary currents of thought that privileged observation, modern curiosity, and reason.

More precisely, in the second part of *Don Quijote*, Master Pedro's puppets (2.25–2.26) engage most bluntly with theatrical practices and, consequently, with the rupture of dramatic illusionism.[2] The novelist chooses Ginés de Pasamonte, a former galley slave that Don Quixote set free in chapter 1.27, as the master manipulator of these marionettes. Ginés, in addition to being a rogue (therefore well acquainted with popular entertainments and petty scams), develops as a multifaceted creator of fictions. Not only is he engaged in writing his autobiography, as he confesses to Don Quijote (1.27), but now, under the fake identity of Master Pedro and hiding behind a green taffeta patch, Ginés orchestrates a trick with a soothsaying monkey and directs a play with puppets.

In all these instances, either the narrator or the characters involved in these performances break with illusionism to expose the deceptiveness and, in some instances, the inaccuracy of fiction. On the one hand, Ginés's autobiography could never be completed in a truthful manner as his life goes on. On the other hand, the narrator reveals the soothsaying monkey trick step by step, a systematic process that is repeated many times throughout the novel, as examined in Chapter 5 of this book in the context of two other performances. Finally, the puppet show turns out to be a creative failure stripped of all artifice. Taking these iconic Cervantine marionettes as the focus of my analysis, I look into how the novelist calls theatrical illusions and authorship into question by extending the act of artistic defacement and its consequences beyond the knight's actions.

Master Pedro's puppet show is inspired by the ballad of the liberation of Melisendra, which reverberates with the anti-Muslim rhetoric we find during the Reconquest.[3] Don Gaiferos rescues his wife Melisendra from the Moors who had imprisoned her in the city of Sansueña (Zaragoza).[4] Carried away by the actions of such enemies and his own ideals of justice, Don Quixote unsheathes his sword to do battle against them, defending the fleeing lovers; however, he ends up destroying the entire stage. While the knight loses himself momentarily in the fiction, he ultimately takes responsibility for his actions by offering to pay Master Pedro for the damage he has caused in his flight of fancy.

FIGURE 2.10. Promotional poster for *Misterio del Cristo de los Gascones*, directed by Ana Zamora (2007). Photograph by Iván Caso, courtesy of Ana Zamora (Nao D'amores).

FIGURE 2.11. Cristo de los Gascones in reclining position. *Iglesia de los Santos Justo y Pastor*, Segovia (Spain). Photograph by and courtesy of Javier Manrique González.

FIGURE 2.12. *Planctus Mariae* (Lament of Mary). *Misterio del Cristo de los Gascones*, directed by Ana Zamora (2007). Iglesia de los Santos Justo y Pastor, Segovia (Spain). Photograph by Esther Candela, courtesy of Ana Zamora (Nao D'amores).

FIGURE 2.13. Christ interacting with one of the musicians. *Misterio del Cristo de los Gascones*, directed by Ana Zamora (2007). Teatro de la Abadía, Madrid. Photograph by Daniel Alonso, courtesy of the Centro de Documentación de las Artes Escénicas y de la Música. INAEM. Ministerio de Cultura y Deporte.

FIGURE 2.14. Judas betraying Jesus. *Misterio del Cristo de los Gascones*, directed by Ana Zamora (2007). Teatro de la Abadía, Madrid. Photograph by Esther Candela, courtesy of Ana Zamora (Nao D'amores).

FIGURE 2.15. Christ in transcendence. *Misterio del Cristo de los Gascones*, directed by Ana Zamora (2007). Teatro de la Abadía, Madrid. Photograph by Daniel Alonso, courtesy of the Centro de Documentación de las Artes Escénicas y de la Música. INAEM. Ministerio de Cultura y Deporte.

FIGURE 3.1. Automaton figure of a monk, South Germany or Spain, ca. 1560; Division of Work and Industry, National Museum of American History, Smithsonian Institution, Washington, DC.

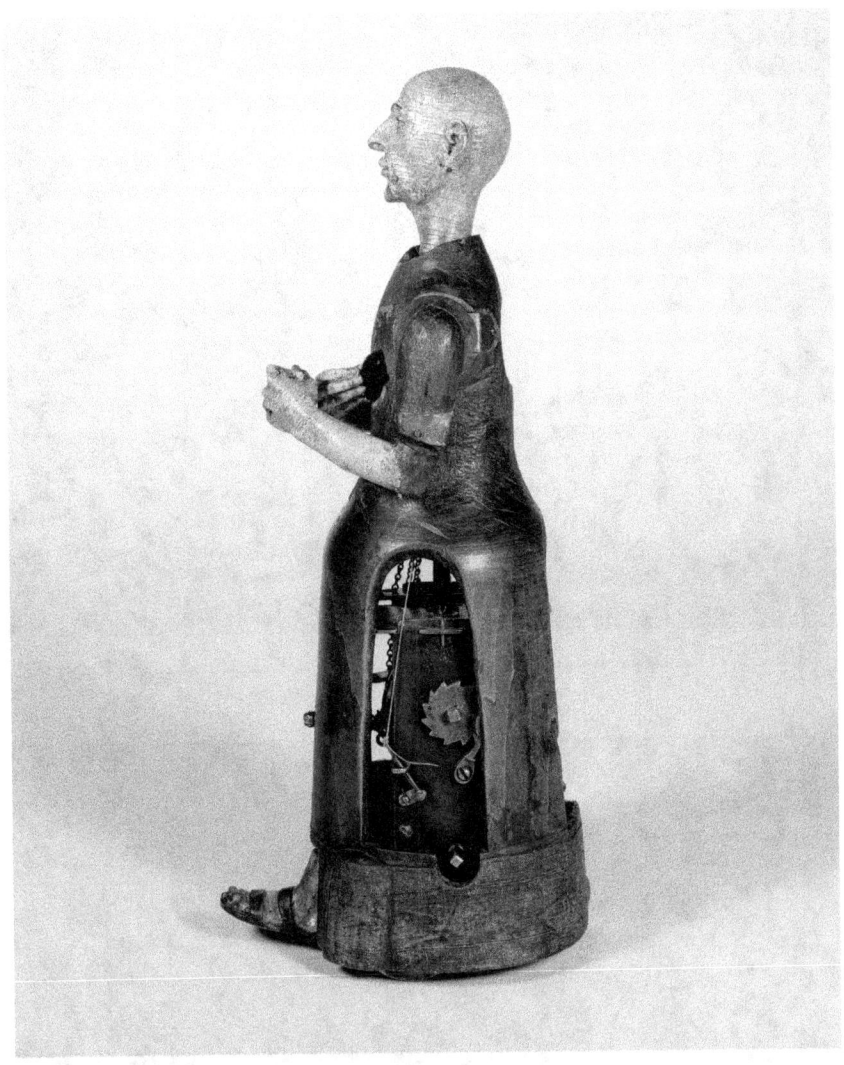

FIGURE 3.2. Automaton figure of a monk, South Germany or Spain, ca. 1560; Division of Work and Industry, National Museum of American History, Smithsonian Institution, Washington, DC.

FIGURE 3.3. Building process of the *retablo* for *El esclavo del demonio*, directed by Jesús Caballero (2009). Photograph by Jesús Caballero, courtesy of La Máquina Real.

FIGURE 3.4. Built-in stage (*retablo*) for *El esclavo del demonio*, directed by Jesús Caballero (2009). Corral de comedias de Almagro, Ciudad Real (Spain). Photograph by Jesús Caballero, courtesy of La Máquina Real.

FIGURE 3.5. Puppets onstage during a performance of *El esclavo del demonio*, directed by Jesús Caballero (2009). Photograph by Jesús Caballero, courtesy of La Máquina Real.

FIGURE 3.6. Contemporary puppeteers manipulating stick puppets from beneath the *retablo* during a rehearsal of *El esclavo del demonio*, directed by Jesús Caballero (2009). Photograph by Jesús Caballero, courtesy of La Máquina Real.

FIGURE 3.7. Sculpted puppet body for *El esclavo del demonio*, directed by Jesús Caballero (2009). Photograph by Jesús Caballero, courtesy of La Máquina Real.

FIGURE 3.8. Sculpted puppet heads for *El esclavo del demonio*, directed by Jesús Caballero (2009). Photograph by Jesús Caballero, courtesy of La Máquina Real.

FIGURE 3.9. Puppet cast for *El esclavo del demonio*, directed by Jesús Caballero (2009). Photograph by Jesús Caballero, courtesy of La Máquina Real.

FIGURE 3.10. Angelio, devil figure in *El esclavo del demonio*, directed by Jesús Caballero (2009). Photograph by Jesús Caballero, courtesy of La Máquina Real.

FIGURE 3.11. Set for the house in *El esclavo del demonio*, directed by Jesús Caballero (2009). Photograph by Jesús Caballero, courtesy of La Máquina Real.

FIGURE 3.12. Set for the town in *El esclavo del demonio*, directed by Jesús Caballero (2009). Photograph by Jesús Caballero, courtesy of La Máquina Real.

However, Don Quixote is not the only one who breaks through fictional illusions in this episode. The narrator also strips the puppet show of its fictional trappings, pushing the dramatic conventions of the time to their limit. In this regard, we could argue that *Don Quijote* is also a novel-in-the-(un)making, or a montage-novel, about reading, writing, and literary criticism, in which fictions are interwoven, each with its own process of creation. Evaluating phenomena by paring circumstances down to their constitutive elements and, therein, tinkering with their operative laws to build anew, Cervantes may have appropriated tactics used by natural philosophers in their quest to probe novel concepts bereft of the benefit of the scientific method to draw a line between fact and fiction (Portuondo 271).

It should come as no surprise that Manuel de Falla, one of Spain's leading composers, became fascinated with the way this show was conceived on the page, straddling popular tradition and performative innovation. Open to experimentation within the field of traditional music, Falla turned Cervantes's imagined puppet show into a cutting-edge operetta, *El retablo de Maese Pedro* (Master Pedro's puppet show, 1923). As a modernist artist living in an interwar society, the composer, no doubt, identified with the tone of disenchantment and skepticism that impregnates the Cervantine performance. Moreover, the modernists' obsession with the threat of the machine as a potential subject saw a compendium for their anxieties in the puppet, which Marjorie Garber summarizes as "the impossibility of verisimilitude, the destabilization of authorship, and ultimately, the vexed status of the subject" (39). Yet, Cervantes had already fleshed out this dread in Master Pedro's puppet show. Thus, in the second part of this chapter, I appraise the critical role that puppetry had in Falla's operetta and how Cervantes's disarticulated animations effectively dialogue with the social anxieties and new aesthetics of the composer's disenchanted opera and era.

The Estrangement of Illusions

In the 1500s, people from the more cultivated echelons of society found themselves ideologically trapped at the intersection between Christian tradition and new scientific and industrial currents (Ferreras 641).

Gradually, remnants of animist and supernatural beliefs were replaced by rationalist thought. The *disarticulation* of theatrical artifice became an effective tool for grappling with this ideological transition in both religious and secular contexts. The public destruction of the Rood of Grace in 1538 epitomized the turn toward a rational conception of animation in sixteenth-century England.[5] This crucifix, kept at the Cistercian Abbey of Boxley in Kent, had a jointed wooden image of Christ affixed to it. With the ongoing Dissolution of the Monasteries in England and Wales in the late 1530s, such crucifixes were denounced as mechanical theatrical mirabilia.[6] John Hilsey, bishop of Rochester (d. 1539), publicly exposed the cross as a fraud in his sermon of 1538 and smashed it, distributing its pieces among the parishioners so they could have material proof of the deceptive artifact.[7]

Peter Burke identifies two examples in seventeenth-century popular European culture that illustrate a comparable demonization of fraudulent performance objects in secular entertainment contexts. Pierre Beurrier, curé of Nanterre from 1634 to 1653, narrates how he shut down a street performance and publicly destroyed all traces of theatrical artifice: "I remember that being warned one feast day that wandering actors were playing a farce on a stage they had erected, I went there with some officers of the law. I climbed onto the stage, *tore the mask* from the face of the leading actor, *took the fiddle away* from the man who was playing and *broke it*, and *made them come down from the stage*, which I had the officers overturn" (qtd. in Burke, *Popular Culture* 214; my emphasis). Archpriest Avvakum Petrovich (c.1620–1682), one of the leaders of the schism of the Russian Orthodox Church, recalled a similar story in his autobiography (1669–1672): "There came to my village dancing bears with drums and lutes, and I, though a miserable sinner, was zealous in Christ's service and I *drove them out* and I *broke the buffoon's mask and the drums* ... and two great bears I took away—one I clubbed senseless but he revived and the other I let go into the open country" (qtd. in Burke 214; my emphasis). In each of these anecdotes, a church representative tore off the deceitful performance object and, in so doing, demystified the illusion in full view of an audience. Such acts of artistic defacement point toward the modern turn, as perpetrators discredit the making of illusions by publicly disclosing their deceptive artifice.

In Master Pedro's puppet show, the novelist presents us with a comparable deed in a fictional context. Although Don Quixote's destructive impulse toward the marionettes arises from a sudden enthusiasm inspired by the ballad, he does not take long to recognize the debacle he has caused and offers to pay for the marionettes he has destroyed: "Let Master Pedro decide what he wants for the *damaged puppets*, for I offer to pay him immediately in good, standard Castilian currency" (*Don Quixote* 634; my emphasis).[8] Later on, he and Master Pedro haggle over the price of every figure and their individual damages. The spelled-out inventory of each of the broken puppets emphasizes their objectification and material value in the eyes of Don Quixote. Therefore, the protagonist's damaging act, which was initially moved by enchantment, leads him to face disenchantment full on, once he acknowledges what underpins theatrical illusionism.

Yet, Don Quixote's attack on the puppets has a much more nuanced and daring artistic meaning than the curé of Nanterre's or the Archpriest Avvakum's public disbandment of the street performances. On the one hand, marionettes are made to embody destruction, as I have argued in Chapter 2, and, as Kenneth Gross has persuasively underscored, "the life of puppets is itself, at its most animated, a world of *destroyed things*" (*Puppet* 95; my emphasis). Master Pedro's broken puppets, then, turn out to be an intrinsic and expected part the show. On the other hand, the narrator and the various spectators watching the performance at the inn, including Don Quixote, actively participate in tearing apart fiction by establishing a critical distance with their comments and constant interruptions. With that, it could be argued that Cervantes conceived of Master Pedro's performance as a thoughtful artistic failure that spurs readers to question fiction and, I would argue, the very novel they are reading.[9]

To achieve this goal, the novelist pushes dramatic conventions to their limits via a remarkable understanding of the metaphorical and technical knowledge of the language of puppetry. *Don Quijote* scholarship has long accepted the allegorical role of the novelist as a master puppeteer because of his skillful manipulation of multiple intertwining narratives. For Cervantes, puppeteering becomes a symbol of authorial control (Percas de Ponseti, "Authorial Strings" 51)[10] and Master Pedro's puppet show a meta-narrative that condenses the structure of his novel as a whole (Haley 163). These figurative interpretations of *Don Quijote* dialogue with a rich tradition of adaptations of the novel into puppet theater, especially from the nineteenth century on. As a matter of fact, condensed versions of the knight's adventures performed by marionettes have been known in Mexico since the 1800s (Beezley 310). And, in the twentieth and twenty-first centuries, renowned directors such as Josef Krofta (DRAK Company, 1971), Art Grueneberger (Puppet Art Theater Company, 2007), Émilie Valantin and Éric Ruf (Comédie Française, 2008), Steven Ritz-Barr (Classics in Miniature, 2010), and Angus Jackson (Royal Shakespeare Company, 2016), among others, have cast puppets in their stage adaptations of *Don Quijote*.

In addition to experimenting with the symbolic meaning of puppetry on a narrative level, Cervantes seemed to be experientially familiar with the technical and social aspects of marionette theater. The novelist was certainly exposed to Sicilian *pupi* during his time in Palermo and Messina in 1574 while recovering from the wounds he suffered at the battle of Lepanto (Díaz-Plaja 143). Thus, it is not a coincidence that there are many Italianisms in the two chapters dedicated to Master Pedro's puppets (Díaz-Plaja 142, 146). Furthermore, the technicalities of the *pupi* no doubt inspired the marionettes portrayed by Cervantes. Italian traditional puppets were manipulated from above using wires that could control very precise movements like the ones alluded to in Master Pedro's show, such as playing backgammon, kissing, spitting, and tearing out their own hair.

In addition to his insightful figurative and technical knowledge of puppetry, Cervantes was familiar with the social implications of being a puppeteer at the time. In his *Novelas ejemplares*, the novelist had already inquired into the precarious lifestyle and depravity of these itinerant artists. In "El licenciado Vidriera," for example, Tomás Rodaja, the protagonist, unabashedly expresses his disdain for those entertainers:

> About puppeteers he said a thousand evil things; he said they were tramps who treated divine things indecently, because with the figures shown in their depictions they turned devotion into laughter,

and they would pack all or most of the figures from the *Old* and *New Testaments* into a sack, and sit on it to eat and drink in cheap restaurants and taverns. In short, he said he was amazed at how it could be that perpetual silence was not imposed on their performances or they were not exiled from the kingdom. (*Exemplary Novels*, Kindle locations 3985–89)[11]

Similarly, in "El coloquio de los perros," the dog Berganza draws on his own experience to denounce a gang of puppeteers who had exploited him when he worked with them as an entertainment dog:

> Greed and envy awoke a desire in the scoundrels to steal me, and they kept looking for the opportunity, for this idea of earning a living without doing any work has many admirers and enthusiasts; that is why there are so many puppeteers in Spain, so many who display retables, so many who sell pins and poems, since their entire property, even if they were to sell everything, is not enough to support them for one day; and even so they don't leave the hostels and taverns all year; which leads me to conclude that the current of their drunkenness flows from a source other than their trades. All these people are idlers, useless, ne'er-do-wells, sponges of wine and weevils of bread. (*Exemplary Novels*, Kindle locations 7881–86)[12]

As these two quotes illustrate, the puppets do not fare as poorly as their handlers, whose lifestyles serve as an excuse for Cervantes to make an incursion into the picaresque, a genre to which the novelist frequently turned in his various works.

This perceptive understanding of the metaphorical, practical, and social aspects of puppetry enables Cervantes to theoretically experiment with the principles of marionette theater in order to revisit the limitations of traditional actor-theater. In fact, most theatrical episodes in *Don Quijote* highlight a series of dramatic innovations that Western playwrights from the eighteenth century to the present have continued experimenting with (Maestro 42).[13] In regard to Master Pedro's performance, from its very beginning, the narrator forecloses the possibility of establishing any realistic illusion. Don Quixote's and Master Pedro's continuous interruptions of the interpreter's narrative, the dehumanized portrayal of the puppets, and Don Quixote's final act of destruction provide the kind of alienation effect that will frame Bertolt Brecht's epic theater in the mid-twentieth century. Like Cervantes, Brecht reminded his audiences that the enactment of reality was not reality itself through what he coined the *Verfremdungseffekt* (A-Effect).[14] This is not to say that Master Pedro's puppet show is a proto-Brechtian performance; on the contrary, the German playwright looked to early modern Spanish drama as a source of inspiration for his epic theater.[15]

Master Pedro's puppet show starts with the narrator exposing the reader to every component of theatrical artifice through an initial distancing act that establishes the conceptual and aesthetic foundation for the rest of the episode:

> Don Quixote and Sancho did as he asked and went to the place where the stage was set up for all to see, and *it was filled with the light of little wax candles* that made it look colorful and resplendent. As soon as they arrived, *Master Pedro went inside the puppet theater, for it was he who would manipulate the figures in the play*, and outside stood a boy, a servant of Master Pedro's, to act as interpreter and narrator of the mysteries on stage; in his hand he held a rod with which he pointed to the figures as they came out. (*Don Quixote* 628; my emphasis)[16]

Following this overview of the deconstructed set, the narrator goes on to develop the process of putting on a small-scale production. Indeed, readers bear witness to the show in the making (see Figure 4.1).

A second distancing effect is the interpreter's interjected narrative by Don Quixote and Master Pedro through their ongoing comments and admonitions during the show (see Figure 4.2). Below, I transcribe the five interpolations as they happen to underline three of the core principles of Cervantes's dramatic theory: clarity, verisimilitude, and distrust of ignorant audiences:

1. "Boy, boy," said Don Quixote in a loud voice, "*tell your story in a straight line* and do not become involved in curves or transverse lines, for to get a clear idea of the truth, one must have proofs and more proofs." (*Don Quixote* 630; my emphasis)[17]
2. And from the interior, Master Pedro also said: "Boy, tend to your business and do what that gentleman says, that's the right thing to do; go on with your plainsong and *don't get involved in counterpoints* that usually break because they're so refined." "I will," responded the boy. (*Don Quixote* 630; my emphasis)[18]
3. At this point Master Pedro once again raised his voice, saying: "*Simplicity*, boy, don't be arrogant, all affectation is bad." (*Don Quixote* 631; my emphasis)[19]
4. "No, that is wrong!" said Don Quixote. "*Master Pedro is incorrect in the matter of the bells, for the Moors do not use bells but drums and a kind of flute that resembles our flageolet,* and there is no doubt that ringing bells in Sansueña is a great piece of nonsense." (*Don Quixote* 632; my emphasis)[20]
5. "Your grace *should not concern yourself with trifles*, Señor Don Quixote, or try to carry things so far that you never reach the end of them. *Aren't a thousand plays performed almost every day that are full of a thousand errors and pieces of nonsense, and yet are successful productions that are greeted not only with applause but with admiration?* Go on, boy, and let them say what they will, for as long as I fill my purse, there can be more errors than atoms in the sun." (*Don Quixote* 632; my emphasis)[21]

These constant interjections tear apart the fictional fabric of the ballad while they expose the novelist's ideas on how to write for the stage, another instance that underlines the inner workings of the dramatic/theatrical experience, a recurrent motive in Cervantes's oeuvre in his frustrated pursuit for recognition as a playwright.

The astuteness of the knight's comments, at this point in the episode, reveals a distanced and critical response, as they prove that Don Quixote can see, in this instance, beyond the fiction presented and clearly identify the show's social and political message better than any of the other spectators at the inn. Even though humor, functioning as another alienation mechanism, distorts the story's ideological implication, the historiography of the Reconquest remains at the heart of the show, although it is downgraded to a ridiculed cast of heroes (Gaylord 123). This subversive reading of the legendary ballad and, to a broader extent, of the Reconquest invites readers and the fictional spectators at the inn to disassociate popular representations from historical truth. Significantly, following Master Pedro's puppet show, the narrator delivers an intricate prolegomenon to chapter 2.27 in which he exposes the puppeteer and the chronicler Cide Hamete Benengeli as untrustworthy artists.[22]

A final estrangement effect rehearsed by Cervantes on the page is the mishandling of Melisendra's puppet. The puppeteer leaves the heroine dangling by her skirt at the exact moment when Don Gaiferos is about to liberate her: "But oh! What misfortune! The lace of her skirt has caught on some of the wrought iron at the balcony, and she hangs in midair and cannot reach the ground. But see how merciful heaven sends help at the moment of greatest need, for here comes Don Gaiferos, and not worrying about tearing the rich skirt, he grasps her and simply pulls her down to the ground, and then in a leap he sets her on his horse's hindquarters" (*Don Quixote* 631).[23] This irreverent twist dehumanizes Melisendra, downgrading her to an unseemly caricature and destroying any empathy the audience may have had for her.[24] The parodic tone of the interpreter's improvisation as he covers for Master Pedro's puppet mishandling shifts the show into the realm of the grotesque. This comical vision of the world—literally a world upside down—ridicules the ballad's overall heroic tone.[25]

Here again we see how Cervantes flaunts his knowledge of puppetry by exemplifying how improvisation goes hand in hand with the marionette's uncanny agency on stage and the importance of improvisation for the puppeteer. Indeed, with the help of the interpreter Master Pedro skillfully turns his mishandling act into a creative scene that deviates from the original story. Even so, "Melisendra's mishap," as John J. Allen refers to the unfortunate incident, could be interpreted as a subversive action on the part of the puppet, which pushes the show toward a new dramatic experience wherein the inanimate object strives for its own artistic agency and evades the manipulator's control. Cervantes had this notion in mind in the second part of the novel and refers to it in several episodes that focus on material performances: Clavileño, the flying wooden horse, and Don Antonio Moreno's oracular head become rebellious artifacts that end up controlling their owners, as I discuss in the next chapter. Moreover, Cervantes confers upon Cide Hamete's pen the autonomy to write the last words of the novel in the ultimate act of creative and authorial subversion: "For me alone was Don Quixote born, and I for him; he knew how to act, and I to write; the two of us are one" (*Don Quixote* 939).[26]

This notion of the unruly marionette becomes a central feature adopted by various early twentieth-century Spanish playwrights who turn to the puppet to denounce human vulnerability and to "experiment with the possibilities and the limitations of anthropomorphic and psychological representation" (Taxidou 10). Among these dramatic creations are Jacinto Grau's *El señor de Pigmalión* (Mister Pigmalion, 1921); Ramón María del Valle-Inclán's *Tablado de marionetas para educación de príncipes* (Tableau of marionettes for the education of princes, 1926); and Federico García Lorca's plays for glove puppets: *La niña que riega la albahaca y el príncipe preguntón* (The girl who waters the basil plant and the inquisitive prince, 1923), *Don Cristóbal y la Señá Rosita* (Tragicomedy of Don Cristóbal and Miss Rosita, ca. 1922), and *El retablillo de Don Cristóbal* (The puppet play of Don Cristóbal, 1931). In all these works—as in Master Pedro's puppet show—the autonomous marionettes break with traditional dramatic conventions by forcing the audience to confront the fact that objects can take full control of their actions and even their creators, a neo-animist threat that is a direct consequence of the dehumanizing effects of industrialization (Bell, "Playing with the Eternal Uncanny" 50).

It might seem contradictory that, despite the novelist's deliberate efforts to critically distance the characters and the readers from the fiction of the show, the puppets still beguile the knight at the end. As might be expected, this happens when enemies enter the narrative, as the interpreter depicts in the following passage:

"Look at the number of brilliant horsemen riding out of the city in pursuit of the two Catholic lovers.... I am afraid they will overtake them and bring them back tied to the tail of their own horse, which would be an awful sight." And Don Quixote, seeing and hearing so many Moors and so much clamor, thought it would be a good idea to assist those who were fleeing: and rising to his feet, in a loud voice he said: "I shall not consent, in my lifetime and in my presence, to any such offense against an enamored knight so famous and bold as Don Gaiferos. Halt you lowborn rabble; do not follow and do not pursue him unless you wish to do battle with me!" (*Don Quixote* 632)[27]

The protagonist empathizes with the puppets at the very moment when the Moors are about to capture the lovers, stressing once again the ballad's social relevance. Nonetheless, as irrational as Don Quixote's aversion to the puppets may seem, in today's society, audiences of all ranks and ages still react to puppets and not so much to puppeteers when a show touches them. The marionette's "residual traces of animism" (Pemberton 20) still abide; therefore, Don Quixote's reaction could be justified to a certain extent in what I consider Cervantes's thorough understanding of the language of puppetry.

When the knight steps out of his temporary state of enchantment, he is able to evaluate his impulsive actions and perceive reality for what it is: a pile of broken puppets. This act of recognition marks an overall turn in the novel and in the protagonist's development. From this point on, Don Quixote and Sancho will engage in much more sophisticated material performances orchestrated by devious characters whose sole purpose is to test their madness and simplicity, respectively. Yet, these dramatic illusions become decreasingly effective and anticlimactic for both the knight and his sidekick, as I explore in Chapter 5. Master Pedro's puppet show presents us, then, with a powerful learning experience for Don Quixote—and for readers, vicariously through him—vis-à-vis dealing with appearances. In a lone episode, the knight is shown coping with illusions in three different ways: from detached philological observation to a blind involvement with fiction and, ultimately, to the final anagnorisis, when he recognizes his transitory error of perception and literally pays for taking appearances at face value, not only in "good, standard Castilian currency" (*Don Quixote* 634) but with the irreversible price of desengaño.

Operatizing the Puppet

The unique theatrical weight carried by this episode in the novel contributed to its development on stage from the eighteenth century on as part of the plays, Spanish operettas, and operas inspired by *Don Quixote* (Huerta Calvo 95). At the turn of the twentieth century, Cervantes's marionettes continued to inspire various Spanish artists, especially playwrights, who included metadramatic scenes with puppets in their plays as an allusion to Master Pedro's show. Some of these works are Jacinto Benavente's *La senda del amor* (The path of love, 1905); Ramón del Valle-Inclán's *Farsa italiana de la enamorada del rey* (Italian farce of the young woman in love with the king, 1920) and his "Prologue" to *Los cuernos de don Friolera* (The horns of Don Friolera, 1921); and García Lorca's *La zapatera prodigiosa* (The shoemaker's prodigious wife, 1926–1930). It is not a coincidence that these writers found inspiration in Cervantes's marionettes as they moved away from realist theater to recreate the human experience and its contradictions using new creative languages for the stage.

The way Cervantes conceived his visionary puppet show dialogued with modernist and avant-garde currents of thought on the ominous agency of objects and the dehumanized society that developed in the aftermath of World War I. Likewise, in *Tres novelas ejemplares y un prólogo* (Three exemplary novels and a prologue, 1920), Miguel de Unamuno (1864–1936) literally evokes Master Pedro to criticize the conformity of realist characters who allow themselves to be manipulated by their authors as if they were automatized machines: "The characters of the realists [writers] tend to be dressed-up mannequins, controlled by strings with phonographs on their chests who repeat sentences Master Pedro picked up in the streets, the plazas and cafés and jotted down in his notebook."[28] This excerpt establishes a suggestive contrast with Augusto Pérez, the controversial protagonist in Unamuno's novel

Niebla (Mist, 1914), who, like Don Quixote and Sancho, is conscious of his fictionality and even rises up against his creator. Although the aforementioned works revived the artistic and conceptual nuances of Cervantes's original puppets, it was actually a composer, Manuel de Falla, who turned Master Pedro's show into a milestone of Spanish twentieth-century culture and the operatic repertoire, achieving the status of Cervantes's most staged *play* over time.[29]

In 1918, Winnaretta Singer, also known as Princesse Edmond de Polignac (1865–1943), commissioned Falla to create a piece for a chamber orchestra of no more than seventeen musicians and a limited number of singers, which was to be performed in her Parisian private salon. Before Falla, Igor Stravinsky (1882–1971) and Erik Satie (1866–1925) composed *Renard* (1916) and *Socrate* (1919), respectively, under similar terms.[30] Even though Falla's piece was among the first commissions by the music patron, it would take him over five years to finish it, and *El retablo* eventually premiered in Paris in 1923. Such a long creation process occurred because Falla aimed to produce a *Gesamtkunstwerk*, or a total work of art, in which he wanted to take charge of writing the musical score and devising its mise-en-scène. This adaptation closely followed the set envisioned by Cervantes, to which the composer added a layer of musical innovation. As an artist fully committed to the ideals of the Generation of 1898, he revaluated folkloric musical traditions and renewed classical molds by adhering to the musical current of neo-classicism, straddling tradition and innovation.[31] This artistic dualism, which runs throughout Falla's oeuvre, was heavily influenced by his personal taste as well as by his intellectual collaborators at the time (Nommick 62).

The books in Falla's library revealed his penchant for early modern Spanish literature. In addition to his interest in *Don Quijote* and the *Novelas ejemplares*, he was also fond of Luis de Góngora (1561–1627), the poetry of the Spanish mystics, and the theater of Lope de Vega and Calderón de la Barca (Torres Clemente, *Las óperas* 289; Persia, *Los últimos días* 146). Calderón de la Barca's plays proved to be especially inspiring for the composer throughout his career. He even considered writing an opera in 1914 based on *La devoción de la cruz* (The devotion of the Cross, 1640) and began preparations for musical scores on *Circe* (1930) and *Los encantos de la culpa* (The enchantments of guilt, 1645), both plays by Calderón de la Barca. Although these projects never reached completion, they acquainted Falla with the baroque aesthetics of seventeenth-century drama (Weber 908).

Besides his knowledge of early modern literature, the composer was also conversant with most avant-garde dramatic experiments that had taken hold in Europe at the turn of the twentieth century. He closely followed new trends in theater and performance, thanks to his friendship with two of the most influential personalities committed to renewing the Spanish stage: Gregorio Martínez Sierra (1881–1947), artistic director of Teatro Eslava, and Cipriano Rivas de Cherif (1891–1967), founder of Teatro Escuela Nueva.[32] Another inspirational collaborator who made a long-lasting impression on Falla's career was García Lorca (1898–1936), a versatile poet and artist imbued in the avant-garde but also a genuine enthusiast of Spanish folk culture. Thanks to his artistic relationship with Lorca, Falla became reacquainted with traditional marionette theater and Spanish balladry, both at the heart of Cervantes's Master Pedro's puppet show.[33] As reflected in their private correspondence, both artists had plans to collaborate in creating an itinerant puppet theater that would travel to the villages of the Alpujarra in Andalusia to perform Moorish ballads and folk tales with puppets (Torres Clemente, "Manuel de Falla" 843–44).

Furthermore, in 1923, Falla teamed up with García Lorca and puppeteer Hermenegildo Lanz (1893–1949) on a children's performance organized by the poet and staged in his house in Granada in honor of his younger sister, Isabel Lorca. The show featured three short plays: *El misterio de los Reyes Magos* (The mystery play of the Three Wise Men, anonymous, 1100s); the interlude *Los dos habladores* (Two talkers, 1600), attributed to Cervantes; and García Lorca's *La niña que riega la albahaca*. While Lorquian scholars have disregarded this event as a purely anecdotal get-together among friends, such a collaborative endeavor was crucial for the careers of the three artists and for the overall conception of *El retablo*. For García Lorca, this project allowed him to experiment as a playwright with puppet theater, a creative vein he would never abandon for the rest of his career (Pérez-Simón 50).³⁴ For Lanz, it meant the start of a fruitful collaboration with Falla, as the composer ended up appointing him as the original marionette designer for the *El retablo* premiere. For Falla, visualizing the set up for this amateur performance helped him to conceive his operetta's spatial and musical composition. The parlor room setting of García Lorca's house bore a resemblance to the intimate design of chamber theaters (Pérez-Simón 49), and the eclectic musical style that Falla devised for the occasion—a mix of semi-toned liturgical chants with Stravinskian ostinatos—would be further developed in *El retablo* (Nommick 62).

Nonetheless, it is fair to say that even before this collaboration took place, the composer already had an overall idea for his opera, as he stated in a personal letter to the Princesse, only a few months after receiving her commission:

> I found this material reading this chapter in the second part of *Don Quixote*, "Maese Pedro's Puppet Show." I'll follow Cervantes's text from the beginning of the performance (performed by puppets in a small theater on the stage). Presumably, the spectators mentioned in the text are in front of the stage. We hear them but we don't see them. It is only at the end that Don Quixote violently goes onstage to punish those who are chasing Melisendra and Don Gaiferos and the scene ends with the words he (Don Quixote) dedicates to the glory of Chivalry. (qtd. in Torres Clemente, *Las óperas* 288)³⁵

Falla ended up making some adjustments that diverged from this preliminary vision. He shortened Don Quixote's and Master Pedro's parts to give greater visibility to the marionettes performing the ballad; he imbued the opera with a more pessimistic tone by omitting Melisendra's spit after the moor's treasonous kiss and her indecorous incident with the skirt (Hess, *Manuel de Falla* 208); and, he included some excerpts from other episodes of the novel.

Nevertheless, Falla's artistic fixation with the mise-en-scène of *El retablo* was with the puppets, whose aesthetics and figurative meaning he would keep revisiting until the end of his life. This was not the first attempt for the composer to combine music and puppetry on stage: Falla's ballet, *El corregidor y la molinera* (The magistrate and the miller's wife, 1917), rewritten later on as *El sombrero de tres picos* (The three-cornered hat, 1919), purposely directed some of the characters to move like puppets. For *El Retablo*'s premiere, in fact, Falla dispensed with actors altogether and replaced all the characters with marionettes, a decision that demonstrates his adhesion to modernist performance trends developed by theater practitioners such as Edward Gordon Craig (1872–1966) and Alfred Jarry (1873–1907). Both Craig and Jarry were known for trying to prove the superiority of the puppet's dramatic qualities over and above the actor's. This "de-individualization" of the character "in favor of the idea" (Fuch 29) can be traced all the way back to the jointed Christ figures and the puppets of the *máquina real*, which we have previously analyzed.

Yet, by exclusively using marionettes to stage the different spatial and temporal layers of the Cervantine episode, the contrast between the spectators at the inn and the puppets starring in the ballad gets lost along with the element of surprise that the marionette generates. In an effort to preserve the dramatic essence devised by Cervantes and break with a homogeneous visual aesthetic, Falla conceived two styles of marionettes with very distinctive traits, as he describes in the stage directions for his opera score:

> The set is divided into two sections corresponding to the main stage and the puppet stage. In the former section the puppets representing the spectators at the inn appear and interact. Of these figures, the puppet representing Don Quixote should be, at the very least, twice the size of the others. The latter section of the set, which is in the background and contains the puppet theater, should give the impression of being completely independent of the former. This is the true theater and should be located at a sensible height above the main stage. (2)[36]

For the premiere, Lanz designed the puppets for the ballad in a cutout (one-dimensional) naive style, inspired by the frescoes in the Alhambra's

Sala de Justicia (Hall of Justice). The marionettes representing Don Quixote, Sancho Panza, Master Pedro, and the interpreter, however, were larger hand puppets with sculpted heads and exaggerated, though realistic, features.[37]

To emphasize the distancing effect that Cervantes created in his show, Falla separated Don Quixote, Master Pedro, and the interpreter from their respective voices and added three soloists to sing each puppet's part (see Figure 4.3). This solution does not break with the puppet's aesthetics; on the contrary, it enhances them, since the opera soloists share with the marionettes a lack of verisimilitude in their voices and the artificiality of their movements (Eruli 12). Consequently, this extra layer of *puppet matter* contributes to the estrangement effect and the dehumanizing aura that closely relates to Cervantes's original vision.[38]

As a result, Falla's set design for his opera superimposed four discontinuous levels of meaning that the audience had to piece together to create a comprehensive interpretation of the plot: 1) the voices of the three soloists representing Don Quixote, Master Pedro, and the interpreter; 2) the marionettes embodying these characters; 3) the silent marionettes of the ballad; and 4) the orchestra, which functioned as an extension of the stage as well as another animated element of the performance. Falla had a very concrete idea about the orchestra's spatial configuration: "The bowed instruments should be to the director's left. Harpsichord and harp should be downstage and to the director's right with the woodwinds, and behind them should be the horns and trumpet, but in such a way that the latter is far away from the flute. The bassoon, close to the horns and the string basses. The percussion: upstage" (qtd. in Persia, *Los últimos días* 149).[39] In addition to incorporating all the dispersed components of the set into a visually logical narrative, audiences also had to search for a coherent melodic flow in what seems, at first, to be a dislocated musical scheme—tested in Isabel García Lorca's home-theater entertainment—that ranged from Spanish folk-inspired rhythms to ultramodern French and Russian melodic patterns.

Over the years, Falla became increasingly inflexible with directors who did not follow his specific instructions for the set and did not hesitate to intervene when actors, instead of puppets, were used to represent

Don Quixote, Sancho Panza, Master Pedro, and the interpreter. In 1942, for example, he deauthorized a production at the Teatro Colón in Buenos Aires that planned to have children playing the parts of the puppets in the ballad. The composer turned, instead, to the famed and at the time exiled Italian puppeteer Vittorio Podrecca (1883–1959) to stage the opera with his renowned Teatro dei Piccoli (Children's Theater) (Persia, *Los últimos días* 147). When actors could not be replaced by marionettes, Falla insisted that they imitate the artificial movements of the puppets by using exaggerated gestures and masks to preserve the alienation effect that Cervantes deliberately intended.[40]

Disarticulated Remediations

In 1941, Argentine film producer Miguel Machinandiarena (1899–1975), the founder of Estudios San Miguel (San Miguel Studios) in Buenos Aires, offered Falla the opportunity to make a motion picture based on his opera. This was not the first time *El retablo* was associated with the film genre. Before Machinandiarena, German conductor Hermann Scherchen (1891–1966) had entertained the possibility of making a film adaptation of the opera, but it never came to fruition (Torres Clemente, *Las óperas* 324). Within the cinematic medium—viewed by experimentalist dramatists like Valle-Inclán as a new form of theater—Falla saw an opportunity to continue experimenting with the aesthetic of his opera.

One idea he contemplated was to precede the story with several still images of the puppets superimposed on the musical score for the overture (Torres Clemente, *Las óperas* 325). This animated audiovisual collage prelude may have been inspired by a wave of experimental performances and ballets that were taking place in the 1910s and 1920s in Europe, such as *Parade* (1917) and *Relâche* (1924). Further, collaborative and eclectic productions by avant-garde artists such as Jean Cocteau, Erik Satie, Léonide Massine, Pablo Picasso, Francis Picabia, and Rolf de Maré combined absurd theatrical performances with disconnected film sequences.[41]

But it was Russian filmmaker Sergei M. Eisenstein (1898–1948) and his approach to the montage technique that was the most instrumental for Falla's film conception. Eisenstein's book *The Film Sense* (1943), along with Manuel Villegas's *El cine: Magia y aventura del séptimo arte* (Cinema: Magic and adventure of the seventh art, 1940), were the two primary sources the composer studied in preparation for adapting his opera to the filmic medium (Del Pino 34). According to Eisenstein, the objective of montage was to highlight the creative process of the visual artwork as a way to promote the spectator's involvement in reconstructing its overall meaning. In the director's own words:

> The spectator not only sees the represented elements of the finished work, but also experiences *the dynamic process of the emergence and assembly* of the image just as it was experienced by the author. And this is, obviously, the highest possible degree of approximation to transmitting visually the author's perceptions and intention in all their fullness, to conveying them with "that strength of physical palpability" with which they arose before the author in his creative work and his creative vision. (32; my emphasis)

Falla found explicit parallelisms between the montage and the collage, as both techniques evoked a similar decimated aesthetic that the audience needed to cognitively reassemble and interpret. Although the film version of the opera was never completed, it gave the composer a broader vision to continue thinking about new ways to experiment with the stage set of *El retablo*.

This almost compulsory revisiting of the mise-en-scène did not stop with the composer; it has continued well into the twenty-first century while simultaneously keeping alive the original innovation of Cervantes's puppet show. Among the most recent Spanish opera adaptations of *El retablo*, Enrique Lanz's version for Títeres Etcétera rekindles the 1923 production most faithfully.[42] Enrique Lanz, the grandson of Hermenegildo Lanz, the designer of the original puppets, premiered his own adaption of *El retablo* in the Gran Teatre del Liceu in Barcelona in 2009 as a personal tribute to the friendship between his grandfather and Falla. Enrique Lanz followed the original artistic and conceptual cues for the staging and design of the puppets, to which he added several sophisticated mechanisms that make them more attuned to modern-day technologies.

In Lanz's contemporary production, Don Quixote, Sancho, Master Pedro, and the interpreter become monumental puppets resembling bronze sculptures between sixteen and twenty-six feet tall, inspired by Diego Velazquez's somber and realistic iconography. Their oversized dimensions, the lethargy of their movements, and their ocher tonalities contrast with the puppets of the ballad. For the latter, the director followed his grandfather's original sketches from 1923. Their smaller size allows them a broader range of motion, and their bright colors make them stand out as animated miniatures from a medieval illuminated manuscript (see Figures 4.4 and 4.5).

This radical contrast in size between Don Quixote, Sancho, Master Pedro, and the interpreter and the protagonists of the ballad had been tested already by American puppeteer Remo Bufano (1894–1948) in his version of *El retablo* that premiered in New York in 1925 and by the production by l'Opéra Comique in Paris in 1926. Remo Bufano created a human-sized puppet whose manipulation techniques were directly inspired by Japanese *kuroko*, the puppet manipulators in Bunraku who dress in black and are nearly invisible on stage while they handle the puppets. At l'Opéra Comique, Spanish painter Ignacio Zuloaga (1870–1945), famous for his depictions of popular and traditional Spanish figures, was in charge of designing the sets, and french painter Maxime Dethomas (1867–1929) carved the puppets (Persia, *Los últimos días* 264). Don Quixote and Sancho Panza performed their roles inside gigantic cardboard figures that make them look like magnified marionettes, following a carnivalesque and distorted aesthetic based on the *gigantes y cabezudos* (giants and big-heads) folk tradition (Llano 229).

Thus, in the 2009 grandiose production by Lanz, reminiscent of Don Quixote's gigantic delusions, the director offered modern-day audiences a revitalized palimpsest, drawing on the creativity of Cervantes, Falla, and his grandfather, that perpetuates a collaborative artistic genealogy spanning four centuries. For the opera's overture, Lanz even recovered the idea of adding some of the preliminary scenes that the composer had planned to include in the film version he was preparing in the

1940s (see Figure 4.6). Falla's *Concierto para clavecín, flauta, oboe, clarinete, violín y violonchelo* (Concerto for clavichord, flute, oboe, clarinet, and cello, 1926) opens this contemporary adaptation, accompanied by a video projected on a backdrop that features the shadow of Master Pedro as he prepares for his show.

Assuming there are as many *Quijotes* as there are readers, we could, then, argue that there are as many retablos as there are directors. Master Pedro's show has bewitched the imaginations of a multitude of artists not only in the theatrical and operatic arenas but also on the big screen. Even though Falla's opera was never adapted for the cinema, Cervantes's marionettes made their way to the cinematic medium as an isolated episode independent from the rest of the novel in a contemporary evocative interpretation. The neorealist film *Paisà* (Paisan, 1946) by Italian director Roberto Rossellini (1906–1977) is a unique example of how Master Pedro's puppet show has assumed a life of its own as a modern sociopolitical adaptation. The film is structured around six vignettes dealing with the German occupation of Italy during the 1940s. In the second vignette, Joe, an African American military police officer, is accompanied by the young Italian orphan rogue, Pasquale, through the streets of Naples. Joe drunkenly rants about his idealized homecoming in the United States and fantasizes about being acknowledged as a war hero. Gradually, he realizes that, upon his return home, he will only resume his dismal, marginalized existence. During one of their perambulations, Joe and Pasquale attend an *Opera dei Pupi* show. Joe immediately identifies himself with the Saracen warriors because of their racial traits and the fierce treatment they receive at the hands of light-skinned Paladins. Carried away by his drunkenness, he does not hesitate to get on the stage to defend them in his delusional state, which is akin to Don Quixote's cathartic intervention.[43]

Rossellini's vignette is a powerful reinterpretation of the message behind Cervantes's puppet show: the misleading illusions of an ineffective marginalized hero and the absurdity of a nation attempting international liberation with soldiers who are themselves victims of discrimination and neglect at home (Amberson 395). Rossellini takes advantage of the language of puppetry to explore the feelings of alienation and dehumanization of World War II, just as Cervantes and Falla did by bringing their retablos to life in their respective disenchanted eras.

For over four hundred years, Master Pedro's puppet show has maintained its original significance as a cautionary tale about the inauthenticity of modern society, to call upon Guy Debord's notion of reality, and the need for individuals to develop skepticism as they navigate it. However, the way the novelist manipulates his puppets can also be read as an audacious contribution to new artistic avenues that might have been too daunting for the stage in his time but perfectly in tune centuries later. In this sense, in his efforts to revitalize the operatic genre at the turn of the twentieth century, Falla found an alter ego in Cervantes's reinvention of the novel. When *El retablo* premiered in 1923, it was misunderstood by traditional audiences and critics who labeled it as a negation of the very essence of opera—just as *Don Quixote* was considered an anti-novel—until it subsequently developed into the greatest Spanish contribution to avant-garde European puppetry (Martínez, "Telón adentro" 100).

As we have seen with Zamora, Caballero, and Landy in the previous chapters, animated performance objects can be culturally recycled and revisited as long as their messages continue to affect contemporary society in a meaningful way. Falla fully contributes to this group of pioneer-artists, since he found regenerative material in Cervantes's puppets to express the schizoid identity of the Generation of 1898—ideologically split between tradition and innovation—in its search for a raison d'être in the disheartened country that Spain became at the end of the nineteenth century.

Cervantes's furious marionettes, as well as Don Quixote, were also direct products of a disoriented era that had lost sight of what was real and what was illusory at the onset of modernity. By the end of Master Pedro's show, the protagonist becomes a disenchanted subject. He accepts responsibility for his ineffective, damaging actions and resorts to using money to settle the affair. This incursion of the supremely outdated knight into a world where everything is calculable is one of the main principles of disenchantment, following Jane Bennett's understanding of the concept (59). It would seem, though, that this blunt step into the modern world prepared the hero for what was yet to come. While physically and psychologically exhausted, Don Quixote is now equipped with the necessary skepticism to navigate the re-enchantments that await him in the rest of the novel, in which science and technology will churn out the main agents of artifice and theatrical illusionism in an increasingly modern world.

5. Technologies of Wonder

> Fortunately, the magical art has not always been characterized by gesticulations into thin air. It has dealt with material things, carried out real experiments and even made its own discoveries.
>
> MARCEL MAUSS, *A General Theory of Magic*, 1950

MASTER PEDRO'S PUPPET show is indicative of a definitive turning point vis-à-vis the material performances featured in *Don Quijote*, not only for the episode's genuine theatrical nature but also because Cervantes bluntly exposes the protagonist to the unmaking of illusions, which inaugurates the knight to a world of skepticism, a marker of identity during the early modern period. Animated props and experimental performances in the novel from this point forward contribute to a sense of doubt and emptiness in the knight as well as the schemers who surround the protagonist and try to control his actions through sophisticated simulated adventures. These devious orchestrators are adept masters of dissimulation who fabricate an artificial chivalric world by means of cold reasoning and material resources (Lee 34). The duke, the duchess, and Don Antonio Moreno are the three principal schemers to whom I refer in this chapter. These characters set the stage for their shows in their private residences, which are comparable to "fortress[es] of solitude" (Eco 5), a fitting allusion to Superman's famous hideout, inasmuch as the Cervantine dwellings share in its isolation, artificiality, and eccentricity. These players reveal themselves to be profoundly dissatisfied individuals who, clinging to their socioeconomic status, attempt to fill their own existential voids at Don Quixote and Sancho's expense. Yet, no matter how extravagant their deceitful performances turn out to be, they do not succeed in fully duping the knight and his squire.

While desengaño was only intimated in the first part of the novel, in the second part—as we have seen already with Master Pedro's puppet show—it becomes a major ideological axis in the plot, as disillusionment is increasingly apparent in the protagonist's weariness, which gradually presages the collapse of his fantasy world. In this regard, David Gitliz has described the second part of *Don Quijote* as "the road to desengaño" (108). The deceptive machinations that befall the protagonist prompt his abulia and sense of personal defeat by the end of the enchanted boat adventure (2.29)—only three chapters after Master Pedro's puppet show—when he declares: "'Enough!' Don Quixote said to himself. It will be preaching in the desert to try to convince this rabble to take any virtuous action. In this adventure two valiant enchanters must have had an encounter, and one hinders what the other attempts: one provided me with the boat, and the other threw me out of it. God help us, for *the entire world is nothing but tricks and deceptions opposing one another. I can do no more*" (*Don Quixote* 652; my emphasis).[1] As these words show, Don Quixote is increasingly self-aware of his ineffectiveness, and, from this moment forward, he resigns himself, for the most part, to the chicanery that others will arrange for him.[2] Don Quixote consciously turns into a passive observer in a society where his selfless heroism has been replaced by transactions, calculations, and skepticism.

For some of these scripted adventures, the orchestrators use animated performance objects to make their artificial illusions more successful at forcing the protagonists to the edge of reason. Within these premade scenarios, Clavileño, the flying wooden horse—devised by the duke, the duchess, and their entourage (2.40–2.41)—and Don

Antonio Moreno's enchanted head (2.62) stand out as recreating the most grandiose and radical wonders of the novel: an interstellar space flight and the quest for absolute knowledge, respectively.[3] Juan Bautista Avalle-Arce has suggested a curious connection between the two props on the basis of the paranormal experiences they promote:

> The moment we take seriously the idea that an enchanted and insolent head exists is the moment when logic comes to an end and we leave the natural world. This type of episode is not abundant in *Don Quijote*; indeed, it is exceedingly scarce. In Part II of the novel, there is only one other episode that openly involves magic and that is the episode of Clavileño. Therein, winged horses exist and they can fly, to the point that one is brought to the palace garden of the duke and duchess and placed at the disposition of Don Quixote and Sancho in order to travel by air to the realm of Candaya to defend justice. And the two of them fly on Clavileño! From this perspective, only the enchanted head in Barcelona can compare with such empirical magic. (56)

Avalle-Arce seems to accept the empirically magical essence of these artifacts, if contextualized beyond all logic and as long as the protagonists and the readers are willing to suspend their disbelief.

I favor, however, a more nuanced interpretation of these *wonderlands* represented by Clavileño and the enchanted head. In my view, both animated and highly theatrical objects function as *technologies of wonder* capable of generating a simultaneous coexistence between the natural and the supernatural, thanks to scientific and technological progress that I read as a type of artificial magic capable of producing marvels (Eamon, *Science* 59). Social anthropologist Alfred Gell and historian William Eamon have claimed in *Art and Agency* (1998) and *Science and the Secrets of Nature* (1994), respectively, that technology and magic are alike in the ways that they manipulate and recombine the occult qualities of things to attain new objectives and results. Thus, in addition to Master Pedro's puppet show, Cervantes turns again to material performances to open yet another avenue for reflecting on the meaning of modernity, this time through emerging technologies that isolate wonder from superstition and frame it as part of the systematic and technical progress of the time.

Making Wonderlands

While the duke, the duchess, and their entourage, as well as Don Antonio Moreno, intend to dupe Don Quixote and Sancho via their duplicitous animated artifacts, the narrator openly reveals what is happening behind the scenes, either while the action is unfolding or immediately thereafter. Such acts of disclosure, however, do not entirely invalidate wonder, as readers are presented with another form of enchantment rooted in the very process of manufacturing illusions through creativity and artistic innovation. Indeed, learning how to assess novel technologies not merely for the elation they arouse but for the scientific progress they represent was a key feature of modernity (Gunning, "Re-Newing" 44). In other words, the modern era did not eliminate magic or the marvelous but re-semanticized and even enhanced its content by appealing to systematic knowledge.

It is debatable whether the two premade adventures of Clavileño and the enchanted head produce the hoped-for results from the protagonists;[4] nonetheless, the conniving masters of ceremonies succeed in deploying two meticulously planned scenarios aligned with Don Quixote's knighthood expectations. The choices of a flying horse and a talking head as the main props for these interactive attractions are expressly informed by magic and adventure.[5] In the fifteenth-century Carolingian romance epic *Valentin et Orson* (Valentine and Orson), both artifacts are present in the plot. In addition, their material history is intrinsically associated with black magic. Flying horses abound in universal folklore, and legendary shamans used them in initiation rites (Padilla 273). Similarly, the oracular head has had a long cultural and literary legacy related to necromancy that is, of note, more complex than that of the flying horse. Its origins can be traced back to a lost ballad about Pope Sylvester II (ca. 946–1003; J. R. Jones 91), but the belief in its magical powers continued to be prevalent until the sixteenth century. Historian Keith Thomas records a daunting case that took place in 1371 before the Court of King's Bench, where a magician was found carrying an actual head of a Saracen warrior that he bought in Toledo to house a spirit with divination powers (274). While some thinkers like the theologian Francisco de Vitoria (ca. 1486–1546) believed in their supernatural potential, others such as Saint Thomas Aquinas, Jesuit Martín del Río (1551–1608), and even Cervantes rejected the magic aura of these divination artifacts.

Notwithstanding, the novelist endows both the wooden horse and the oracular head with artificial supernatural qualities, and the paranormal sheens lose their luster in no time for any reader or audience acquainted with the leisure activities that combine playfulness and science so in vogue since the sixteenth century. Indeed, both artifacts evoke the rich tradition of automata, hydraulic devices, and animated toys that became a favorite courtly entertainment during the Renaissance and continued throughout the baroque era in Spain. This taste for kinetic artifice was partially due to the Neoplatonic humanists' fascination with Egyptian civilization and its advanced knowledge in building automata.[6]

In addition to these frivolous uses of scientific advances, technology began to have a greater presence in various aspects of everyday life owing to the increase in trade and urbanization over the course of the seventeenth century. Of note, some entertainment artifacts were refurbished by the scientific community to improve living conditions and advance the industry. An illustrative example is the similitude between the mechanisms that activate the enchanted head in *Don Quijote* and an air-conditioning system that inventor Jerónimo de Ayanz y Beaumont (1553–1613) designed, which astounded leading scientists and engineers of the time (Paz Gago 73–74).

In choosing props that fit Don Quixote's chivalric expectations that were likewise rooted in the material and cultural trends of the period, Cervantes underlines the concept of rational wonder. Furthermore, these fantastic scenarios are literally and figuratively moved by techniques that point to the artificiality of their staging. The first strategy is rhetorical persuasion. In the case of the flying horse, the Dueña Dolorida (dolorous duenna), one of the sidekicks in the ducal entourage, starts by relating the magical origins of Clavileño and its supernatural powers:

> Malambruno obtained him through his arts, and has him in his power, and uses him on the journeys that he takes from time to time to different parts of the world: today he is here, and tomorrow in France, and the next day in Potosí; and the good thing is that this horse doesn't eat or sleep or need shoes, and he trots through the air without wings, and his gait is so smooth and even that whoever rides him can hold a cup full of water in his hand without spilling a drop. (*Don Quixote* 715)[7]

It is needless to say that the much longer and more elaborate story than what is quoted above requires a histrionic performance that matches this larger-than-life tale that the duenna does not hesitate to deploy to her full potential.[8]

Don Antonio, for his part, also deploys a thoughtful, persuasive speech, describing the paranormal powers of the talking head:

> This head, Señor Don Quixote, has been fabricated and made by one of the greatest enchanters and wizards the world has ever seen, a Pole, I believe, and a disciple of the famous Escotillo, about whom so many marvels are told; he was here in my house and for a thousand *escudos*, which I paid him, he fashioned this head, which has the property and virtue of responding to any question spoken into its ear. He determined the bearings, painted the characters, observed the stars, looked at the degrees, and finally completed this with all the perfection that we shall see tomorrow, because the head is mute on Fridays, and since today is Friday, we shall have to wait until tomorrow. (*Don Quixote* 866)[9]

Don Antonio's self-fashioning as a conjurer and the atmosphere of illusion that he recreates around his persona find curious historical parallelisms with the aura of eccentricity that virtuoso Juan de Espina (1583–1642) cultivated throughout his life (García Santo-Tomás, *Refracted* 122). This famous Spanish collector of curiosities was known for inventing a specific narrative and a customized display for each of the bizarre objects he had in his Madrid villa (García Santo-Tomás, "Visiting the Virtuoso" 133).

In both of these preambles, the duenna and Don Antonio manage to leverage persuasion by wrapping the artifacts in a fantastic rhetorical patina perfectly adapted to the type of simulated attraction that will follow. The duenna performs an overacted thriller solo that prepares the protagonists for the interstellar journey they are about to undertake.[10] For his part, Don Antonio's enigmatic tale lures the knight into the occult sciences field and the paranormal realm (Reed, "Ludic Revelations" 193), making him an active participant in this immersive experience from the very beginning, as the following proves:

> Don Antonio *walked with Don Quixote* around the chamber, *circling the table many times*, and then he said: "Now that I am certain, Señor Don Quixote, that *no one is listening, and no one can hear us*, and the door is closed, I want to tell your grace about one of the strangest adventures, or I should say marvels, that anyone could imagine, on the condition that whatever I tell your grace must be *buried in the deepest recesses of secrecy*." (*Don Quixote* 865; my emphasis)[11]

The emphasis on secrecy enhances the eerie atmosphere of the overall setting and the power of the schemer, yet it also alludes to the importance of safeguarding inventions, a practice shared among the early modern scientific community (Eamon, *Science* 356). To that end, let's not forget that the uniqueness of Clavileño and the enchanted head is located in the ways in which Cervantes enmeshes reason and entertainment technologies in what purport to be two magical experiences.

The supernatural realm artificially created around these two artifacts by the duenna and Don Antonio through their speech acts is emphasized by the settings these masters of ceremonies choose to frame their interactive mise-en-scènes: the garden where the Clavileño adventure is staged and the home theater-laboratory where the talking head is displayed. As in the preparatory speeches we just examined, these two alternative stages are similarly and thoroughly conceived to engage the viewers' creative imaginations vis-à-vis the devices they are about to experience firsthand. The duke's garden and Don Antonio's parlor deliberately function as liminal milieus between the natural and the artificial, the mundane and the supernatural, and the controlled and the disorderly.

Clavileño's flight is intended to be staged in a garden at night, which, at the time, was considered a site for displaying the ways in which nature could be restrained by man's artistry but remained open to the potential threat of chaos and the occult. Il Sacro Bosco (Garden of Bomarzo), in Viterbo, Italy, built in 1552 by Vincenzo Orsini (1523–1580), epitomizes the kind of mannerist garden that John Onians has described as a "theatre of astonishment" (16). Similarly, in the Orti Oricellari (Rucellai Gardens) in Florence, Bianca Cappello (1548–1587), second wife of Francesco I de' Medici (1541–1587), organized performances in which fear and spectacle went hand in hand, just as in the mise-en-scène of Clavileño. Celio Malespini describes a specific enactment whose similarity to the performances staged outdoors and outside of the duke and the duchess's castle—Clavileño's flight being one of them—is quite astounding:

> Assembling in the Oricellari after midnight, the group was met by a necromancer, whose appearance before them was accompanied by "infinite voices and laments, strange yowlings, gnashing of teeth, hands clapping, shaking of iron chains, cries, sighs, and infinite fireworks that exploded from all sides, issuing forth from many holes dug with marvelous artistry." At a signal from this bizarre figure, a trap door in the ground, camouflaged with grass, suddenly opened to reveal a cavernous hole, into which the guests promptly fell. Awaiting them at the bottom were servants dressed up as devils, who were, however, soon expelled from the garden and replaced by beautiful girls wearing perfume, fine jewels and little else. (qtd. in Morgan 1–2)

Il Sacro Bosco, the Orti Oricellari, and the fictional ducal gardens in *Don Quijote* do not conform to the utopian Arcadia model; rather, they evoke an artificial *locus horridus* (hellish place), opposite the *locus amoenus* (pleasant place), where the supernatural and the monstrous end up making their artificial appearance, operated by human ingenuity.

Indeed, mechanical animals and other novel technological artifacts like the *engiens d'esbattement* (frolicsome engines) were displayed in these gardens as in an open-air museum of science (Sawday 190; Knoespel 117).[12] As such, it is worthwhile to consider the comparison drawn by Alfredo Aracil between the garden and the automaton, an illuminating correlation that stresses the uncanny experience surrounding Clavileño's adventure: "Paradise in some cases, universe in others, [the garden] was the scene and refuge of some of the objects and manifestations that sew together our overview: automaton, labyrinths, fiestas, collections. But we should also consider the garden as a giant automaton in itself, a sophisticated device that imitates, recreates and, at times, surpasses nature" (16; my emphasis). Jessica Riskin also highlights the fact that Renaissance gardens were larger-than-life spaces that blurred the border between the human and the fantastic, recreating a "magico-mechanical feast" ("Machines" 36)—just like the other animated artifacts we have examined up to this point. Accordingly, when Clavileño makes its first appearance, the horse is escorted by "four savages, all of them dressed in green ivy" (*Don Quixote* 718).[13] These fantastic creatures emerge as part of the natural space, as if it has assumed a life of its own to intensify the unsettling presence of the horse and its potential for rebellion (i.e., the potential for a machine to go "haywire"). Here, the *hombre selvático* (wild man), taking the form of a myrtle figure—the conceptual opposite of the marble statue—evokes the potential threat of the wilderness to distort the human world (Rodríguez de la Flor, *Pasiones* 125).[14]

In contrast to the outdoor mechanized setting that frames the adventure of Clavileño, the enchanted head is displayed in a parlor in Don Antonio's residence, which is expressly designed to suit the technical needs of the automaton. This exhibition space shares a good number of characteristics with the aforementioned Juan de Espina's private gallery of mechanical figures in Madrid as well as the famous *Wunderkammer* (cabinet of curiosities) curated by scientific collector Juan de Lastanosa (1607–1681) in his residence in Huesca.[15] De Espina, in particular, remained concerned throughout his life with "the performative and material aspects of knowledge, with hidden information that led to ultimate revelations, and with the power of the secret and the double" (García Santo-Tomás, *Refracted Muse* 122).

Driven by a similar interactive approach to knowledge and curiosity, Don Antonio acclimatized a chamber in his house comparable to the private exhibition spaces where European collectors displayed their bizarre findings. Javier Moscoso's description of the *Wunderkammer* is enlightening as it emphasizes its theatrical nature (discursively and spatially), reminiscent of Don Antonio's ingenious show around the oracular artefact: "What had been the most private place, most removed from the mundane, became a center for conversion in the seventeenth century, a refuge for conversation, *a genteel theater* in which one could simultaneously cultivate a curiosity for the most prized objects in both nature and art" (275; my emphasis). Thanks to the cabinets of curiosities and their virtuoso keepers, wonder in seventeenth-century Europe found a legitimate space for active observation and elucidation, where select viewers attempted to figure out hypothetical links among the objects on display, completed their stories, and learned how to read the artifacts' performativity.[16] Thus, these *disciplined spaces* could be interpreted as the origin of scientific inquiry, as they were open to novelty and rarity with the intent of promoting knowledge through conversation and the exchange of ideas (Eamon, *Science* 338). Don Antonio seems well aware of the new collaborative meaning of modern *curiosity* when he expressly invites two of his best friends to test the enchanted head for the first time, just as in a legitimate scientific experiment where collective witnessing was required to prove reliability.[17]

Once the oracular head and Clavileño have been properly contextualized within their simulated backgrounds, the novelist then reveals the inner workings of their supernatural powers. The animation of Clavileño and the oracular head are specifically envisioned to conceal technologies whose disclosure will debunk black magic in favor of the technological systems applied to entertainment.[18] Even though Clavileño's only automatic key mechanism is a wooden peg in its forehead through which it activates a false takeoff, the systematic staging orchestrated around its virtual flight makes the horse an "inert automaton" (Aranda 65) and part of a long-lasting tradition of zoomorphic artifacts. Robert I, count of Artois (1216–1250), for example, entertained his guests in his Hesdin Castle in France with mechanical beasts that could greet, scold, or soak visitors with water (Cave and Dihal 474). Likewise, among his curiosities, Lastanosa collected animal-shaped automata made from patent leather (Paz Gago 52). This trend continued well into the eighteenth century when Jacques Vaucason (1709–1782) designed the famous *canard digérateur* (digesting duck) in 1739. With four hundred moving parts, the duck could bend his neck to eat, swallow grain, and defecate pellets (Boehn 12–13).[19]

Cervantes was well aware of the innovative mechanical artifacts of his time when he envisioned Clavileño as a flying machine. Arial devices were becoming increasingly popular in early modern Western fiction.[20] They appear, for instance, in Juan Maldonado's bestseller *Somnium* (The dream, 1532), Robert Greene's *Friar Bacon and Friar Bungay* (ca. 1589), Francis Bacon's *Sylva Sylvarum; or, A Natural History, in Ten Centuries* (1627), and Francis Godwin's *The Man in the Moone, or a Discourse on a Voyage Thither, by Domingo Gonsales the Speedy Messenger* (1638). Further, Johannes Kepler's *Somnium, seu opus posthumum de astronomia lunari* (The dream, or posthumous work on lunar astronomy, 1634) and Francis Godwin's *The Man in the Moone* are considered the first two literary works of European science fiction, as they include cosmic voyages, explorations to the moon, aliens, and critical engagement with astronomy and physics (Poole 57–58).

Early modern "space-colonizing fiction," as Mari-Tere Alvárez has called this literary trend (13), was politically meaningful in Spain after the Treaty of Tordesillas (1494), which established the country as a global superpower.[21] The treaty and its implications did not go unnoticed by English writers who started portraying Spain as the innate colonizer of the moon (Álvarez 12). At the beginning of the seventeenth century in England, there were even rumors that the Jesuits had a plan to reach the moon. John Donne (1572–1631), inspired by such an extraordinary enterprise, wrote *Ignatius His Conclave* (1611), a satire of Saint Ignatius of Loyola (1491–1556), telling the story of how the founder of the Jesuit order was instructed to carry out a lunar mission after having gone through hell.[22]

Clavileño's virtual flight alters the conceptions of time and space and combines the fascinations for mechanization and futuristic explorations into the unknown, not without a dose of subversion, as was to be expected from Cervantes's pen (see Figure 5.1).[23] In the garden of the ducal estate, the servants prepare a journey into outer space for the knight and the squire. Both protagonists are forced to ride the wooden horse blindfolded, while the reader fully participates in each of the steps implied in this humiliating aerial simulation.[24]

In this episode, the first special effect is the launching of the horse. The fake duennas persuade Don Quixote and Sancho that they are taking flight—although they never leave the ground—through the power of suggestion enhanced this time via the horse's articulated peg and the retinue's histrionic farewell:

> Both *were blindfolded*, and Don Quixote, *sensing that everything was as it should be, touched the peg*, and as soon as he had placed his fingers on it, all the duennas and everyone else present *raised their voices*, saying: "May God be your guide, valiant Knight!" "God go with you, intrepid squire!" "Now, now you are in the air, moving through it faster than an arrow!" "Now you are beginning to amaze and astonish everyone looking at you from the ground." "Hold on, valiant Sancho, you're slipping! Be careful you don't fall, because your fall will be worse than that of the daring boy who wanted to drive the chariot of his father, the Sun!" (*Don Quixote* 722; my emphasis)[25]

This virtual takeoff is followed by a series of tricks that vividly recreate the sensations of wind, with bellows, and heat, with flaming mops waved in front of the protagonists' faces:

> "Friend, banish your fear, for in fact the matter is proceeding as it should, and we have the wind at our backs." "That is true," responded Sancho. "On this side the wind's so strong it feels like a thousand bellows blowing on me." And there were *large bellows blowing the air* around him, for this adventure had been so well planned by the duke and the duchess and their steward that no element was lacking to make it perfect. Then, with some *tow-cloth on a reed that was easy to light and extinguish, their faces were warmed from a distance*. Sancho, who felt the heat, said: "By my soul, we must be in that place of fire already, or very close to it, because a good part of my beard has been

singed and I'm ready, Señor, to take off the blindfold and see where we are." (*Don Quixote* 723; my emphasis)²⁶

Shortly thereafter, the retinue stages the impact of landing back on Earth with the aid of pyrotechnics: "and desiring to conclude the strange and carefully made adventure, they set fire to Clavileño's tail with some tow-cloths, and since the horse was full of fireworks, it suddenly flew into the air with a fearsome noise and threw Don Quixote and Sancho Panza to the ground half-scorched" (*Don Quixote* 724; see Figure 5.2).²⁷

While it is tempting to interpret Clavileño's flight as a trivial comical extravaganza, Cervantes based this theatrical interlude on contemporary literary and cultural currents that influenced social circles at the time. Writers, natural philosophers, and scientists found in fiction writing a medium that, in Portuondo's words, "shared with science a desire to recreate experiences and experiments and share observations so that the reader both witnesses and vicariously partakes *in the knowledge making process*" (71; my emphasis). Furthermore, the novelist uses this exploratory surreal journey to point out that the technology behind entertainment succeeds in creating artificial wonder and materializing futuristic imagination.²⁸

By the same token, the enchanted head, although presented to Don Quixote as a paranormal divinatory experiment by keeping once again its mechanisms concealed from the protagonist's sight, is revealed to the reader as a compendium of instructions for building a device capable of transmitting the human voice. Athanasius Kircher (1602–1680) designed a similar talking bust that could move its eyes and emit guttural sounds through a resonating tube system hidden inside a building's walls (see Figure 5.3).²⁹ From the very first description of the talking head, the narrator focuses on its external appearance, which implies the existence of a concealed reality beneath its facade: "Don Antonio took Don Quixote by the hand and led him to a side room where the only furnishing was a table, *apparently of jasper*, on a base of the same material, and on it there was a head, made in the fashion of the busts of Roman emperors, *which seemed to be* of bronze" (*Don Quixote* 865; my emphasis).³⁰

Moreover, as soon as the deception ends, Cide Hamete discloses to the reader, in minute detail, the artifact's concealed technologies "in order to curb the astonishment of those who might think that some magical and extraordinary mystery was contained in the head" (*Don Quixote* 871).[31] Cide Hamete notes:

> It was constructed in this fashion: the tabletop was of wood painted and varnished to look like jasper, and the base on which it rested was made of the same material, with four eagle's talons projecting from it for greater stability. The head, which resembled a carved portrait bust of a Roman emperor cast in bronze, was completely hollow, as was the table top into which it fit so perfectly that there was no sign of their joining. The base of the table was also hollow, corresponding to the throat and chest of the head, and all this connected to another chamber beneath the room where the head was located. Through the entire hollow of the base, the tabletop, throat, and chest of the portrait bust ran a tube of tinplate that was very precisely fitted and could not be seen by anyone. Posted in the corresponding chamber below was the man who would respond, his mouth up against the tube, so that, as if the tube were an ear trumpet, one voice would travel down and the other would travel up in clear, well-articulated words, and in this way, it was not possible to discover deception. Don Antonio's nephew, an astute and clever student, was the responder; having been told by his uncle who would come into the room with him to question the head that day, it was easy for him to respond quickly and accurately to the first question; he responded to the others by conjecture and, since he was clever, with cleverness. (*Don Quixote* 871–72)[32]

Although the narrator explains away any possibility of sorcery, by uncovering the technology that activates the oracular head, he simultaneously triggers a sense of *modern wonder* in the reader. That is to say, the wondrous experience is made possible by the conditions of modernity, rooted in curiosity and rationality.

To a certain extent, modern wonder is similar to what Gell has termed the "technology of enchantment" with respect to the work of art. As Gell states, "the *technology of enchantment* is founded on the *enchantment of technology*. The enchantment of technology is the power that technical processes have of casting a spell over us so that we see the real world in an enchanted form" (44; my emphasis). This theory may be applied most suitably to the talking head if we consider that such a device is a scientific *and* performative work of art. Considering that the word *art* in early modernity also referred to science (Díaz Santiago 13), such an argument is defensible. Furthermore, according to Guillaume Budé's *Lexicon Graeco-Latinum* (1554), one meaning for the term *technologia* at the time was also *art* or *treatise on the art(s)* (from *tekhnē*, art or craft, and *-logia* [-logy], treatise or discourse). In another vein, we must also interpret the divination séance as a joke of knowledge, or a *lusus scientae*. Following Cory Reed's interpretation of this episode, the revelation of the enchanted head's hidden mechanisms—just like the description of the behind-the-scenes events in Clavileño's flight—represent another facet of modern wonder in light of the technical skills required for the artifact's operative system.

Furthermore, in his definition of modernity, Tom Gunning considers technology as a pragmatic tool for performing a task in a way that would have seemed magical in the past ("Re-Newing" 45). Thus, if we appreciate all of the aforementioned facets of wonder as science, as *technē*, as art, as joke, as tool, etc. in a grand epistemic confluence, we can properly frame our understanding of Clavileño and the oracular head as processes of spectacular technology. The disclosure of the systems that set in motion both artifacts leads readers to experience a modern re-enchantment—a "wow" effect, if you will—based on discerning the very mechanisms that create animation. For the protagonists, as we shall see in the next section, their engagement with technology in relation to both simulated adventures is much more nuanced, as the novelist does not expose them directly to the revelation of the jokes as he does with his readers.

Enchantment Interrupted

The performances around Clavileño and the talking head are representative of cultural modernity not only because of their spectacular creativity and the technicalities they display, as I have argued thus far, but also because they foreshadow artistic, ideological, and mechanistic futurities. Like Francis Godwin (1562–1633) or Johannes Kepler (1571–1630), Cervantes was ahead of his time in embracing and understanding scientific thought. By highlighting the liminal positions of his two automata, straddling the supernatural and the natural, the novelist portends some of the social anxieties of industrial society concerning the autonomy of objects/machines, which were mentioned in the previous chapter regarding Master Pedro's puppet show.

Clavileño and the enchanted head prefigure a series of literary automata at the turn of the twentieth century that rebel against their creators, such as the lifelike doll Olimpia in E. T. A. Hoffmann's "The Sandman" (1816), the robots in Karel Capek's *R.U.R.* (*Rossum's Universal Robots*, 1921), and the mechanical figures in Jacinto Grau's *El señor de Pigmalión* (Mister Pygmalion, 1921). Films like Segundo Chomón's *El hotel eléctrico* (The electric hotel, 1908) and Fritz Lang's *Metropolis* (1927) also contemplate the loss of control over humanity's mechanical creations, which may be seen as a portentous prefiguring of modern complexity and, further still, the resultant hyperreality of the postmodern in the late twentieth and early twenty-first centuries.[33]

Animist beliefs about the agency of premodern objects that were overcome in early modernity via the Scientific Revolution arose again at the beginning of the twentieth century; this time, however, they revolved around the threat of technological and industrial innovations. This contemporary new age of machinery in the Western world, which Walter Benjamin (1892–1940) famously examined in art, would translate to the concept of the uncanny as a way to control on an emotional level what is uncontrollable on a material one. Although Ernst Jentsch (1867–1919) and Sigmund Freud (1856–1939) approached the notion of uncanny from different perspectives, both thinkers associated it with a dark feeling of uncertainty and alienation in the presence of objects that are *strangely* familiar (e.g., simultaneously familiar and unfamiliar, or *heimlich/unheimlich*) to us, bespeaking a properly modern preoccupation with estrangement.

Cervantes had already delved mockingly into the agency of the inanimate object with the Melisendra puppet, of whom Master Pedro loses control. Nonetheless, it is with Clavileño and the enchanted head that the novelist further explores human anxiety triggered by mechanical animacy. Both of these artifacts end up turning against their manipulators and, ultimately, are discarded as "the most obvious way to cope with the danger of automata" (Strauss 193). In Clavileño's case, the narrator provides a step-by-step explanation and compendium of theatrical mechanisms that simulate the wooden horse's flight. However, when Sancho assumes control over the discourse by narrating the aerial experience in his own terms, the artifact acquires a life of its own. In this respect, Mario Martín-Flores points out, "Sancho recounts his dizzying journey in such a way as to maintain the deception intact. Sancho, in this case, sees himself transfigured into a mythical hero who plays a central role in this adventure, similar to Daedalus and Icarus" (58). Carlos Orlando Nállim is even more categorical about the leading role of the squire in this space adventure when he states: "Practically the entire 'story' of Clavileño the horse belongs to Sancho. He imagines, he speaks, and the others attentively listen to a new work of literary art that is based on a long tradition of the horse, the flying horse" (84). I would even add that in his space-travel tale, Sancho weaves in his own notions of astrology: at the time, astrology was not dismissed as a delusional belief but was considered a legitimate field of study with an inner logic and intellectual coherence (Walsham 504).

In the bizarre world recreated by the duke and duchess, perhaps the only logical response is the one that Sancho suggests, wherein he deploys an even more extravagant narrative that defies the deceivers' expectations, transforming them into the deceived ones.[34] By the end of Clavileño's adventure, both protagonists assert their roles as co-creators of the fantastic: Sancho through his journey into space, and Don Quixote in his underground exploits in the Cave of Montesinos, as the knight recalls in the words that end the chapter: "Sancho, just as you want people to believe what you have seen in the sky, I want you to believe what I saw in the Cave of Montesinos. And that is all I have to say" (*Don Quixote* 727).[35]

The enchanted head follows a similar course vis-à-vis its uncanny autonomy. On the one hand, the artifact demonstrates an agency similar to that of Clavileño's by defying its owner. Hilaire Kallendorf explains:

> Like the autonomous protagonists of this first great novel in world literature, *the enchanted head metaphorically leaps from the page to take on a life of its own*. In this respect, the enchanted head may be seen as a synecdoche for the work as a whole: like the book it suddenly writes, it seems not to be Cervantes' son but rather his stepson insofar as the enchanted head surpasses the limits of fiction and, in a meta-literary sense, begins to speak for itself. (180; my emphasis)

On the other hand, after putting the talking head to the test before Don Quixote and having exhibited it among his closest friends, Don Antonio is forced to dispose of it: "but the word spread throughout the city that Don Antonio had an enchanted head in his house that would answer every question asked of it, and fearing that rumors would reach the ears of the alert guardians of our Faith, he informed the inquisitors of the matter and was ordered to dismantle it and not to use it in the future lest it cause turmoil among the ignorant common people" (*Don Quixote* 872).[36] This act of dispossession reveals the apprehension this pseudo-virtuoso faces when he sees that his trick has escaped his control (Kallendorf 180).

During the Counter-Reformation, oracular heads were either denounced as diabolical devices or explained in mechanistic terms as the narrator does in this episode. Let us not forget—as we mentioned at the beginning of the chapter—that the novelist was among the thinkers who rejected the magical powers of these artifacts. It is, therefore, not surprising that Cervantes purposely turns Don Antonio into a frustrated trickster, just as he did with the duke and duchess in the Clavileño adventure. First, Don Antonio feels obliged to destroy his diabolical toy, a common course of action that appears in most narratives featuring similar artifacts. For example, in Greene's *Friar Bacon and Friar Bungay*, the protagonist, Fray Bacon, works on crafting a talking head for seven years, but a magic hand that suddenly appears

FIGURE 3.13. Michael Landy, *Saint Jerome*, 2012. Installation view, The National Gallery, London. Photograph courtesy of Michael Landy.

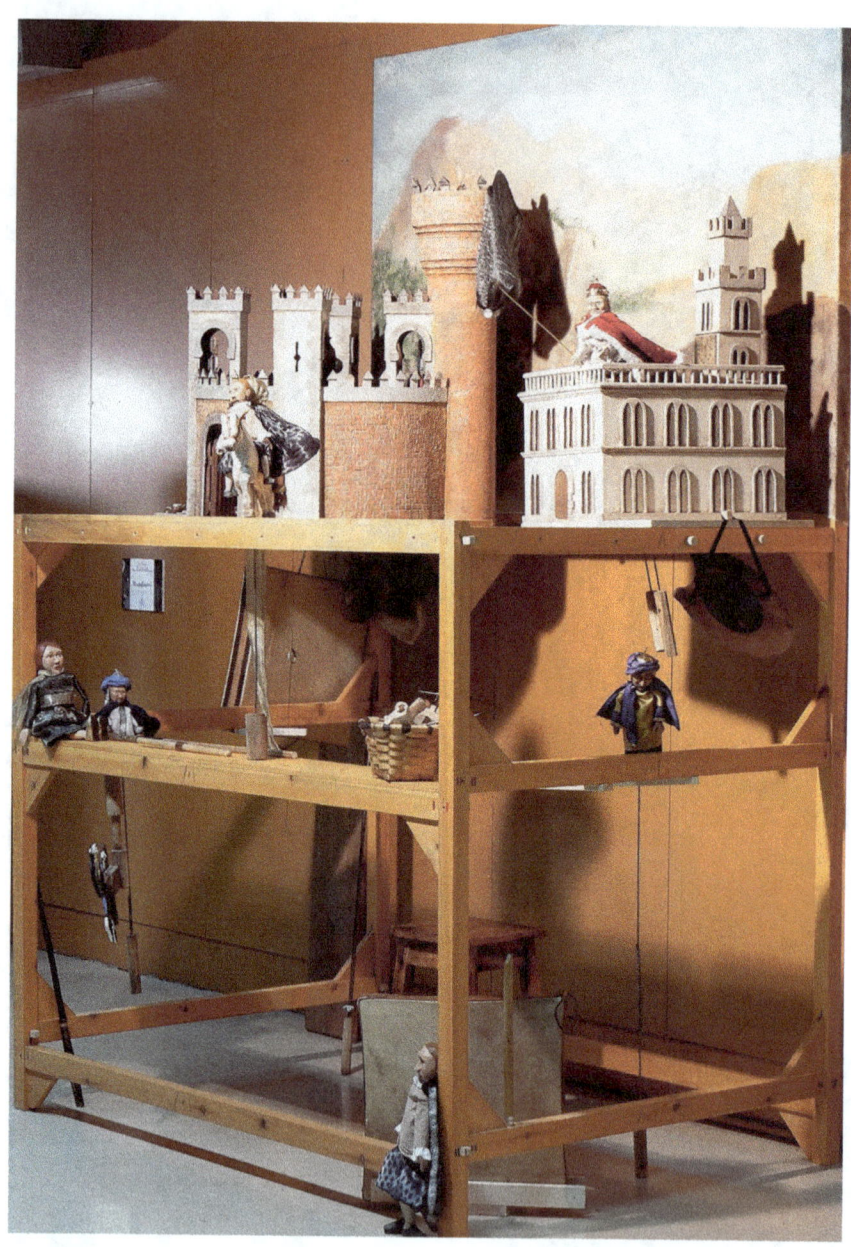

FIGURE 4.1. Contemporary reproduction of Master Pedro's puppet show set as described in *Don Quijote de la Mancha* (2.26). Photograph by Jesús Caballero, courtesy of La Máquina Real.

FIGURE 4.2. Don Quixote interrupting the young interpreter (*Don Quijote*, 2.26). Annotated edition by Nicolás Díaz de Benjumea and illustrated by Ricardo Balaca, Barcelona, Montaner y Simón (1880–1883). Biblioteca de la Facultad de Derecho y Ciencias del Trabajo, Universidad de Sevilla. Wikimedia Creative Commons.

FIGURE 4.3. Soloists in *El retablo de Maese Pedro*, directed by Enrique Lanz (2009). Gran Teatre del Liceu, Barcelona. Photograph by Enrique Lanz, courtesy of Títeres Etcétera.

FIGURE 4.4. *El retablo de Maese Pedro*, directed by Enrique Lanz (2009). Gran Teatre del Liceu, Barcelona. Photograph by Enrique Lanz, courtesy of Títeres Etcétera.

FIGURE 4.5. *El retablo de Maese Pedro*, directed by Enrique Lanz (2009). Gran Teatre del Liceu, Barcelona. Photograph by Enrique Lanz, courtesy of Títeres Etcétera.

FIGURE 4.6. Opening scene of *El retablo de Maese Pedro*, directed by Enrique Lanz (2009). Gran Teatre del Liceu, Barcelona. Photograph by Enrique Lanz, courtesy of Títeres Etcétera.

FIGURE 5.1. Don Quixote and Sancho flying on Clavileño, Ricardo Balaca (19th c.). Wikimedia Creative Commons.

FIGURE 5.2. Don Quixote and Sancho "fly" with the fireworks inside Clavileño, Ricardo Balaca (ca. 1870). Wikimedia Creative Commons.

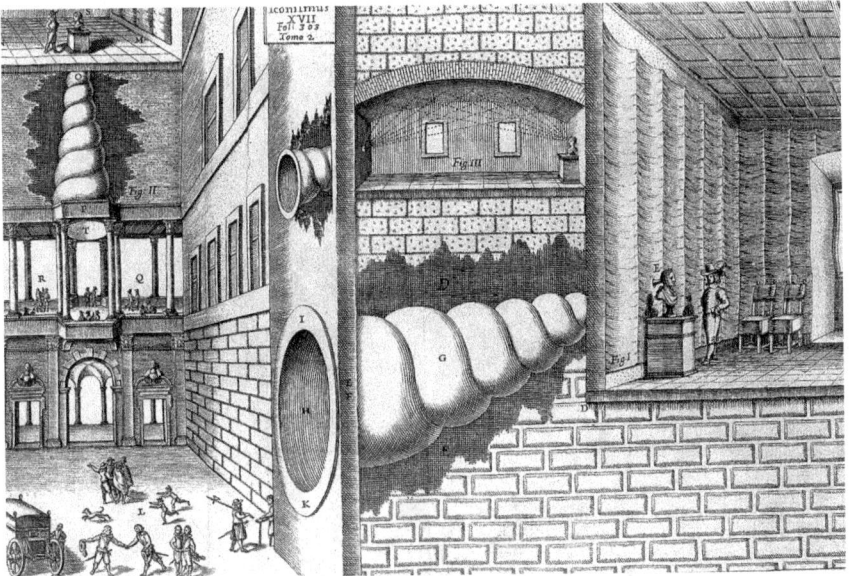

FIGURE 5.3. The *panacousticon* (speaking-trumpet) in Athanasius Kircher's *Musurgia Universalis* (The universal musical art, 1650).

FIGURE 5.4. A woodblock engraving of Miles playing the tambour while Friars Bacon and Bungay sleep and the Brazen Head speaks, "Time is. Time was. Time is past." From the 1630 edition of Robert Greene's *The Honorable Historie of Frier Bacon, and Frier Bongay*. Anonymous woodblock engraver. Wikimedia Creative Commons.

FIGURE 5.5. Exitazo Tournée Roca (Big success Roca tour) promotional poster, 1900–1910. Photograph courtesy of Museu de les Arts Escèniques (MAE), Barcelona.

FIGURE 5.6. *La dama de la fortuna* (The fortuneteller, n.d.). Photograph by Jesús Martínez Atienza, courtesy of Museu de las Arts Escèniques (MAE), Barcelona.

FIGURE 6.1. *La dama duende*, directed by José Luis Alonso de Santos (2000). Teatro de la Comedia, Madrid. Photograph by Daniel Alonso, courtesy of the Centro de Documentación de las Artes Escénicas y de la Música. INAEM. Ministerio de Cultura y Deporte.

FIGURE 6.2. *La dama duende*, directed by Helena Pimenta (2017). Teatro de la Comedia, Madrid. Photograph by Marcos GPunto, courtesy of the Centro de Documentación de las Artes Escénicas y de la Música. INAEM. Ministerio de Educación, Cultura y Deporte.

FIGURE 6.3. Caricature by Julio Cebrián. *ABC* (Espectáculos). April 30, 1981, page 67. Photograph courtesy of ABC.

FIGURE 6.4. *El galán fantasma*, directed by José Luis Alonso Mañés (1981). Teatro español, Madrid. Photograph by Jesús Alcántara, courtesy of the Centro de Documentación de las Artes Escénicas y de la Música. INAEM. Ministerio de Educación, Cultura y Deporte.

FIGURE 6.5. Julia in the garden. *El galán fantasma*, directed by José Mariano de Paco (2010). Teatro Principal, Zamora (Spain). Photograph by Pedro Gato, courtesy of Secuencia 3 and Eduardo Galán.

FIGURE 6.6. Astolfo crossing the tunnel in *El galán fantasma*, directed by José Mariano de Paco (2010). Teatro Principal, Zamora (Spain). Photograph by Pedro Gato, courtesy of Secuencia 3 and Eduardo Galán.

onstage ends up destroying the artifact with a hammer with no further justification than what the following stage direction asserts: "lightning flasheth forth, and a hand appears that breaketh down the head with a hammer" (xi, 75). For Todd Andrew Borlik, these supernatural acts of destruction are "a stern judgment not only on contemporary fantasies of technological dominion, but also on drama itself as an aesthetically and morally dubious form of animation" (120–30). The supposed diabolical origins of such animated objects, associated with their Islamic craftsmanship (Sawday 195–96; LaGrandeur 410) and the boldness of scientists seeking to rival God, make them obvious targets for acts of vandalism (see Figure 5.4). Although I read Don Antonio's enchanted head primarily as an apologia for the new technologies of entertainment, by having Don Antonio discard it, the novelist points to these prevailing contemporary anxieties and, as he did with Master Pedro's puppets, satirizes the illusion of animacy and strips it of all superstitious aura.[37]

Don Quixote's listless response to the head's prophetic powers is not what Don Antonio has envisioned as the outcome of his cautiously schemed joke. Indeed, the artifact's unsatisfying answers regarding the disenchantment of Dulcinea make the Don refuse to ask any more questions—"I do not wish to know more" (*Don Quixote* 870)[38]—as if he feels he has to choose between trusting the supernatural powers of the head and evading the issue. Such an attitude illustrates how the automaton was perceived at the time, precisely as a "technology of belief as well as deception" (Kimmel 219). It is significant that Don Antonio takes Don Quixote and Sancho to a printing press right after experiencing the fake powers of the oracular artifact. For Barbara Maria Stafford, mass production, like the automaton, straddles trust and deceit as it "breaks down the division between *pure* essence and *impure appearance, model and imitation*, to vindicate the authentic image without proper parentage" (105; my emphasis). Moreover, we can read the visit to the printing press as another act of dismantling the world of chivalry on the novelist's part. Mass production trivialized fiction by reducing it to a mere commodity that could be reproduced, bought, and discarded with no major consequences—just as Master Pedro's broken puppets are easily replaced with money.

Modern Re-enchantments

Whereas Clavileño and the enchanted head foreshadow the same anxieties that would emerge centuries later as a result of rampant industrialization and mechanization, the two artifacts also predate new entertainment trends from the eighteenth century onward. On a purely visual and experiential level, the way Cervantes conceives of the flying horse adventure evokes the first cinematic experiments in the 1900s that created a degree of hyperrealism that was perceived as threatening for non-initiated audiences in the new medium.[39] Pushing the hyperreal potential of Cervantes's episode even further, the adventure of Clavileño and all the other theatrical performances organized at the ducal estate garden are part of a *tunnel of terror*, where the world of chivalry transforms into a grotesque show in which Don Quixote and Sancho are forced to participate. Grottoes in Italian Renaissance gardens were already theatricalized spaces designed to stage social feasts where guests played an active role engaging with automata and other hydraulic engines in what, by contemporary standards, could be considered a simulated haunted attraction. At the Villa di Pratolino in Tuscany built by Francesco I de' Medici (1541–1587), its mannerist landscape housed the famous Dining Grotto (also known as the Grotto of the Samaritan) where the Grand Duke hosted spectacular gatherings with hydraulically powered moving statues, mechanical birds that sang, and a mechanized wheel that served food as if by magic, among other fantastic diversions (Tigner 150). The connection we can draw between these elaborate ruses, including the ones conceived by the duke and duchess, and modern theme parks and haunted attractions is evident.

These interactive attractions originated in Europe in the 1700s and have evolved to delight and astonish audiences but also to reflect contemporary anxieties. The audio-animatronic technology of theme-park attractions in the twenty-first century, for example, immerses the public firsthand in a simulated supernatural world that blurs the line between reality and fantasy. Even more akin to Clavileño's feigned flight is the popular contemporary ride "The Amazing Adventures of Spiderman" at Universal Studios' Islands of Adventure in Orlando,

Florida. This interactive show transforms visitors into reporters and lets them take part in one of the superhero's exploits through a multisensorial ride that "lures the audience into various layers of 'reality' by displaying a variety of technologically conjured effects—in the process, setting itself up as *a new kind of techno-spatial experience*" (Ndalianis, "Architectures of the Senses" 368; my emphasis).

In a more techno-scientific context, Chad M. Gasta documents how, in the twentieth century, the Clavileño adventure functioned as a referent for the space race between the United States and Russia. In 1962, Luis Cavanillas Ávila published an article in the newspaper *La nueva democracia* (The new democracy) under the title, "Don Quijote y Sancho: Los primeros 'cosmonautas' del mundo" (Don Quixote and Sancho: The world's first "cosmonauts"), wherein he compares the space voyage described by Sancho with the testimony of Yuri Gagarin (1934–1968) after he orbited the earth in 1961 (Gasta 51–52). Likewise, spaceships, flight simulators, virtual reality, artificial intelligence systems, mobile technology, digital television, and information networks are contemporary inventions that share characteristics with Clavileño's flight (Paz Gago 54). Cervantes seemed well aware of the futuristic reach of his simulated space adventure when he put the following words in his protagonist's mouth: "Pay no attention to that, Sancho, for since these things and these flights are outside the ordinary course of events, at a distance of a thousand leagues you will see and hear whatever you wish" (*Don Quixote* 722–23).[40]

As the creative, commercial, and scientific potential of Clavileño-like experiences developed over the centuries, the enchanted head also fostered a peculiar progeny of speaking androids from the beginning of mechanized society up to the present. Oracular automata, in particular, continued to be a popular form of entertainment well into the nineteenth century (Strauss 199), and mechanisms for reproducing the human voice reached a high degree of sophistication during the 1700s. Wolfgang von Kempelen (1734–1804) built the first speech synthesizer and describes the technology behind it in his book *Mechanismus der menschlichen sprache nebst beschreibung seiner sprechenden maschine* (Mechanism of the human language together with a description of its speaking machine, 1791).

In the nineteenth century, when the fantastic continued to be questioned from a scientific perspective but had also infiltrated everyday life, performances featuring enchanted heads became very popular throughout Europe. Showmen publicized such artifacts as paranormal objects, presuming that eerie advertising would be key to bringing in audiences. Nonetheless, what truly attracted people to those shows was the opportunity to admire the mechanical sophistication of such androids. In Victorian England, for example, stage magician John Nevil Maskelyne (1839–1917) created Psycho, known in popular culture as the whist-playing automaton, and it was one of the most famous androids in the nineteenth century.[41] The artifact was mainly reduced to a bust—as its legs were crisscrossed under a table and hardly perceivable—but could perform all kinds of human actions from the torso up, such as nodding, bowing, giving a masonic grip, smoking, doing mathematical calculations, and playing whist. Maskelyne's show featuring Psycho had over four thousand performances from 1873 to 1905 and became a permanent attraction in London's Egyptian Hall, the first long-running magic theater in London (During 156).

Similar commercial amusements took place in Spain during the same period and are key in our attempt to understand the development of the oracular and talking heads over time. However, what spectators were most excited about was not the magic they displayed but, again, the possibility of discovering their underlying tricks. Newspapers featured humorous anecdotes that illustrate how spontaneous audience participation transformed these supposedly transcendental magic shows into comic sketches. One account, for example, recalls a member in the audience throwing a rock at the foot of the table where the oracular head was displayed to see if it moved. As a result, several mirrors in the set were unintentionally broken. In another incident, a spectator shouted a false fire alarm, and the table that was holding the magic head moved across the stage to reveal the legs of the actor hidden underneath (Goñi Pérez 226–27). In all of these modern shows, like in Cervantes, the true wonder ironically lay in their deconstruction.

The enchanted head also relates to the first experiments in ventriloquism that originated in Spain in the nineteenth century, where a voice was projected inside a box or a closet containing the artificial head.[42] These illusionistic shows reached their peak in popularity in the 1930s with spectacular mise-en-scènes that also featured mechanical dolls housed in a cabinet, collectively known as *gabinetes de muñecos* (doll cabinets; see Figure 5.5). Caballero Ariñano (n.d.), Caballero Felip (n.d.), Francisco Sanz (1872–1939), Francesc Roca (?–1945), and Wenceslao Moreno (1896–1999; known as Señor Wences in the United States) were among the most famous Spanish ventriloquists and magicians who worked with these heads throughout the first half of the twentieth century (see Figure 5.5).[43] Coin-operated fortune tellers are remnants of these attractions and still exist as vintage oddities or, as Linda M. Strauss puts it, as the "last relics of a functional tradition" (199) in a long genealogy of artifacts that points to the origins of artificial intelligence and robotics (see Figure 5.6).

In a novel that introduces modernity from a wide array of perspectives, Cervantes presents an inert automaton (Clavileño) and an oracular head to reveal how stagecraft technologies and innovative currents in scientific and mechanistic knowledge create what Simon During has called "secular magic" (1). Whereas Don Quixote and Sancho are not fully aware of the natural explanations behind these artifacts, their firsthand experience with them implies a critical interaction. By this point in the novel, the knight has become increasingly weary: both he and Sancho, I argue, start to question the fiction they are living, even going so far as to deceive themselves by playing along with it.

Gasta rightly states that Cervantes is a writer interested in the Scientific Revolution and its impact on society:

> There is no way of knowing for sure what Cervantes thought about the great scientific advances of his own day, but the many scientific references in his works suggest he was at least conversant about what was transpiring, and understood how such discoveries were shaping the manner in which people viewed their own world. . . . The novelist was aware of contemporaneous science even if he relayed that knowledge in an often funny or irreverent way, yet still firmly grounded in sound scientific principle. (79–80)

Clavileño and the enchanted head are good examples of techno-scientific progress and can be seen as commitments to futurity that developed in early modern Europe. Both artifacts materialize the supernatural through rationality and promote skepticism in the two protagonists as well as in the readers of *Don Quijote*.[44]

The 1600s were known as a *siglo maquinístico* (machinist century; Jalón Calvo and Crespo 155); therefore, by riding this wave of modernity, these two automata enabled Cervantes to recreate the otherworldly through innovative performance practices and emergent technologies of leisure informed by contemporary social anxieties. While the novelist dismantles the agency of performance objects in the two episodes examined throughout this chapter, he simultaneously re-enchants his readership by crafting a modern type of entertainment that fills the *horror vacui* of the baroque while concurrently inquiring into the startling art of illusions. After all, as Javier Ordoñez rhetorically asks, thinking about the meaning of applied science in *Don Quijote*, "what is technology but another dream?" (250).

6. Trapdoors to *Desengaño*

> How many times poets-painters, in their prisons, have broken through walls, by way of a tunnel! How many times, as they painted their dreams, they have escaped through a crack in the wall!
>
> GASTON BACHELARD, *The Poetics of Space*, 1958

IN THE SECOND part of *Don Quijote*, Cervantes engages with the *technology of entertainment*, or the inner workings of artificial animated things, to initiate his protagonists into the experience of wonder mediated through curiosity and inquiry. By retaining the artificial marvelous in his novel, Cervantes meticulously guides characters and readers through the process of making illusions that, at the time, was gradually migrating into the realm of artistic production and imagination. In these creative arenas, the supernatural still took many creative forms and even was appropriated for personal, pragmatic, and social uses.

Calderón de la Barca, the dramatist who best embodied the baroque ethos and molded the notion of desengaño for the stage, no doubt had these Cervantine teachings in mind when he explored the articulation of the otherworldly in his plays. Literary critics have documented the presence of Cervantes's works and, specifically, the influence of *Don Quijote* in Calderonian drama.[1] Aside from the lavish fantastic settings of his mythological plays, driven by sophisticated technologies reserved to flaunt the means of the courtly stage, in two of his *comedias de capa y espada* (cloak-and-dagger plays)—*La dama duende* and *El galán fantasma*—Calderón de la Barca goes a step further than Cervantes in his conceptualization and manipulation of modern wonder, by bringing it closer to the everyday and trivializing its magical aura, reducing it to a "do it yourself" brand of illusionism.

For the playwright, I argue, the supernatural becomes a purely performative and artificial construct within everyone's reach, which temporarily provides respite from social injustice. Therefore, the "secular magic," harking back to Simon During's terminology (1), deployed by Cervantes becomes a *practical magic* in Calderón de la Barca's hands, where it is more attuned to the personal needs of his protagonists, who use it to resist social norms, if only fleetingly.

On the home front in Spain, the vitality and idealism of the Renaissance gradually gave way to seventeenth-century malaise, and the essence of desengaño operated on all levels of society, as assessed in the previous chapters. Thus, fantasy and distortion of reality became escapist antidotes for a wonder-seeking society that took shelter in pious and entertainment technologies. In *La dama* and *El galán*, two plays considered sister *comedias* because of their faux spectral thematic, the playwright refurbishes domestic settings to empower his protagonists as they become illusionists of their everyday lives.[2] Here, we are no longer dealing with the Cervantine wonders orchestrated by third parties for the sake of pure entertainment. On the contrary, Doña Ángela in *La dama* and Astolfo in *El galán* are self-made artists who perceptively appropriate the remnants of superstitious beliefs and a general longing for the marvelous to recreate a homemade technology of the fantastic to overcome their discontent.[3]

As I will discuss, both protagonists find a literal opening in their confined existences to envision alternative ways to survive through creative acts around their own personas. In other words, in an era when Spain was going through one of its more profound crises and its people fully embraced "a magical sense of existence" (Caro Baroja, *Teatro popular* 35), these Calderonian heroes created their own magic shows as an artistic mechanism for social resistance.

The secret portals Doña Ángela and Astolfo find available in their immediate surroundings—an *alacena movil* (movable cupboard or a secret door) in *La dama* and a trapdoor to a *mina* (underground tunnel) in *El galán*—become thresholds of wonder through which the protagonists fashion their identities into ghostly beings. Both characters generate, in their respective homes, a space similar to a *temporary autonomous zone* (TAZ), recalling Hakim Bey's strategy, where one exists in those areas to evade social control without directly confronting the oppressor.[4]

In dramatic literature, as Andrew Sofer argues in *The Stage Life of Props* (2003), it is not uncommon for certain props to have their own agency on the page and onstage to the point that they motivate action, absorb dramatic meaning, or become fetishized by protagonists (26). The cupboard and the tunnel trapdoor belong to this category of objects, as Doña Ángela and Astolfo lead double lives organized around each object. These portals function as conduits between the protagonists' everyday struggles and the artificial otherworldly dimension they refashion to move more easily on the margins of society and recuperate some of their agency. In this way, a literal bridge between reality and illusion is instantiated via the concealed technologies of the animated thresholds that Doña Ángela and Astolfo learn to operate to their own advantage.

For Jonathan Sawday, "illusion, machinery, and magic were intimately linked to one another through the idea of 'motion' in Renaissance aesthetic culture" (187). The cupboard and the tunnel trapdoor—with their hinging mechanisms—come to exemplify Sawday's triad of concepts working in unison to manipulate and resist oppressive social strictures from the stage. Subsequently, Calderón de la Barca's theater of wonder becomes experiential, as in some Shakespearean plays with magical elements, "a site for the complex modulation of audience identification and detachment, making the 'between' of the theatrical performance a space of semiotic and psychological experiment, through which the audience, like the characters, must negotiate a way" (Bishop 41).

In *La dama*, the cupboard—the *primum mobile* of the plot (Varey, *Cosmovisión* 323)—functions as a secret portal connecting Doña Ángela's bedroom with Don Manuel's, the guest with whom she falls in love. The playwright specifically highlights the artifact's capacity for motion when the protagonist and her maid, Isabel, pass through it for the very first time, as illustrated in the following stage direction: "Doña Ángela and Isabel enter by *unhinging* the glass panel" (*The Phantom Lady* 226; my emphasis).⁵ Similarly, the tunnel in *El galán* operates as an internal passageway, connected to the ground via trap doors (or chutes) that link Carlos's house with Julia's garden. (Carlos is Astolfo's best friend, and Julia is Astolfo's lover.) By inhabiting these threshold spaces, both protagonists literally put into motion what William Egginton regards as a "major strategy of the baroque" that "assumes the existence of a veil of appearances and then suggests the possibility of a space opening just beyond those appearances where the truth resides" ("The Baroque" 144).

Doña Ángela and Astolfo are characterized from the beginning of the plot as socially challenged individuals. The use of impairment as a symbol of social dysfunction follows David T. Mitchell and Sharon L. Snyder's notion of "narrative prosthesis" that refers to disability as a metaphor of individual and social collapse (47). This concept is relevant in that both protagonists have been pushed literally to the margins of society. Moreover, Doña Ángela and Astolfo belong to an extensive catalog of Calderonian heroes who hover in a liminal space, forced upon them by others, between life and death, just like Segismundo, the imprisoned prince in *La vida es sueño* (Life is a dream, 1635). Yet, these two characters are well aware of the reasons for their confinement and lean on the power of illusions to break free by deceiving those around them.

Taking the protagonists' phantasmagoric performances around secret trapdoors as the focal point of this chapter, I first analyze the dysfunctional conditions of Doña Ángela and Astolfo, who are stripped of their identities and rendered *unhuman* to and by society. The protagonists build on their alienation by inhabiting the aforementioned secret passages to turn them into prosthetic aids through which they refashion themselves as spectral illusions, processes that merit thorough attention, as they give a material presence to the impossible onstage. Finally, and as I have been doing vis-à-vis other animated artifacts examined in this book, I consider the contemporary afterlives of the cupboard and the tunnel in a series of Spanish productions of *La dama* and *El galán* over the last forty years. Interestingly enough, most modern directors have established an interpretive tradition in which the *articulation of wonder* in these plays has lost touch with the original sociocultural context of the baroque era, more than in any of the other case studies evaluated herein. Most contemporary adaptations interpret Doña Ángela's and Astolfo's illusionistic tricks from a one-sided perspective, as theatrical mechanisms at the service of love entanglements, ignoring the daring creativity imbued in them and distorting the essence of both plays, which are so grounded in desengaño.[6]

Plays such as *La dama* and *El galán*, where the making of illusions was very much informed by the social realities of the time, paved the way for the creation of the *comedia de magia* (magic play), as I argue in the Conclusion. This genre gained popularity on the Spanish stage toward the end of the seventeenth century and remained active well into the nineteenth century. Its crosscutting interdisciplinarity between literature, science, and technology introduced new reformist ideas that emerged during the reign of Charles II (1661–1700) and developed further during the eighteen century. As ironic as it may seem, the *comedia de magia*, indeed, came to be a definitive testing ground to scrutinize secular wonder and to assess the basic premise of the baroque—i.e., the divide between appearance and truth—that had been falling apart for quite some time.

Barely Humans

La dama duende is a cloak-and-dagger play that unfolds in seventeenth-century Madrid, where family honor becomes Doña Ángela's main antagonist, depriving her of her identity. Debt inherited from her deceased husband has forced the young widow to remain behind closed doors in the strict care of her two brothers, Don Juan and Don Luis, until the family can cope with her financial situation.[7] Her challenge throughout the plot is to recuperate her visibility. Finding herself unable to fit in beyond the confines of her own room, which she compares to a mausoleum, Doña Ángela sees herself as the living dead:

> DOÑA ÁNGELA. Here, Isabel, give me back
>   my widowhood, worse luck!
>   And wrap me up again

> in that black shroud; as cruel fate
> will have it, *I must be buried
> in this way, alive.* (*The Phantom Lady* 215, my emphasis)[8]

The protagonist's unnatural existence extends to the bond she has with her two brothers, a relationship that borders on the incestuous and the necrophilic (Aranda 152).[9] The power that Don Juan and Don Luis hold over their sister is such that even in the privacy of her own room, they dictate the way she must dress and behave.

Added to this chronically diminished existence is Doña Ángela's widowhood, a status that renders her even more fragmented in society's eyes. In *Tratado del govierno de la familia y estado de las viudas y donzellas* (Treatise on the guidance of families and estates of widows and maidens, 1597), Jesuit theologian Gaspar Astete (1537–1601) defines *widow* as "the end of two"—that is to say, a widow is a not truly an individual, nor is she societally palatable without her consort (Boyle 50). In this sense, Doña Ángela is incomplete insofar as her widowhood creates an inherent lack in her being that invalidates her identity and integrity in both the private and social spheres. The mourning attire she wears during most of the play is evidence of her erasure, as the headcloth and veil blur and deface her true being. Additionally, the only time she goes outside incognito is at the beginning of the play, but the veil she wears can be viewed as a "portable house" that still keeps her locked up, if we follow Antonio de León Pinelo's interpretation of the accessory as misogynistic in this instance (240–41).

Furthermore, to protect her anonymity once inside her house, when she is about to be discovered by Don Manuel, Doña Ángela avoids all gallantries by rhetorically portraying herself as a non-being:

> DOÑA ÁNGELA. Do not compare me to the dawn
>   whose fixed smile I do not share,
>   for *I am not* frequently so blissful.
>   *Nor am I* like the early morning
>   light in shedding pearly tears;
>   I hope you have not found me weeping

> *nor can I* like the sun divide
> the light of truth I love
> into so many parts.
> And so, although *I cannot say*
> exactly what I'm like,
> I only know *I'm not* the dawn,
> the morning, or the sun of day.
> At least I cannot think I am
> the sunlight all aglow,
> or weeping like a stream. (*The Phantom Lady* 265; my emphasis)[10]

The protagonist, nonetheless, does not resign herself to this counter-portrait she improvises to confuse Don Manuel in a moment of *force majeure*, nor does she flounder in passive incompleteness throughout the play; instead, she leverages her invisibility as an act of resistance to create a new enigmatic identity.

The power of her *duende* (or magic spirit), into which the heroine leans, ironically resides in being ethereal, indecipherable, and impossible to confine, traits that Don Manuel notices when he glimpses her for the very first time:

> DON MANUEL. There was something ghostly in the way
> she suddenly appeared
> in that fantastic light,
> but there was also something human
> in the way she avoided
> being seen and touched—
> something mortal in her fear,
> something feminine in her distrust.
> Yet she simply came apart
> like an illusion, and
> like a spirit vanished in the air. (*The Phantom Lady* 262)[11]

Since her *humanness* does not go unnoticed by Don Manuel, Doña Ángela uses her human/non-human liminality to transform into a *vanishing lady*, a trick that she keeps improvising with slight variations in each of her disappearance acts.[12]

The protagonist learns how to melt into space at a moment's notice: at the beginning of the play, for example, Cosme compares her to a *torbellino* or "whirlwind" (*La dama* v.113; *The Phantom Lady* 209) because of the speed with which she vanishes in the street the first time he and Don Manuel gaze upon her veiled visage. In the second act, when her identity is about to be discovered, she performs an even more challenging trick of escapology from an apparently closed room, leaving both master and servant utterly disconcerted.[13] But all of this is only possible thanks to the cupboard, the metatheatrical threshold stage from where Doña Ángela deploys her *practical magic*.

The secret hinged mechanisms of the artifact are crucial for turning Don Manuel's bedroom into an early version of today's escape rooms, luring him into solving the enigma Doña Ángela has devised for his eyes only.[14] Don Manuel, driven by curiosity, succumbs without hesitation to the conviviality of this mystery house charade. Like Doña Ángela, he is saddled with a sordid past of his own and is on a quest to reclaim his own identity. Such a personal and spiritual search is a recurring characteristic of Calderón de la Barca's most tragic heroes (Wardropper 182). Doña Ángela falls into this category as well, even if the play is not a tragedy in the strictest sense of the word. The theater of wonder she orchestrates around the movable cupboard is expressly designed to fill a personal void—her invisibility. The moment that Doña Ángela becomes aware of her paranormal game's influence on Don Manuel, she intensifies her vanishing powers to fully embody another subversive role: the invisible mistress (Armas, "Por una hora" 120).[15]

Astolfo's initial characterization in *El galán*, where he is portrayed as "stumbling in the shadows of [his] death,"[16] is utterly similar to Doña Ángela's incomplete and socially dysfunctional identity. In this case, the play unfolds in the Saxon court around a love triangle between the two young paramours, Julia and Astolfo, and the antagonist, the duke of Saxony. Whereas family honor has diminished Doña Ángela to an invisible being, the duke's jealousy forces Astolfo into a precarious nonexistence. It is Julia, however, who persuades him to temporarily disappear to avoid suspicion:

> JULIA. And so I beseech you
>   not to come see me, or pass by
>   either openly or under cover
>   anywhere near my threshold.
>   Let several days pass
>   without anyone seeing you
>   to dispel suspicions
>   your worries are in vain.
>   And so I come thus
>   to persuade you, to beseech you,
>   Astolfo, do not try to see me,
>   husband, do not try to speak to me,
>   I know you will do it.[17]

Astolfo disregards Julia's advice and, in a confrontation with the duke, is severely wounded. All those close to him, with the exception of his father and sister, believe he is dead. Thanks to the care of a physician, he survives, though his recovery is guarded in firm secrecy by his relatives for his own protection.

Later on, Astolfo observes his own funeral, devised by his father, who acts as a stage magician over the course of the play as he orchestrates his son's fake burial and resurrection:

> ASTOLFO. Hardly, then, a new life
>   I'm poorly compensated
>   when my father, from this
>   voluntary prison cell
>   takes me out in the darkness of night
>   at the same time as I hear
>   in another room of my house
>   sad funeral rites and lamentation.

> The threshold of a door
> I feverishly touch,
> when from the other door emerges
> a sumptuous burial.
> "Who is the deceased?" I ask
> my father and he replies, doubtfully
> "You are the one and the same."[18]

While Astolfo's human and social existence is put to an end in this moment, a new isolated life in the realm of the quasi-paranormal awaits him. He, like Doña Ángela, has no choice but to become a nonentity and accept the barely human existence that is forced upon him. Yet, in the concealed interstices both protagonists inhabit, they find a way out of their predicaments as phantasmagorical beings. In so doing, they daringly orchestrate a game of illusions that simultaneously trivializes the supernatural.

Animated Thresholds

The cupboard and the tunnel are part of a long list of secret passageways—basements, doors, trapdoors, hatches, and partitions—very common in cloak-and-dagger plays, as Tirso de Molina hits upon in this following excerpt from his *comedia*, *En Madrid y en una casa* (In Madrid and in a house, 1625):

> ORTIZ. Where there are *basement* lovers,
> a phantom lover, a phantom lady,
> *hatches*, houses with two *doors*,
> false partitions,
> they will pilfer from the stages
> plots that extract certain
> already lost hopes. (my emphasis)[19]

Like Calderón de la Barca, Tirso de Molina was a great aficionado of such dramatic thresholds, as reflected by the titles of some of his plays, such as *Los balcones de Madrid* (The balconies of Madrid, 1624), *En Madrid y en una casa*, and *Por el sótano y el torno* (Through basement and hatch, 1635).[20] However, in all these comedias and in Calderón de la Barca's *Casa con dos puertas, mala es de guardar* (A house with two doors is difficult to guard, 1629), such deceptive portals belong strictly to the domestic and urban spheres without fully crossing into the magical realm as they do—artificially—in *La dama* and *El galán*. Nonetheless, before Doña Ángela and Astolfo put the cupboard and the tunnel to their own fantastical (re)use, the playwright makes sure to endow both threshold spaces with a functional life history that illuminates their pragmatic uses. Calderón de la Barca first legitimizes their connections with the real world then builds on their simulated supernatural auras.[21] In relation to the cupboard, Rodrigo, Don Luis's servant, reveals that the secret door was originally installed as a deceit mechanism to hide the entrance to other rooms in the house:

> RODRIGO. Besides, special pains were taken
>   to make the door to his apartment
>   lead into the street. Then,
>   to conceal the second doorway,
>   which leads into the other rooms,
>   while allowing for its later use,
>   a paneling of glass mirrors
>   has been installed in that space.
>   And the panel has been designed
>   so that no one would suspect
>   there'd ever been another door there. (*The Phantom Lady* 215)[22]

Here, the dematerialization of space achieved through the cupboard is similar to the architectural strategies employed at the time in the so-called *casas a malicia* (malice houses). Such spacious households were made by their owners to look purposely smaller to avoid hosting court officials, who had the right to be accommodated in Madrid's wealthiest residences.[23] Noelia Cirnigliaro explains: "Madrid homeowners resorted to notoriously theatrical methods, comparable to the makeup, wardrobes, and set changes used on the stages of the *corrales*, but in this case for the purpose of concealing signs of spaciousness and room partitions inside the houses, and thus being called upon to provide lodging" (35–36). Doña Ángela's magical refurbishing of the cupboard echoes this unique practice in Madrid's urban history.

Moreover, when both plays were being written, Madrid was a site open to legends, as recorded in Jerónimo de Barrionuevo's *Avisos* (Notices, 1654–1658). In this sense, Frederick A. de Armas compares the magical atmosphere that reigns in Doña Angela's quarters with the feel of the Escorial palace: "Like the house where a *duende* seems to live, El Escorial was considered a marvelous place, a place of magic, an axis mundi. Its construction was begun at a propitious time according to astrology and hagiography of the period" ("Por una hora" 125). Specifically, it is this banalization of fantasy in daily life (and political life, even, following de Armas's reading) that Calderón de la Barca explores through the secret cupboard in *La dama*.

In a similar fashion, the tunnel in *El galán* was a space with its own practical genealogy before becoming Astolfo's illusionistic attraction. During a civil war in Saxony, one of Carlos's ancestors hired an engineer to design the tunnel as an offensive mechanism to be used in a surprise attack against his enemy, who happened to be none other than Julia's father. This explains why the tunnel directly connects Carlos's house to Julia's garden:

> CARLOS. He looked for an engineer
> who, digging the earth skillfully,
> to mitigate the offense
> which was impossible for his sword
> and, trusting me,
> as my house was positioned
> closer to his aspirations,
> more conveniently for his attack,
> the man began from the house
> to design the models
> for digging a tunnel

to that very room, which was
easy for him, because
he was of the Flemish nation,
the school where bravery
competes with ingenuity.[24]

Moreover, the military use that Calderón de la Barca ascribes to such a passageway is inspired by a real strategy used during the sixteenth and seventeenth centuries to plant gunpowder kegs underground, where they could be detonated during battle. Further, in other historically oriented plays, our playwright mentions similar underground passages also used for military purposes, such as in *Amar después de la muerte* (Love after death, 1633), *La aurora en Copacabana* (Dawn at Copacabana, ca. 1664–1665), and *Origen, pérdida y restauración de la Virgen del Sagrario* (The origin, loss, and restoration of the Virgin of the Sanctuary, ca. 1617–1629). At the other end of the spectrum, these tunnels were very popular among the nobility for purely extravagant entertainment, analogous to the illusionistic shows displayed in the aforementioned Renaissance grottoes (Iglesias Iglesias, "El jardín" 67).

In addition, Calderón de la Barca stresses that the tunnel's and the cupboard's designs were informed by the science of engineering, another instance that serves to highlight their practicality and connection to the real.[25] Carlos describes how an engineer devised the tunnel, and Doña Ángela refers anecdotally to the famous inventor Turriano when she explains the trick of the cupboard.[26] Such connections to the applied sciences set the stage for the phantasmagorical experiments that both protagonists carry out through the technologies of the everyday, or what they have at hand. However, as in most seventeenth-century *comedias*, their plots conclude with the lovers hurriedly reunited and without directly implicating all the other characters in the reassessment of the roles that the two animated thresholds played in the protagonists' fantastical schemes. In point of fact, both the cupboard and the tunnel end up giving way abruptly, bringing Doña Ángela and Astolfo back to their own reality without the plot detailing the process of the dismantling of illusion.

Spatial Prosthetics

The cupboard and the tunnel function in both plays as support mechanisms for the protagonists' survival, helping them to *move through* their incomplete existences. As if they were prostheses, these passageways are inextricably tied to their owners' deficiencies and, at the same time, perfectly adjusted to their supernatural identities. Just as with any prosthetic mechanism, the similarity between the human and the artificial is what makes the apparent disjunction between the organic and the inorganic surmountable (Johnson 88).

The glass panel that covers the surface of the cupboard comes to epitomize the fragility of Doña Ángela's honor. Don Luis, obsessed with his sister's integrity and good name, does not overlook the furniture's flimsy characteristic, as shown in the following lines:

> DON LUIS. And do you suppose all this
>   will reassure me? Such precautions
>   only double my uneasiness
>   for what you tell me, in effect,
>   is that the only thing now standing
>   as bulwark to my sister's honor
>   is a frame of glass a single blow
>   will shatter in a thousand pieces. (*The Phantom Lady* 215)[27]

Don Luis is invested in the reinstatement of such a threshold, but the protagonist traverses it at will and, in doing so, perturbs the heteronormative constructs and expectations of the feminine that her two brothers have been trying to enforce so firmly throughout the plot.

Besides its obvious fragility, glass can also be an emblem of the unattainable and a conduit of melancholy (Rodríguez de la Flor, *Pasiones* 190), two qualities that closely relate to Doña Ángela's temperament. What's more, the cupboard's interior location and its deceptive appearance represent the protagonist's false confinement throughout the play. As Anthony Cascardi has noticed: "Rarely was Calderón so concerned with the selection and placement of stage properties. Two rooms, a mysteriously moveable cabinet and door separating them, a travelling bag, and a basket of clothes: *all are powerful images of inwardness.* They are *dense with the intimate lives* of the characters around them, laden with desire" (30; my emphasis).[28] By the same token, fragility, enclosure, and deceitfulness are attributes associated with sprites and, therefore, perfectly attuned to the protagonist's fashioning as a *duende*: according to Spanish folklore, *duendes* choose secluded rooms in private residences as their preferred spaces in which to live (Caro Baroja, *Algunos mitos* 150–56).[29]

This perfect coupling of the cupboard's material properties and Doña Ángela's identity markers is paralleled in the correlation that exists between the tunnel and Astolfo. The invisibility that society imposes upon him corresponds to the inwardness of the underground passageway and the excruciating secret of his supposed death. Indeed, some of Calderón de la Barca's plays feature tunnels that are figuratively associated with violent births and the burdensome consequences of keeping secrets.[30] Therefore, the first time Astolfo goes through the tunnel symbolizes his urge to disclose his underground existence and to regain his life, albeit in the form of an imposter ghost.

The cupboard and tunnel are so closely entwined with the protagonists' twofold nature (i.e., the real and the fantastic), which implies that both props will evolve along with the characters until finally acquiring a life of their own and revealing their latent animacy—just as Doña Ángela and Astolfo will do by the end of both plays when they disclose their covert insubordination.[31] In the case of the cupboard, Doña Ángela and Isabel easily control its hinges at the beginning of the play when they enter the guest's room for the very first time:

ISABEL. Do you agree there's
   no difficulty getting in?
DOÑA ÁNGELA. Yes, Isabel. I was so wrong
   to doubt it. Why, there's nothing to it.
   The panel moves so easily,
   we can go in and out this way
   without the slightest fear
   of being seen by anyone. (*The Phantom Lady* 226)[32]

Up to this point, Doña Ángela traverses the cupboard with two purposes in mind: to express her gratitude to Don Manuel for saving her from being discovered in the street by her brother, and to initiate a live-action game to escape from her oppressive circumstances. Given the harmlessness of her initial intentions, moving through the cupboard is simply frivolous mischief. Isabel's command, "Open sesame!" (*The Phantom Lady* 228), demonstrates the easy access that the cupboard provides at first. These words correspond in the original Spanish to "alacena *me fecit*" (*La dama* v.892), an expression that refers to the intrinsic bonds and synchronous workings between the two women and the cupboard.[33]

Yet, as Doña Ángela's infatuation intensifies, her entrances and exits from Don Manuel's bedchamber become increasingly compromised and, consequently, crossing through the secret door turns out to be riskier than it was in her initial use (de Armas, "Por una hora" 124). An example is when Doña Ángela enters Don Manuel's room and finds herself trapped inside because Isabel has latched the cupboard from the other side by mistake. The protagonist has no other choice but to let herself be seen in the half-light, and she is on the verge of revealing her identity when she finally manages to escape.

Doña Ángela relies so much on the cupboard for perpetuating her phantasmagoric existence that the artifact eventually detaches itself from the wall in the third act and ends up unveiling her game and dishonor. Vivian Sobchack points out: "Such transfer of human agency to our technologies allows our artifacts to come back with a vengeance" (212). The moment the trick of the cupboard is revealed and Doña Ángela's ghostly identity collapses, her situation is even more precarious than at the beginning of the play. Now, marrying Don Manuel seems the only alternative for her to survive her dishonor or even death at the hand of her brothers.

However, Don Manuel's feelings about whether to protect her remain ambiguous until the very end. His decision to marry Doña Ángela appears to arise more from compassion than true love, as we see him riddled by a moral dilemma:

DON MANUEL. Then what am I supposed to do?
   If I reject her, I am a villain.
   If I defend her, a thankless guest;
   And fiendishly inhuman
   if I yield her to her brother.
   Say I decide to protect her:
   that makes me a false friend;
   and if I free her, I violate
   a noble trust; if I don't free her,
   I violate the noblest love.
   Whichever way I turn, I'm in
   the wrong. So, I'll die fighting. (*The Phantom Lady* 283–84)[34]

Even though Doña Ángela is infatuated with Don Manuel, her marriage portends a bleak outcome, as she has no other choice but to depend on her benefactor in order to reintegrate into society.[35] She is "rescued" from social invisibility and recuperates her "substantial being," but at the expense of the possibility for future freedom.

As with other animated objects examined up to now, the cupboard rebels against its activator. Beginning as a prosthetic aid that gives the protagonist certain freedom of movement to recover her identity, the cupboard ultimately exposes its mechanisms. As a result, Doña Ángela is expelled from her game and brought back under patriarchal surveillance. This is, however, a reflection on the instability of appearances, a harsh turn toward desengaño—a creatively barren realm—that may suggest that the reality behind kinetic illusionism and spectacular animations is still far from changing. And when I say *reality* in the context of Calderón de la Barca, I refer to the ways he typifies the social and political sentiments and beliefs of a narrowly restricted historical era.

Reminiscent of Calderón de la Barca, only two and a half centuries later, realist novelist Benito Pérez Galdós (1843–1920) denounced some of the ills in need of regeneration in Spanish society. He returned to the idea of female oppression in literal dialogue with physical disability in his novel *Tristana* (1892). His heroine, after struggling for her freedom and rights, loses one leg to illness and settles down with her crafty protector, Don Lope, seeking refuge in religion and domesticity.[36] Pérez Galdós closes Tristana's story with a scathing question that we could also ask with respect to the marriage of Doña Ángela and Don Manuel: "Were they happy, the two of them?... *Perhaps*" (169; my emphasis).[37] A similar reservation can be raised at the end of most *comedias* that conclude with hasty and dubious marital unions, but in the case of *La dama*, it is even more mordant because Doña Ángela—as with Tristana—strove for survival on her own. Stagnant social values end up getting in their way and disempowering both female protagonists.

In *El galán*, the tunnel follows a similar development throughout the play. At the beginning, it provides Astolfo with an alternative metatheatrical stage for recreating a ghostly identity that will help him temporarily navigate society while remaining invisible. After its completion, it had fallen into disuse and obscurity.[38] For this reason, when Astolfo crosses the tunnel for the first time, he neither is aware of the apocalyptic spectacle his underground transit could cause on the surface, nor does he foresee that Julia will be in the garden at that specific moment:

> JULIA. Pregnant, the earth wants,
> while scratching its entrails,
> the birth or explosion
> of wonders; don't you see, don't you see
> how everything trembles?
> Don't you see the plants and branches
> either trembling or moving?[39]

When the protagonist exits, he is blanketed by soil as if the subterranean world has taken possession of his persona: "A trapdoor opens and Astolfo enters, covered with dirt."[40] This moment could allude symbolically to the supernatural rebirth of the protagonist, who will have no choice but to lead a public ghostly existence in order to remain close to his beloved.[41]

In addition to being unaware of the effects caused by his first crossing, Astolfo improvises with the powers of his newly acquired phantasmagoric identity when he prevents the duke from raping Julia:

> DUKE. (*To Julia*) So you saw Astolfo, tell him to come / to defend you. (Astolfo leaves in such a way that the duke does not see him and kills the light.)
> ASTOLFO. Yes, I'll arrive in that way.
> DUKE. The light is gone and I hear a voice. [. . .]
> ASTOLFO. (By the heavens, by not being seen I have quelled his vigor, I'll hide again.)
> DUKE. Where are you hiding, voice? If you call me, why don't you answer me?[42]

Like Doña Ángela, Astolfo, in this scene, transforms his invisibility and nonexistence into the trademark of his ghostly identity and strength. And, once he is aware of the impact his spectral presence has on the others, he begins to refine his otherworldly self, with Julia collaborating as the artistic director of his charade:

> JULIA. And I, to assure you
> of time which shall be short
> and will even seem short to you,
> today with ingenious study
> I will cover this opening
> *with a panel* in such a way
> that, with plants and flowers
> continuing the adornments
> of the garden, they can deceive
> the south wind, the north wind, and the tide.
> In this way, you will *come speak to me*
> *at night*, known only
> by a gardener, to whom our secret
> I will entrust. (my emphasis)[43]

Julia's garden becomes, then, the main stage for the couple's paranormal performance. The liminality of the garden—between the natural and the supernatural—as we saw in the previous chapter with the staging of Clavileño's adventure, transforms itself into a convivial backdrop for the lovers (a *locus amoenus*) and simultaneously into a hostile space (*locus horridus*) for all the other characters, who do not dare trespass for fear of encountering Astolfo's specter.

In this dual setting, Astolfo and Julia start turning their relationship into a spectacle of spectrophilia, a love affair between a human and a ghost, that attracts as well as repels the duke's retinue. In this respect, Julia and Porcia's exchange is imbued with significance:

> PORCIA. How is it possible that you could have
>   such manly strength
>   as to love a dead person,
>   and speak to him?
> JULIA. In me
>   there is no fear, because there is love.
> PORCIA. Well, in me, Señora, yes:
>   there is no love, because there is fear.
>   But tell me only this:
>   Do the dead show affection?[44]

The notoriety of this bizarre relationship fashions Astolfo into a legendary ghostly lover throughout Saxony, as the duke explains:

> DUKE. It was at Julia's house,
>   where he goes every night,
>   from the moment I saw him,
>   he has never been absent
>   and all of Saxony
>   knows of this.[45]

Whereas the tunnel initially takes full control of Astolfo when he first crosses it, over the course of the plot, he gradually manages to inhabit it fully. Nonetheless, the tunnel only provides temporary relief for the protagonist's chronically dysfunctional existence. As with the cupboard, this spatial prosthesis is revealed once it is lived in and used at maximum intensity, and Astolfo has no choice but to disclose his deceitful identity and re-enter social normativity.

The duke ends up forgiving the lovers with the stipulation that they leave Saxony for good. Banishment plunges the protagonist yet again into a state of nonexistence, but this time, he drags Julia with him into permanent exile. It is difficult to imagine that Astolfo could ever feel like a complete being again.[46] His reinsertion into society depends on enduring exile, that is, non-belonging, just as Doña Ángela's life depends on agreeing to and re-entering patriarchal subjugation through marriage. Their paranormal performances are ultimately overcome by the social order, and the stage props they use to move at ease against oppression reveal their mechanisms and return them to the starting point of their struggles. The circular plots of both plays confine the protagonists to the exhausted structure of a society that was still clinging to archaic concepts of honor, superstition, and despotism in its many facets.

Nonetheless, Calderón de la Barca's protagonists succeed in leaving a solid footprint on how to use the mechanics of the threshold to create critically engaging scenarios that explore the breach between appearance and truth. This *destabilization* of illusions is similar to the ones we have already seen in previous chapters in relation to other material performances; however, in the playwright's hands, it becomes a more social and everyday life practice.

Secret Passageways Refurbished

Since the mid-1960s, literary critics have recognized a tendency toward social denunciation behind the restless *comings and goings* of Calderonian protagonists in cloak-and-dagger-plays. At the same time, most contemporary directors have felt the need to cleanse the playwright's image of fundamentalist Catholic and patriarchal prejudices that have built up around Calderon de la Barca's dramaturgy and persona. Influential writers and playwrights for the country's national identity such as Cervantes, Lope de Vega, and Calderón de la Barca, among others, have been exploited over the centuries by the different political regimes that have appropriated them for their own agendas, distorting their genuine personalities and ideological and artistic values.

On the three hundredth anniversary of Calderón de la Barca's death in 1981, Spain was a country newly experiencing democracy and trying to avoid any cultural products tinged with authoritarian reminiscences; here, the-cloak-and-dagger plays performed for the occasion purposely stressed their comic elements (Rodríguez Cuadros). This cheerful interpretation of what critics regard as Calderonian comic plays has continued to this day. Thus, subsequent performances of *La dama* and *El galán*, associated with this lighthearted category of dramatic works, have tended to overlook their social significance. Indeed, instead of focusing on the protagonists' disaffection, most contemporary productions lean toward portraying Doña Ángela and Astolfo as carefree heroes with superficial happy endings. Such readings relegate the cupboard and the tunnel to visually spectacular props at the service of love imbroglios, while they fail to delve into their metaphorical prosthetic meanings, intricately tied to the protagonists' resilience, social denunciation, and struggle for survival.

In the most notable Spanish productions of *La dama*, despite slight variations, the cupboard is animated with a revolving-door mechanism. In 1942, director Cayetano Luca de Tena (1917–1997) conceived the most dynamic and creative scenography for its time. He devised a revolving platform system that allows performers to transition from Doña Ángela to Don Manuel's rooms and vice versa without slowing down the pace of the play (Luca de Tena 46).[47] Theater critic Alfredo Marquerie compared this kinetic stage to a "naive and primitive mechanism of the carousel and the music box" (2). While such an analogy emphasizes the innovative mechanization of the set for its time, it also downgrades the overall tone of the *comedia* to a children's pastime. On the other side of the spectrum, Antonio Girau (1939–2001) directed *La dama* in 1979 and sacrificed all sense of motion for a static and simultaneous view of both rooms throughout the entire performance. The director devised a low wall dividing the stage into two adjoining spaces (Marquerie 170). This wider panoramic vision overlooks, once again, the true essence of play in the way that it distances the audience from Doña Ángela's deceitful intimacy. These early 'maladjusted' stagings, nonetheless, illustrate the centrality of the cupboard as a driving force that even escapes the director's control.

Most contemporary adaptations have continued to set the play in the seventeenth century, although, for the most part, they often include gratuitous anachronistic details drawn from the eighteenth and nineteenth centuries. In his 2000 adaptation, director Alonso de Santos (1942–) featured Llorenç Corbellá's set design, in which the walls were made of a spongy, glittery texture that heightened the production's eerie atmosphere (see Figure 6.1). In his review for the newspaper *El País*, theater critic Eduardo Haro Tecglen stresses this sublime and extravagant aesthetic, devoid, however, of any deeper meaning: "As if written by Marivaux, with garlands and nude statues, which are in reality painted young women who breathe and move ever so slightly, trembling, as in England when the first nudes appeared in theaters and were obliged by law not to move" ("Frontera"). This move toward the palpable supernatural is something that Helena Pimenta has thoughtfully explored in her 2017 adaptation in a way that is more aligned with the social implications of the play.[48]

Pimenta is one of the few contemporary directors who dares to move away from the superfluous comicality of the play to propose a more reflective interpretation, but not without controversy. Her more sober characterizations of the *comedia* genre in general have cost her the approval of critics and audiences in some cases.[49] For *La dama*, Pimenta dives into a gothic illusionism set in the late Victorian era and enfolds the play in a dark mood that arises from giving serious scrutiny to the patriarchy and to an obsolete system of superstitious beliefs. The director brings out the play's most unsettling aspects by establishing a fitting dialogue with the culture of dwelling and optical illusionism that parallels seventeenth-century misogyny and man-made fantasy in a modern context. Her adaptation displaces the obscurantism of superstitions with an approach to natural magic based on the scientific principles that gave rise to new optical-illusion tools such as the magic lantern, kinetoscope, and phantasmagoria.[50] The scenography alludes to the cinematic techniques of the Lumière brothers (Auguste Marie Louis Nicolas, 1862–1954, and Louis Jean, 1864–1948) and to the fantasies of Georges Méliès (1861–1938), which serve to re-semanticize and modernize the Calderonian *duende* through the lens of modern entertainment (see Figure 6.2).

Pimenta also relates patriarchal oppression to the suffocating, miniaturized universe of a Victorian dollhouse, melding the baroque period with fin-de-siècle themes. The production set is inspired by the so-called *Boîtes*, created by Charles Matton (1931–2008), which are scale-model boxes of approximately two cubic feet in which the artist builds miniaturized interior spaces that question appearances by experimenting with perspectivism. Pimenta, for her part, adopts a similar disquieting atmosphere by transforming all the characters in *La dama* into figurines caught up in the uncanny environment of a toy theater.[51] As she describes it:

> Everything is related to the end of the nineteenth century, which extends from Romanticism to illusionism. It is an escape to a place where there is fear, like riding a train of terror. . . . Carnivals and circuses suggest two types of feelings to us, from the happiest to the most bitter. Why do they go together? I don't know. Because there is a space for mystery, danger, a space for humility and suffering, a space for masks, clowns, a space for risk. It is the illusion of the child and the adult. (48–49)

Within this context, Doña Ángela exudes rebelliousness and courage as she becomes a master of appearances, creating a funhouse where the borders of reality and fantasy bleed into one another, and humor leaves a bitter aftertaste.

The director interprets the cupboard as an illusionist trick that literally assumes a life of its own, as it seems to conceal a disturbing, mysterious inner world. This effect is visually achieved through a stage fog that rises every time the door opens and via the perception of spatial depth that contributes to Doña Ángela's esoteric presence as she carries out her game of illusions. Stage designer Esmeralda Díaz explains: "We started with a kind of invisibility for the cupboard. . . . The intensity increases as the play progresses, and little by little the interior can be seen with all its complexity, with compartments, with movements, revealing its private spaces and its true nature" (59). Díaz interprets the cupboard as an extension of Doña Ángela, gaining agency as the plot progresses and simultaneously amplifying its uncanny aura. In no other production of *La dama*, to my knowledge, does the cupboard have such depth and symbolic meaning, especially if we compare it to its original representation in the *corrales*, where it would have been set flush against the back of the stage between the dressing rooms and covered by curtains (Varey, "*La dama*" 171).

Overall, Pimenta's adaptation of *La dama* illustrates a more nonconformist message about female confinement than most contemporary productions discussed here.[52] The director successfully challenges an established performative tradition that has relegated the stage life of the play to facile comicality and the cupboard to a superficial prop at the service of the amorous imbroglio. Pimenta overtly sides with Doña Angela and builds for her a perfect deceit mechanism, beyond one-dimensional animation and interpretation. However, I do not think that Pimenta's reading will continue to be carried on or further developed on the contemporary stage. The darker, more insightful notes with which she infuses the plot and the characters cannot compete with a prevalent tradition that still clings to a lighthearted, entertaining vision of the mechanics of the *duende*.

Although it was staged in the eighteenth century and continued to be adapted in the twentieth and twenty-first centuries, *El galán* has been overall less impactful in Spain's performance history compared to *La dama*. While in some cases it has been performed alongside *La dama* by the same company on consecutive days, it has never achieved the status of one of Calderón de la Barca's primary *comedias*. Its trajectory on the stage has remained generally faithful to its original setting—more so than *La dama*—but the design of the tunnel has gradually acquired a greater visual presence, stressing the play's fantastic theatricality.

In 1981, José Luis Alonso Mañés (1924–1990) premiered *El galán* in Madrid at the Teatro Español. This was the first production of the *comedia* in the twentieth century, and what critics tended to notice in their reviews, as in *La dama*, was its playful tonality. For Haro Tecglen, the production was a "laughing, mocking Calderón, *El galán fantasma* is one of those entangled Spanish plays that anticipate what later became known as vaudeville: The dead are not dead, ghosts are not ghosts, confusion of ladies, gallants, *embozados*, entrances and hurried exits abound, ridiculous jealousies, lovers ever dissatisfied" ("Sencillez"). Similarly, journalist Lorenzo López Sancho found the production to be a breath of fresh air in comparison to the other famed tragic works by the playwright (55). Oddly enough, none of these reviews mentions the tunnel as a central mechanism for the plot. It would seem that because it was not a blatantly visible element on the stage, unlike the cupboard, critics overlooked its theatrical and conceptual function. Only one caricature by Julio Cebrián that illustrates López Sancho's note for the *ABC* newspaper captures better than any critic the presence of the tunnel as a privileged metatheatrical stage. The cartoonist positions the tunnel at the very center of his drawing with its two secret entrances framing the rest of the characters (see Figure 6.3).

Alonso Mañés staged the tunnel using an *escotillón*, or trapdoor, just as would have been done in the seventeenth century. Indeed, all playhouses at the time had this seamless hinged opening flush against the surface of the stage, which was used mainly for sudden appearances and disappearances of the characters.[53] Hence, the supernatural gist in Mañés's adaptation resides, primarily, in the protagonists' words and in the audience's imagination. The director's overt effort to materialize the eerie atmosphere occurred through the staging of the garden surrounding the tunnel, represented by a cloth that moved every time Astolfo was about to emerge from underground. Nonetheless, Mañés took the liberty of including the scene when the protagonist contemplates his own funeral. While Astolfo only gestures to that experience in the original version of the play, Mañés comes to terms with the protagonist's new existence as a spectral being by fully capturing it onstage. Wonder in this production, then, lies more with the hero than with the set that stays true to the seventeenth-century metonymic decor of the *corrales* (see Figure 6.4).

In the 2010 production of the play directed by Mariano de Paco, the most visually striking staging of *El galán* to date, the tunnel regains its visual prominence, enveloped in a wondrous nocturnal atmosphere similar to Shakespeare's *A Midsummer Night's Dream* (1595–1596; see Figure 6.5). Each time Astolfo emerges from the passageway, the stage floor rises up as if it were swelling. Here, while the tridimensional animation of the tunnel brings to life the spectacular visual texture of

Calderonian dramaturgy, it also overrides its original essence as a torturous labyrinth and pushes the plot away from being a sociohistorically charged drama to becoming a survival thriller or a neo-baroque rom-com (see Figure 6.6).

All of these productions are illustrative of the ways in which directors and audiences have weighed the role of the artificial animation in *La dama* and *El galán* throughout the twenty and twenty-first centuries and the difficult task of regulating its nuanced meaning beyond purely playful mechanics. As with other artifacts studied in this book, the two-hinged portals show how the concept of artificial animacy changes and adjusts to different sensibilities over time but does not lose its essence to fascinate while always maintaining some of its original eerie principles that escape superfluous interpretations.

Going back to Calderón de la Barca and the original effects of illusionism in the two *comedias* studied, the playwright grants simulated life to the two secret passageways in an era "where confusion predominates and deception is generalized about the true status of reality" (Rodríguez de la Flor, *Pasiones frías* 31). Within this climate of contrived fantasy, he dismantles the supernatural, as Cervantes did with Clavileño and the enchanted head; however, in the playwright's case, he delves deeper into the meaning of desengaño in dialogue with everyday life and the social crisis that spanned Spain in the seventeenth century.[54]

In this context, the cupboard and the tunnel function as prostheses inasmuch as the protagonists appropriate them to fully move in otherworldly spheres of their own creation where otherness is the norm. Moreover, we could even argue that these alternative metatheatrical scenarios function as *mise en abymes* of Doña Ángela's and Astolfo's individual tragedies—tales of entrapment, isolation, and invisibility. While these protagonists "play" to change their lives, their creativity and *ingenio* (wit) can only momentarily alleviate their situations without completely breaking away from the patriarchal, tyrannical systems that oppress them.

The seventeenth century came to an end with the death of the last Habsburg ruler, Charles II, in 1700, appropriately nicknamed "El hechizado" (The bewitched), and led to a renewed attraction to magic, exorcism, and witchcraft. It is precisely during this time that theologian and Capuchin friar Antonio de Fuentelapeña (1628–ca. 1702) wrote *El ente dilucidado* (The entity elucidated, 1676), a unique pseudo-scientific treatise that explores the existence of fantastic creatures (e.g., goblins, gnomes, and sprites) in an era when the visible and the invisible were beginning to be revisited from theoretical and experimental scientific approaches.[55] Likewise, Calderón de la Barca's visionary protagonists engage with the supernatural in a systematic way, through the creativity implied in their homemade secular magic shows. In their hands, animation turns into a thoughtful spectacle of social survival as they perform baroque escape acts—à la Houdini—but well *avant la lettre*.[56] Nevertheless, we will have to wait until the eighteenth century for a more explicit engagement of the otherworldly with social order, when magic plays start featuring professional *magos* and *magas* (male and female wizards) that overtly articulate illusions around technical innovation, à la Cervantes, and in dialogue with social dissent, à la Calderón.[57]

Conclusion.
When Statues Move

> I suppose the body to be nothing but a statue or machine made of earth.
>
> RENÉ DESCARTES, *Traité de l'homme*, 1662

> JUAN. My lady, wait
>   and you will presently see
>   how Cesar, my Prince, will be
>   enchanting inanimate beings.
> MARGARITA. How so?
> JUAN. To amuse you,
>   he will blow the breath of life
>   into the sturdiest wood
>   and the hardiest of marbles. (vv. 819–26)
>
> JOSÉ DE CAÑIZARES Y SUÁREZ, *Don Juan de Espina in Milán*, 1713

AT THE TIME of Calderón de la Barca's death in 1681, innovative currents of thought had emerged under the influence of the so-called *novatores* (innovators) who sought to debunk the perception that late seventeenth-century Spain was a period devoid of cultural and intellectual life. This group of scientists and humanists welcomed, not without polemic, a modern curiosity that brought with it new trends in scientific, philosophical, and artistic knowledge and opened interdisciplinary dialogue among these fields.[1] Once Philip V assumed the throne in 1700 and Bourbon power settled in Spain, the efforts to open and revitalize society continued, but the nobility and the clergy still adhered to stagnant Counter-Reformation ideals and questioned any initiative they considered somewhat rooted in the Protestant ethic. Therefore, the devaluation of the Catholic faith in favor of atheistic rationalism, the rise of science and reason, the emphasis on education, and the implementation of social reforms still had a long way to go in Spain in comparison to other European countries.

Nonetheless, following the postulate that theaters could open new ways of understanding the world (Veltruský 91), eighteenth-century playwrights found in the *comedia de magia* an engaging vehicle to endorse the secularization of thought and disseminate alternative views of a new order that highlighted anthropocentric faith, reason, and social democratization.

In this sense, the root and subsequent popularity of magic plays can be justified in the decline of *comedia de santos*, which, by the end of the seventeenth century, had turned into a secular mass entertainment stripped of all pious didacticism. Many defining aspects of Christian wonder in the saint plays were revamped as products of natural magic in the *comedia de magia*. The magician replaced the saint, and the incantation substituted the miracle.[2] Strategically, when magic plays ran the risk of being banned during Lent, they were publicized as scientifically based entertainment to avoid prohibition (Fuente Ballesteros).

Moreover, many of the magician protagonists in these dramas were characterized as studious scientists engaged in philanthropy, as they devoted much of their knowledge and power to serving the greater good and those in need. Due to their self-imposed isolation and vocation for a contemplative intellectual life, they became invisible to society (Álvarez Barrientos, "Introducción" 17). Yet, just like Doña Ángela in *La dama duende* and Astolfo in *El galán fantasma*, these protagonists used their conditions as outsiders to live with greater freedom and to distance themselves from the restrictive social order.[3] Their independence and unconditional dedication to knowledge exemplifies the possibility of living in a more democratic, egalitarian society (Álvarez Barrientos, *La comedia* 246; Contreras Elvira, "Ciencia" 154).

It was to be expected, though, that in a culturally isolated country reluctant to embrace progress, the most traditional thinkers rejected revolutionary or non-conformist takes on magic that, moreover, required technically sophisticated staging.[4] In *La poética* (The poetics, 1737), poet and critic Ignacio de Luzán (1702–1754) denounced the *comedia de magia* specifically for these reasons and for doing "much violence to the comprehension and imagination" (7). Thus, what Luzán did not seem to have taken into consideration was that rather than deceiving their audiences, these plays offered the possibility for considering new ideas behind visual and conceptual illusions—in other words, offering viewers a way to look beyond appearances to break with the deceit of the senses. Perhaps, then, the true magic of these *comedias* resided in revealing as possible what hitherto had been regarded as impossible.

Among the many peculiarities shared by the animated artifacts examined in this book, there is a trait especially crucial because of its connection to the rise of modernity: the correlation between art and technology, which *articulates* religious, ideological, and social concepts from an engaging perspective. The *jointedness* that animated objects have exhibited is an intrinsic part of their aesthetic. Moreover, their visible interstices and the struggle involved in their manipulation are precisely what activate reflexive experiences and a critical understanding of new realities behind long-standing appearances.

There is, however, one object rather common in magic plays that I intentionally excluded from this cabinet of curiosities, and that is the animated statue. Even though it would appear to be an obvious choice to display in this collection, the moving statue has two features that make it distinct from the other artifacts curated in this book: the lack of joints and its purely fantastic nature. By definition, statues are jointless and are sculpted in one individuated piece. Unlike the articulated Christ-figure, the religious and secular puppet, the automaton, and the secret trapdoor, the stone figure does not have the necessary hinged mechanisms through which I have developed my theoretical approach to modern animation. Further, even if contemplation and human interaction can figuratively infuse life into inert matter, these objects still belong entirely to the realm of the fantastic—with no strings attached to reality.[5]

And yet, I did not want to close this study without mentioning them, especially because the most iconic animated statue in literature, the stone guest (Don Gonzalo de Ulloa, commander of the Order of Calatrava), comes from the seventeenth-century play *El burlador de Sevilla y convidado de Piedra*, attributed to Tirso de Molina. To a certain extent, my investigation is not complete without invoking its animation in a book about illusions in early modern Spain.

Notably, the most pressing question to ask about the function of the moving statue at the rise of modernity has already been put forth by Kenneth Gross: "What does it mean for a statue to step down from a pedestal (assuming we know what that is), to enter the sphere of the human or natural, to lose its isolation and aura?" ("Moving" 5). Gross responds to this inquiry with an answer that merits quoting in its entirety:

> It can seem both a fall and a resurrection, a descent and a transcendence into the human, both an enchantment and a disenchantment, the killing of a thing which lives a different life and the restoration of a dead sign to use and relation. It can be, as in Shakespeare (and to a certain degree in Ovid), an image of the most profound, gratuitous restitution, a figure not just for erotic recovery but for a recovery of the world, an awakening of the self to its objects, a return of objects themselves from their alienation. And yet in numerous texts the life which a statue takes on is partial, daimonic, unnatural, a violation rather than a recovery of the world—calling into question our naively benign pictures of metamorphosis. The statue's animation may be awakening into nightmare, a birth into nonlife—a state in the statue itself can become a Medusa (goddess of sculptors). ("Moving" 5)

Many of these ideas encompass what I have already discussed in relation to other animated artifacts in previous chapters. The biggest challenge in considering the animated statue as part of a study that aims at rationalizing illusions in the theatrical culture of the sixteenth and seventeenth centuries, however, is finding a way to bring these statues back to the realm of the real. And, this is precisely where the *comedia de magia* stages its ultimate stunt.

Since the rise of Hermetism in the 1400s, Renaissance humanists and philosophers have probed the relationship between art and religion through the notion of agency. The *Asclepius* (2nd c. CE), ascribed to the mythical Hellenistic figure Hermes Trismegistus, became, for example, a reference book containing wisdom for hermetic thinkers. The text gave detailed instructions for creating statues capable of incorporating spirits and, in so doing, turning the statues into gods (Strauss 199). Saint Augustine (354–430 CE) severely criticized these ideas and considered such figures to be deceitful and more akin to devilish creations than to divine iterations. Over the course of the seventeenth century, the moralizing revenant immortalized by Tirso de Molina kept its spectacular agency intact, although it gradually lost its religious dimension.

In mythological plays such as *La fiera, el rayo y la piedra* (The beast, the lightning, and the stone, 1652) and *La estatua de Prometeo* (The statue of Prometheus, 1669), both by Calderón de la Barca, the characters struggle to dominate their human passions and long for the sense of control that these supernatural sculptures came to epitomize.[6] As the eighteenth century drew closer, the animated statue furthered the dressage of chaos, order, and balance. The neoclassical taste for Greek sculpture contributed to these measured ideals, and magic plays featuring animated statues promoted these values and beliefs. The fascination inspired by the moving figures even translated into a real entertainment in Europe at the time. People enjoyed promenading at night in areas where sculptures reflected the light of nearby lanterns, which created the illusion of movement (Contreras Elvira, "Ciencia" 154).

In the *comedia de magia*, the moving statue coexisted with the magician in his daily life and made spectacular appearances that inspired a unique sense of awe to amuse his social entourage. These artifacts acted as subservient creations that obeyed their creators.[7] From a performance perspective, there were three different methods to represent such artificial characters onstage: 1) the so-called *estatuas de recortado* (cut-out statues), which were silhouettes cut from flat boards that moved along rails onstage; 2) mechanical artifacts similar to automata (Aranda 19); and, 3) actors who specialized in mimicry.[8] Such artists were no doubt familiar with and trained in *commedia dell'arte* techniques. The soi-disant Compañía de los Trufaldines (Trufaldines Theater Company) that moved to Madrid in 1702 from Italy played a critical role in the development of the *commedia dell'arte* in connection to the *comedia de magia* and the professional training of its interpreters at the time in both genres.[9]

Contrary to other artifacts mentioned in previous chapters, which exemplify the taming of wonder through the exposure of their inner workings, the moving statue rationalizes the supernatural through the control that the magician exerts upon it.[10] Even the actor that embodied the stone had to demonstrate a rigorous discipline over his body to realistically impersonate the non-human.[11] The self-controlled appearance of the modern *homo artificialis* (artificial man), symbolically embodied in the moving statue, stresses once again the idea that illusions are technical, scientific mechanisms. In Joaquín Álvarez Barrientos's words:

> The exterior, the appearance, ceased to identify with reality, with the motionless and the finished, to conclude, thanks to philosophical experiences of sensism, that reality was within the individual. The magic, or its "apparent" reflections, was an instrument to externalize that image of reality, that utopia that each one carried inside, which made it the "most necessary, / most useful and most perfect science" as the magician Fileno defended in *Lo que quería ver el marqués de Villena* (What the Marquis of Villena wanted to see). ("Apariencia" 349)

This demonstrates, as I have argued in this book, that subjects as well as objects are *made*, and theatrical illusions, particularly animation, were critical in shaping material and social history in early modernity.

For Bruno Brulon Soares, it is precisely at the breach between the real and the fantastic were the most profound social discoveries are made (17). And, that is why all the performance objects and scenarios discussed up to this point have functioned as artistic agents that articulated new ideas while awakening skepticism and modern curiosity among the real and fictional audiences that interacted with them. The jointed Christ figures, the marionettes of the máquina real, Master Pedro's puppets, Cervantes's automata, the secret trapdoors devised by Calderón de la Barca, and, to a certain extent, the moving statues had the power to critically link illusion, machinery, and magic, the three key elements in bringing to life the principle of animation in early modernity (Sawday 187).

The goal of this book has been to recover each one of these prop's micro-histories, mainly throughout the seventeenth century while also tracing their cultural and social agency up to the present. The study of how these artifacts developed over time, the narratives that their handlers recreated around them, and the reflexive experiences they evoked in viewers and readers help illuminate the inner workings of art, literature, and social history in Spain's early modernity from a novel perspective. Nonetheless, as I pointed out in the Introduction, this is but a humble beginning to a much broader study on animation and imagination vis-à-vis Western thought that must continue to be explored from a transnational and transhistorical perspective within material and performance cultures.

I opened this conclusion with two epigraphs that may seem, at first glance, to be disconnected. The first, by René Descartes, refers to the mechanistic philosophy through which the natural philosopher explains man's physiology using the allegorical precision of the machine, into which I delved in the first chapter. The second quote, from a *comedia de magia* by José de Cañizares y Suárez (1676–1750), alludes to the process of infusing stone with artificial life, a deed I have just addressed in these closing remarks. Reading both quotes side by side, they trace the intellectual breadth of the journey I have undertaken in this book, from inwardness to outwardness, from creation to revelation, from the supernatural to the natural, and, above all, from life to the stage—and vice versa.

NOTES

INTRODUCTION

EPIGRAPH. "Todo es arte, y todo lo alcança el hombre." Unless otherwise indicated, all translations are by the author.

1. The Carambolo is a municipality three kilometers away from Seville where the treasure containing the Astarté statuette was found in 1958.
2. By animation, I mean the act of giving movement and, to a certain degree, life to an inanimate performance object by direct manipulation or through concealed technologies.
3. The *Diccionario de la lengua española* defines the term *illusion* as a nonreal representation suggested by the imagination or a deception of the senses. The concept is also defined as hope.
4. The culture of science started to change and expand in early modernity thanks to cooperative research methods, the replication of experiments, and group witnessing.
5. See Richard H. Popkin, *The History of Scepticism from Erasmus to Spinoza*.
6. Throughout this book, I will use the words *marionette* and *puppet* interchangeably.
7. Early modern philosophers, unlike medieval scholastics, were driven to discover the "hidden causes of things" (Eamon, *Science* 291). During the 1600s, curiosity was considered a modern virtue that promoted scientific inquiry; it was not considered a vice that endangered the soul, as it was perceived in the Middle Ages. For an analysis on the evolution of the notion of curiosity in relation to scientific knowledge, see William Eamon's *Science and the Secrets of Nature: Books of Secrets in Medieval and Early Modern Culture*.

CHAPTER 1

1. See Charlene Villaseñor Black and Mari-Tere Álvarez's introduction to their edited volume, *Renaissance Futurities: Science, Art, Invention* (1–8).
2. The term *motion* in early modernity also referred to a puppet show and was shorthand for puppet (Garber 39).
3. Thomas Hobbes (1588–1679), René Descartes (1596–1650), John Wilkins (1614–1672), Robert Boyle (1627–1691), and Isaac Newton (1642–1727).
4. For a detailed analysis of these allegorical readings, see José María González García, Metáforas del poder (160–72). In addition, its sophistication and precision for timekeeping made the clock an essential tool to control navigational longitude in the shipping trade (Elizabeth King, "Clockwork Prayer" 12).
5. See Enrique García Santo-Tomás, *The Refracted Muse: Literature and Optics in Early Modern Spain*.
6. See Stephen Rupp, "The Soul under Siege: Strategy and Neostocism in Calderón de la Barca's *El sitio de Bredá*." In Chapter 6, I return to this idea in relation to *El galán fantasma*.
7. To engage beyond the materiality of illusions also relates to the philosophy of stoicism that took hold in Spain during the seventeenth century in the fields of political theory, culture, and religiosity because of its commonalities with Catholicism (Reula Baquero 145).
8. Basil Jones is one of the co-founders of the Handspring Puppet Company. In collaboration with Adrian Kohler, they created the much-acclaimed puppets for the original stage performance of *War Horse* (2007). Their unique, life-sized marionettes reveal the processes of animation and manipulation through their bare structure.
9. Sacred objects in the Middle Ages were highly adaptable and mobile, which means that they could serve a variety of purposes beyond the one for which they were originally intended (Buc 101–2).
10. In *The Stage Life of Props*, Andrew Sofer examines how iconic dramatic props develop their own afterlife through subsequent performances.
11. In contrast to Jiří Veltruský, Steve Tillis considers the very instant when the prop assumes movement or speech as the moment it transforms into a puppet ("The Actor Occluded").
12. Ernst Jentsch in "On the Psychology of the Uncanny" (1906) and Sigmund Freud in "The Uncanny" (1919) engage with the fascination that puppets still inspired at the turn of the twentieth century.
13. Caroline Walker Bynum devotes a fascinating study to the dynamics of what she calls "dissimilar similitudes" in religious artefacts. See *Dissimilar Similitudes: Devotional Objects in Late Medieval Europe*.

14. "Ce n'est plus de la pierre ni du bois enluminé, c'est une peau humaine (on le dit du moins), rembourrée avec beaucoup d'art et de soin. Les cheveux sont de véritables cheveux, les yeux ont des cils, la couronne d'épines est en vraie ronce, aucun détail n'est oublié. Rien n'est plus lugubre et plus inquiétant à voir que ce long fantôme crucifié, avec son faux air de vie et son immobilité morte; la peau, d'un ton rance et bistré, est rayée de longs filets de sang si bien imités que l'on croirait qu'ils ruissellent effectivement. Il ne faut pas un grand effort d'imagination pour ajouter foi à la légende qui raconte que ce crucifix miraculeux saigne tous les vendredis" (50–51).
15. Saint Bridget of Sweden's *Revelations* (1492) contributed to the dissemination in Europe of this excruciating vision of the body of Christ.
16. See Jonah Coman, "No Strings Attached: Emotional Interaction with Animated Sculptures of Crucified Christ."
17. This normalization of the animated object will resurface again in nineteenth-century fantastic fiction, where the supernatural is enmeshed in everyday life.
18. Within a broader European context, the no-longer-extant fourteenth-century Virgin from Saint Mary's Church in Rostock, Germany, could weep by virtue of the movement of water housed in a tank that was concealed in the Virgin's head, wherein a fish, when swimming close to the orifices of the eyes, pushed water outward, creating the illusion of falling tears (Kopania 180). In 1501, a French engineer from Rabastens, near Toulouse, designed a prototype of an elevator to recreate the Assumption of the Virgin. The children of the region were quick to build their own homemade versions of this device (Riskin, "Machines" 22).
19. There are local processions nowadays in Spain that display articulated Virgins, such as the Virgin of Jubrique in Málaga, whose manipulation techniques have been passed down for generations within the same family.
20. See Rosa M. Rodríguez Porto, "Knighted by the Apostle Himself: Political Fabrication and Chivalric Artifact in Compostela, 1332."
21. Cervantes immortalized two of the most famous retablos in Spanish literature in his interlude *Retablo de las maravillas* (The marvelous pageant, 1615) and in Master Pedro's puppet show in *Don Quijote*. Writer Ramón del Valle-Inclán (1866–1936) portrays a dehumanized version of these shows in his *Retablo de la avaricia, la lujuria y la muerte* (Altar-piece of avarice, lust, and death, 1927), a collection of five symbolist short plays in which most of his human characters are devoid of a spiritual dimension.
22. The original figures of this nativity scene were sculpted in the mid-1700s to decorate the altarpiece of the church. Only later were they refurbished to become animated as part of the nativity scene.

23. This United Nations proclamation started in 2001 as a way to raise awareness and to protect unique cultural expressions among local communities.
24. Calderón de la Barca used this type of celestial imagery as part of the scenery in some of his *autos sacramentales* (short religious plays). See Ana Suárez Miramón, "La correspondencia de las esferas en el universo de Calderón."
25. For a detailed analysis of the symbolism implied in this celebration, see Joan Castaño García, "Los símbolos de la Festa o Misterio de Elche."
26. The *gigantes* and *cabezudos* were part of the Corpus Christi festivities and remain an attraction in popular festivals to this day. They are made with papier-mâché. The giants have a disproportionate height, and the big-heads are shorter with oversized heads.
27. On the date and conditions concerning the entry of the manuscript to the Escorial, see Víctor de Lama's "Un antecedente de Celestina a finales del siglo XIII: El teatro de sombras de Ibn Dāniyāl."
28. Another form of puppetry in Spain, probably rooted in the Arabic tradition, was the *bavastells*. These were small, wooden, medieval warrior figurines suspended horizontally on strings. One end was tied to a fixed object, and the other was tied to the leg of the puppeteer, who tautened the string by moving his leg to make the puppet pirouette. The earliest existing engraving of the *bavastells* is in the *Hortus deliciarum codex* (12th c.).

CHAPTER 2

EPIGRAPH. Translation by Deborah Tarn Steiner in Images in Mind: Statues in Archaic and Classical Greek Literature and Thought (115).
1. For a detailed catalog of these figures, see Jessica Riskin, *The Restless Clock*.
2. See Nigel Llwellyn, "Baroque Sculpture: Materiality and the Question of Movement."
3. In devotional contexts the animated Christ figure erases the distinction between the earthly and the heavenly while maintaining a certain reverential distance. Ana Zamora reconstructs this complex visual language of the devotional object while infusing it with an inclusive and global meaning that goes beyond any specific religious beliefs.
4. Peter Lombard's compilation of theological sources functioned as a forum for debating other theological ideas among intellectuals of the period.
5. Romano Guardini (1885–1968), one of the most influential Catholic intellectuals of the twentieth century, also considered the liturgy as a "sacred game which the soul plays before God" (71).

6. Honorius Augustodunensis (ca. 1080–1154), Hugh of St. Victor (ca. 1096–1141), Sicardus of Cremona (1155–1215), Innocent III (ca. 1160–1216), John Beleth (ca. 12th c.), Durandus of Mende (ca. 1230–1296), Thomas Aquinas (1225–1274).
7. For a detailed analysis of "Del sacrificio de la misa," see Pedro M. Cátedra's edition of Gonzalo de Berceo's *Obra Completa* (Complete works).
8. During her pilgrimage to Rome in 1414, English mystic Margery Kempe (ca. 1373–1438) met a woman carrying a chest with a baby Jesus doll (Moshenska 47). See Joe Moshenska's chapter on "Dolls" (41–67) and Ulinka Rublack's "Female Spirituality and the Infant Jesus in Late Medieval Dominican Convents."
9. Andrew Sofer dedicates chapter 1 in his book *The Stage Life of Props* (31–50) to the interpretation of the Host as theater prop.
10. Samuel Sharp (ca. 1700–1778) in *Letters from Italy* (1767) recounts an anecdote that illustrates this tendency of transforming the cross into a puppet. In the Largo del Castello in Naples, a monk was preaching on the street near a Pulcinello puppet show. Since no one paid attention to him and passers-by were immersed in watching the puppeteer, he held up the crucifix and screamed, "Ecco il vero Pulcinella" (Here is the true Pulchinello; Sharp 183–84; qtd. in Moshenska 75).
11. Leanne Groeneveld mentions the "preacher Christs" as a type of figurine that some celebrants used to highlight the theatricality of their sermons. See Groeneveld, "'lyke unto a lyvely thyng': The Boxley Rood of Grace and Medieval Performance" (200–201).
12. A pin joint refers to a pin that joins two pieces together and creates a pivot point for articulation on a single plane. In many instances, this kind of articulation in puppets is achieved using a variation of the pin joint called a rotating mortise and tenon joint.
13. Moshenska goes on to argue how Incarnation, Crucifixion, and Resurrection are the three most majestic stages in Christ's life but irrational, too, if interpreted from a worldly perspective (78–81).
14. Devout modernist writers such as Anatole France (1844–1924), Maurice Bouchor (1855–1929), Paul Claudel (1868–1955), and Michel Ghelderode (1898–1962) sought to recover the majestic spirituality and sacred innocence of puppets when writing their symbolist neo-mysteries for marionettes. Bouchor's introduction to his *Mystères bibliques et chrétiens* (Biblical and Christian mysteries, 1920) stresses this unique ability of the puppet to represent "all impression of the supernatural" without losing any of its human qualities (7–8).
15. Around 923–924, the *Visitatio* was adapted into the *Quem quaretis* (Whom do you seek?) in the French monastery of Saint Martial at Limoges. The trope subsequently spread throughout Europe. The *Elevatio* was also dramatized but

much less frequently than the *Visitatio*.

16. At the intersection of material culture and medieval Christianity, the wound on Christ's side was sometimes depicted in the iconography of the period as "a stand-alone object, independent of his body" (Dailey 280). See also Caroline Walker Bynum, "Violent Imagery in Late Medieval Piety."

17. Many more *Cristos articulados* were made in the sixteenth century, when their popularity increased coinciding with the endorsement of the twenty-fifth session (1563) of the Council of Trent (1541–1563).

18. In medieval Bohemia, up to three sculptures were used to represent the various stages of Christ during the Crucifixion, Descent, and Resurrection. This was the case in the Augustinian cloister of Olomouc and in the monastery of Saint Thomas in Prague (Uličný 47–48).

19. Franciscan missionaries introduced this rite in Mexico in the sixteenth century. See Octavio Rivera Krakowska and Estrada David Aarón's "Títeres en Nueva España en el Siglo XVI."

20. "Vnos se ocupan en miradas lizinziosas, otros en conversaziones mundanas, otros en voces destempladas y otros (quando mas) en unos suspiros y lagrimas materiales que, como agua de tormenta, pasan luego sin umedezer y fecundar la tierra del corazon, sacadas maquinal mente de los ojos a fuerza de artifizios y Esterioridades, como son dar rezios golpes con el martillo para desenclavar el Cadáver del Sr. por la tramoia (así se debe llamar). Que se usa en algunos pueblos de subir y bajar con un cordel las manos de la Ymagn. de Nª Sª de la Soledad para limpiar los ojos y Recivir la corona y los clabos que le han a ofrezer los minsas. y otras imbenziones ajenas a la seriedad con que se debe celebrar este tierno paso."

21. In the earliest iconographic representations of the Descent, Joseph of Arimathea and Nicodemus were the only ones present in the scene, apart from the crucified Christ. By the late Middle Ages, due in part to the influence of the *Meditationes Vitae Christi* (Meditations on the life of Christ, 14th c.) and the medieval mystery plays, more characters were added to the background (Viladesau 54).

22. Of note, the canvas is currently housed in the monastery of Santa María Magdalena in Medina del Campo (Valladolid).

23. For various analyses of the symbolic elements of the painting, see Antonio Sánchez del Barrio, "La función del Desenclavo en un cuadro de 1722" and "La Función del Desenclavo" as well as Manuel Arias, José Ignacio Hernández Redondo, and Antonio Sánchez del Barrio, *Semana Santa en Medina del Campo. Historia y obras artísticas.*

24. Recovered Depositio ceremonies that still take place today can be found in the towns of Ahigal, Peraleda de Mata, and Robledillo de Gata (Cáceres); Vivero (Lugo); Pollensa (Mallorca); Palencia; Santiago de Cangas do Morrazo and

Tui (Pontevedra); Salamanca; Nava del Rey, Cuenca de Campos, Valdenebro de los Valles, and Villavicencio de Caballeros (Valladolid); and Bercianos de Aliste (Zamora).

25. For footage of one of these surviving Depositio ceremonies in Peraleda de la Mata (Cáceres), see www.youtube.com/watch?v=ZKvhgEMQCMI.
26. See Julio Vélez Sainz, "De teatro primitivo a primer teatro clásico," for a detailed analysis of Ana Zamora's pioneering career. A full list of her productions can be found on the company's webpage: www.naodamores.com/.
27. In addition to Zamora, other directors and companies specializing in a premodern Iberian repertoire are Manuel Canseco, Rafael Álvarez "El brujo," Teatro Dran, and Teatro da Cornucópia.
28. For more historical and cultural background on the Abadía Theater, see Simon David Breden, *The Creative Process of Els Joglars and Teatro de la Abadía: Beyond the Playwright* (157–76 and 209–22).
29. Although the figure is considered a Romanesque piece, the face belongs to the Gothic period. This combination of artistic styles implies that the wood carving was refurbished at some point in its history (Díez González 93).
30. "En esta çiudad hay una calle que nonbramos Cal de Gascos. Esta calle poblaron gascones y dellos tomó el nonbre. Eran obligados a representar cada año la Pasión de Nuestro Señor."
31. "¡Ay dolor, dolor, / por mi fijo y mi señor! / ¡Ay dolor!" (Zamora, *Misterio* 23).
32. See also Martin Stevens, "Illusion and Reality in the Medieval Drama."
33. See Richard Cenier, "Bocetos para un espacio escénico," in the online dossier for *Misterio del Cristo de los Gascones*.
34. David Freedberg illustrates the function of the statue's gaze, taking as an example the *nētra pinkama* (the ceremony of the eyes), a consecration rite celebrated among Ceylonese Theravada Buddhists. In this celebration, the statue of Buddha comes to life only when the eyes are painted on the figure (110).
35. See Shelley and Pamela Jackson's *The Doll Games* project website at www.ineradicablestain.com/dollgames/.
36. See Shelley and Pamela Jackson's Josh McBig slide at www.ineradicablestain.com/dollgames/josh.html.

CHAPTER 3

EPIGRAPH. Translated in Segel (93).
1. For a detailed genealogy of other references to marionette theater in Spanish literature, see John E. Varey, *Historia de los títeres en España (Desde sus orígenes hasta mediados del siglo XVIII)*.

2. See Susan Young, *Shakespeare Manipulated: The Use of the Dramatic Works of Shakespeare in teatro di figura in Italy.*
3. The database on performances of Spanish classical theater, *Base de datos de comedias mencionadas en la documentación teatral* (CATCOM), attributes this play to an anonymous author since there is no record of any *comedia* under this specific title.
4. "Un dragón todo el desnudillo pintado plateado y dorado . . . las alas de hilo de alambre; una caveça grande de dragón que se entrava a una mujer en la caveça; un león todo entero vestido de pelo con sus garras y caveça vaciado; un pescado grande y puro aroz en él."
5. For a study on the professional conditions for artists working in a máquina real, see Francisco J. Cornejo Vega, "Primeros tiempos de la máquina real de los títeres: Los actores maquinistas (hacia 1630–1750)."
6. See Alejandro García-Reidy, "The Technological Environment of the Early Modern Spanish Stage."
7. See Kenneth L. Woodward, *Making Saints: How the Catholic Church Determines Who Becomes a Saint, Who Doesn't, and Why.*
8. Portuguese poet Manuel de Faria e Sousa (1590–1649) records the case of a young woman who, after seeing a performance of *La Baltasara* (1634), was brought to God, inspired by the example of the anchorite protagonist. Similarly, actress Manuela de Escamilla (1648–1721) was known for inducing a devotional response in the audience and for wearing multiple amulets onstage (Aparicio Maydeu, "La comedia" 65).
9. Jesuit theologian Gian Domenico Ottonelli (1584–1670) stressed this idea in his treatise *Della christiana moderazione del teatro* (On the Christian moderation of the theatre, 1652). In Spain, several puppeteers were imprisoned after an inquisitorial trial in Valencia in 1619 for staging a show mocking the Dominican friars on the same day that they held a procession in honor of their patron saint (Varey, "Titiriteros" 243).
10. In early modern English literature, references to marionettes were used to denigrate Catholic morality for its tendency to idolatry. The interplay of the words *Pope/puppetry* was common in these contexts (Butterworth 126–27).
11. Philip Butterworth mentions the use of dummies to materialize the soul on stage in English mysteries plays (148).
12. The Sicilian *Opera dei Pupi* (19th c.) is a compelling example of the relationship between puppetry and violence. The warrior marionettes cut their enemies in half, and the mutilated limbs return to life on stage (Morse 149; See also Baird 118–29).

13. This is one of three monk/saint automata that we know of from around the world. The other two are in the Deutsches Museum in Munich and in the Iparmuvészti Múseum in Budapest (Elizabeth King, "Clockwork Prayer" 6–7).
14. See Sarah Macmillan, "Phenomenal Pain: Embodying the Passion in the Life of Elizabeth of Spalbeek."
15. The Jesuits used clockwork automata as one of their instructional tools for spreading the Christian doctrine. Athanasius Kircher (1602–1680) contributed to this missionary call with his hydraulic mechanical religious sets (Riskin, "Machines" 29).
16. Theater companies in countries with a millenary tradition in marionette theater have recently undertaken similar efforts to recover their original puppetry arts. See Katia Légeret, "Mettre en scène le danseur et la marionette: Les conditions d'émergence en Inde d'un nouveau musée de l'art vivant."
17. See my two interviews with Jesús Caballero, "La máquina real en el siglo XXI: Entrevista con Jesús Caballero" and "Recovering the Intangible Art of Baroque Puppetry: Interview with Jesús Caballero."
18. See José Sánchez-Arjona in *El teatro en Sevilla en los siglos XVI y XVII: Estudios históricos* for a full account of the tragic event (193–99).
19. For a performance review of this production, see Sergio Adillo Rufo's "Classical Theater and Puppetry: La máquina real" and Esther Fernández's "*Lo fingido verdadero* de Lope de Vega."
20. "figuras contrahechas, al modo de títeres, representaban unas *comedias* con tanta propiedad y artificio, y las figuras tan pulidamente vestidas, dándoles los movimientos con unos alambres tan al vivo y con tal tenor de voz y acciones, que era cosa de grandísima admiración."
21. A similar technique was used for sculpting the so-called *imágenes de vestir* (dressed images). These types of figures were refurbished medieval statues of the Virgin and Child from a seated to a standing position. The clothing was a crucial accessory to cover their originally severed bodies (Donahue-Wallace 145).
22. In cultures with a long-standing puppet theater tradition like Java, puppeteers are considered to have magical and divine qualities.
23. In her review of *El esclavo* (2009), Elizabeth M. Petersen goes into detail about the manipulators' work behind the scenes and their strenuous physical efforts to keep the puppets alive at all times during the show (264).
24. For an inventory of the artistic belongings of a máquina real, see Piedad Bolaños, Mercedes de los Reyes Peña, Vicente Palacios, Juan Ruesga Navarro, and Francisco J. Cornejo Vega, "La magia de los títeres en el teatro áureo español: La Máquina Real en el Corral de Montería de Sevilla."

25. "(1) Sale don Gil abrazado con una muerte, cubierta con un manto; (2) Descúbrela [la muerte], y luego se hunde; (3) Vuélvese una tramoya, aparece una figura de demonio, y disparando cohetes y arcabuces, se va Angelio; (4) Desaparece la visión, suenan trompetas, aparece una batalla arriba entre un ángel y un demonio, en sus tramoyas y desaparecen; (5) Descúbrese Lisarda con música, muerta de rodillas, con un Cristo y una calavera, en un jardín."

26. Concerning the role of illusions created by music and sound on the English stage, see chapter 5, "Magic Through Sound: Illusion, Deception and Agreed Pretence," in Butterworth's *Magic on the Early English Stage* (98–112).

27. As the seventeenth century developed, there were several attempts to ban saint plays as they gradually turned into pure spectacle devoid of all moral and religious teachings.

28. In Michael Landy's exhibition/performance *Break Down* (2001), all the artist's possessions were catalogued, subsequently destroyed, and sent to a landfill over a fourteen-day period. Landy was left with only the clothes that he was wearing. I mention this particular exhibit because it closely relates to the process of destruction to which Landy returns in *Saints Alive* (2013).

29. In the 1960s, Bruce Lacey experimented with similar interactive robotic assemblages as a critique of consumer society.

30. See Wiggins, et al., *Michael Landy: Saints Alive* and Alice Dailey, "Stigma and Stigmata: Medieval Hagiography and Michael Landy's *Saints Alive*," wherein Dailey applies medieval theories of the stigmata to Landy's work.

31. *The Doll Games* project (1970–1976) by Shelley and Pamela Jackson can be interpreted as part of the artistic trend that revisits violence and disjointedness vis-à-vis the holy, especially through the figures of Josh McBig, the "sorrowful, suffering Christ," and Laurie, "the martyred saint." See Chapter 2, notes 36–37.

CHAPTER 4

EPIGRAPH. Translated in Segel (93). "El caballo de don Gaiferos, en su galope vertiginoso, va abriendo tras su cola una estrella de vacío: en ella se precipita una corriente de aire alucinado que arrastra consigo cuanto no está muy firme sobre la tierra. Y allá va volteando arrebatada en el vórtice ilusorio, el alma de don Quijote, ingrávida como un villano, como una hoja seca. Y allá irá siempre en su seguimiento cuanto quede en el mundo de ingenuo y de doliente" (Ortega y Gasset, *Meditaciones* 209).

1. *Don Quijote* has been associated with the dramatic genre in multiple studies. Francisco Fernández-Turienzo, for example, considers the novel as the play Cervantes always aspired to write (26).

2. Bruce Burningham argues that Cervantes positions Master Pedro's puppet show along a continuum of popular performances that illustrates a microcosm of early Spanish theater (181).
3. The Muslim echoes of the puppet show evoke the Christian Reconquest that gradually forced Spanish Muslims to take refuge in the south of the Peninsula and reduced the kingdom of Granada to the last bastion of Moorish civilization until it fell to Christian rule in 1492 under the Catholic monarchs.
4. For John E. Varey, a possible source for this show could have been the "Danza de don Gayferos y rescate de Melisendra" (Dance of Don Gayferos and rescue of Melisendra) performed by actors during the procession of the Corpus Christi in Madrid in 1609 (*Historia* 234, 236).
5. While the Protestant Reformation is considered one of the major motivators of modernity, secularization, and rationalism, Alexandra Walsham stresses the long and gradual process it took for these ideas to gel in society (500–501). See Walsham, "The Reformation and 'The Disenchantment of the World' Reassessed."
6. In "A Theatrical Miracle: The Boxley Rood of Grace as Puppet," Leanne Groeneveld discusses the controversies surrounding the crucifix's miraculous nature. Jessica Riskin also points out the Rood's doubly illusionistic experience: before approaching the cross, the faithful had to go by a remote-controlled Saint Rumwold who administered his benediction ("Machines" 20).
7. English historian John Foxe (ca. 1516–1587) condemned the deceitful crucifix in his influential *Book of Martyrs: Acts and Monuments of the Church* (1563; Conti 97). See also Margaret Aston, "Iconoclasm in England: Official and Clandestine," 56–57.
8. "Vea maese Pedro lo que quiere por las figuras deshechas, que yo me ofrezco a pagárselo luego, en buena y corriente moneda castellana" (*Don Quijote* 853).
9. On autopoiesis in *Don Quijote*, see *Cognitive Approaches to Early Modern Spanish Literature*, edited by Isabel Jaén and Julien Jacques Simon.
10. Helena Percas de Ponseti interprets the Master Pedro's puppet show as a burlesque *auto sacramental* (short religious play) about humanity created by a god-puppeteer. Similarly, David Gitliz reads this episode as a religious allegory in "La ruta alegórica del segundo *Quijote*" (115).
11. "De los titiriteros decía mil males: decía que era gente vagabunda y que trataba con indecencia a las cosas divinas, porque con las figuras que mostraban en sus retablos volvían la devoción en risa, y que les acontecía envasar en un costal todas o las más figuras del *Testamento Viejo y Nuevo* y sentarse sobre él a comer y beber en los bodegones y tabernas; en resolución, decía que se maravillaba de cómo quien podía no les ponía perpetuo silencio en sus retablos, o los desterraba del reino" (Cervantes, "El licenciado Vidriera," *Novelas ejemplares* 66).

12. "La codicia y la envidia despertó en los rufianes voluntad de hurtarme, y andaban buscando ocasión para ello; que esto del ganar de comer holgando tiene muchos aficionados y golosos; por esto hay tantos titiriteros en España, tantos que muestran retablos, tantos que venden alfileres y coplas, que todo su caudal, aunque le vendiesen todo, no llega a poderse sustentar un día; y con esto los unos y los otros no salen de los bodegones y tabernas en todo el año; por do me doy a entender que de otra parte que de la de sus oficios sale la corriente de sus borracheras. Toda esta gente es vagabunda, inútil y sin provecho; esponjas del vino y gorgojos del pan" (Cervantes, "El coloquio de los perros," *Novelas ejemplares* 333).
13. See "La profecía de la bruja (El coloquio de los perros)" by Edward Riley and "Comedias" by Bruce Wardropper.
14. Whereas Bertolt Brecht does not directly discuss puppet theater in his theoretical writings, artists working with marionettes have often drawn on Brecht's dramatic theory to conceptualize their shows (Osman 19).
15. In addition to seventeenth-century Spanish drama, Brecht also found inspiration in medieval mystery plays, Jesuit theater, and Asian theater (C. A. Jones, "Brecht" 40, 42, 48).
16. All the English extracts from *Don Quixote* come from Edith Grossman's 2003 translation. "Obedeciéronle don Quijote y Sancho, y vinieron donde ya estaba el retablo puesto y descubierto, lleno por todas partes de candelillas de cera encendidas que le hacían vistoso y resplandeciente. En llegando, se metió maese Pedro dentro dél, que era el que había de manejar las figuras del artificio, y fuera se puso un muchacho, criado del maese Pedro, para servir de intérprete y declarador de los misterios del retablo: tenía una varilla en la mano, con que señalaba las figuras que salían" (*Don Quijote* 845).
17. "—Niño, niño—dijo con voz alta a esta sazón don Quijote—seguid vuestra historia línea recta y no os metáis en las curvas o transversales, que para sacar una verdad en limpio menester son muchas pruebas y repruebas" (*Don Quijote* 848).
18. "También dijo maese Pedro desde dentro:—Muchacho, no te metas en dibujos, sino haz lo que ese señor te manda, que será lo más acertado: sigue tu canto llano y no te metas en contrapuntos, que se suelen quebrar de sotiles.—Yo así lo haré—respondió el muchacho" (*Don Quijote* 848).
19. "Aquí alzó otra vez la voz maese Pedro y dijo:—Llaneza, muchacho, no te encumbres que toda afectación es mala" (*Don Quijote* 849).
20. "—¡Eso no!—dijo a esta sazón don Quijote—. En esto de las campanas anda muy impropio maese Pedro, porque entre moros no se usan campanas, sino atabales y un género de dulzainas que parecen nuestras chirimías; y esto de sonar campanas en Sansueña sin duda lo que es un gran disparate" (*Don Quijote* 849–50).

21. "—No mire vuesa merced en niñerías señor don Quijote, ni quiera llevar las cosas tan por el cabo, que se le halle. ¿No se representan por ahí casi de ordinario mil comedias llenas de mil impropiedades y disparates, y, con todo eso, corren felicísimamente su carrera y se escuchan no sólo con aplauso, sino con admiración y todo? Prosigue muchacho, y dejar decir, que como llene mi talego, siquiera represente más inapropiedades que tiene átomos el sol" (*Don Quijote* 850).
22. See *Quixote* (636–37) and *Don Quijote* (855).
23. "Mas, ¡ay, sin ventura!, que se le ha asido una punta del faldellín de uno de los hierros del balcón, y está pendiente en el aire, sin poder llegar al suelo. Pero veis cómo el piadoso cielo socorre en las mayores necesidades, pues llega don Gaiferos y si se rasgará o no el rico faldellín, ase de ella y mal su grado la hace bajar al suelo y luego de un brinco la pone sobre las ancas de su caballo" (*Don Quijote* 849).
24. Cervantes animalizes some of his characters in the two anecdotes that precede Master Pedro's puppet show: the braying adventure and the divinations of the soothsaying monkey. The novelist uses these episodes to explore the concept of dehumanization (Haley 149).
25. In Luis de Góngora's ballad, "Desde Sansueña a París" (From Sansueña to Paris, 1588), Melisendra is satirically portrayed and could have been a source of inspiration for her ridiculed characterization in Cervantes's puppet show.
26. "Para mi sola nació don Quijote, y yo para él: él supo obrar y yo escribir, solo los dos somos para en uno," (*Don Quijote* 1223). Wilma Newberry considers these excerpts to be particularly crucial vis-à-vis "the materials of creation and the self-conscious artist" (10).
27. "—Miren cuánta y cuán lucida caballería sale de la ciudad en siguimiento de los dos católicos amantes. . . . Témome que los han de alcanzar y los han de volver atados a la cola de su mismo caballo, que sería un horrendo espetáculo. Viendo y oyendo, pues, tanta morisma y tanto estruendo don Quijote, parecióle ser bien dar ayuda a los que huían, y levantándose en pie, en voz alta dijo:—No consentiré yo que en mis días y en mi presencia se le haga superchería a tan famoso caballero y a tan atrevido enamorado como don Gaiferos. ¡Deteneos, mal nacida canalla, no le sigáis ni persigáis; si no, conmigo sois en la batalla!" (*Don Quijote* 850).
28. "Las figuras de los realistas suelen ser maniquíes vestidos, que se mueven por cuerda y que llevan en el pecho un fonógrafo que repite las frases que su Maese Pedro recogió por calles y plazuelas y cafés y apuntó en su cartera" (13).
29. Other episodes from *Don Quijote* were transposed into operas, operettas, and symphonies from the eighteenth century on. The most popular chapters for

such musical adaptations were the knight keeping vigil for his arms, his first sally, the enchanted inn, the adventures in Sierra Morena, Camacho's wedding, the encounter with the duke and duchess, Sancho as governor of Barataria, and the battle with the Knight of the Mirrors (Hess, *Manuel de Falla* 307–08).

30. In her role as music patron, the Princesse Edmond de Polignac continued commissioning works that have become decisive in the history of European music: Germaine Tailleferre's *First Piano Concerto* (1924), Darius Milhaud's *Les malheurs d'Orphée* (The misfortunes of Orpheus, 1924), Francis Poulenc's *Concerto for Two Pianos and Orchestra* (1932), Kurt Weill's *Second Symphony* (1933), and Jean Françaix's *Sérénade pour douze instruments* (Serenade for twelve instruments, 1934) and *Le diable boîteux* (The devil on two sticks, 1937) (Kahan 417–18).

31. The writers and intellectuals belonging to the Generation of 1898 were profoundly affected by the loss of the last Spanish colonies in the Spanish-American War (1898). The group collaborated to find a path to spiritual renewal and the recovery of a national consciousness by reclaiming Spanish cultural heritage while introducing new European trends in literature and thought (Shaw 22–31).

32. The mission of Teatro Nueva Escuela was to support artistic works that could be performed as chamber operas and small-scale productions.

33. Manuel de Falla was an enthusiast of puppet theater since childhood, and Don Quixote was among his favorite characters (Martínez, "Orígenes" 30). Born and raised in Cádiz, he was no doubt familiar with *Los títeres de la tía Norica* (Aunt Norica's puppets, ca. 1790), one of the oldest extant traditions of puppet theater in Spain.

34. Andrés Pérez-Simón in *Baroque Lorca: An Archaist Playwright for the New Stage* dedicates the second chapter, "Of Human and Puppets" (45–66), to the role that puppetry had in Lorca's career. Pérez-Simón also studies Cervantes's influence on the poet's experimentation with marionettes and comic theater.

35. "Este tema lo encontrará leyendo el capítulo de la segunda parte de *Don Quijote*, 'El retablo de Maese Pedro.' Seguiré el texto de Cervantes desde el comienzo de la representación (hecha por marionetas sobre un pequeño teatro situado sobre la escena). Se supondrá que los espectadores citados en el texto se encuentran delante del retablo. Los escucharemos, pero no los veremos. Es solamente al final cuando don Quijote sube violentamente a la escena para castigar a aquellos que persiguen a Melisendra y don Gaiferos, terminando la representación con las palabras que él dedica (don Quijote) a la gloria de la caballería."

36. "La escena está dividida en dos secciones que corresponden al proscenio y al retablo. En la primera sección aparecen y accionan los muñecos representativos de las personas que se hallan en la venta. De estas figuras, la que representa a don

Quijote ha de ser, por lo menos, del doble tamaño que las restantes. La segunda sección de la escena, o sea el fondo, ocupado por el retablo, debe dar la impresión de algo independiente en absoluto de la primera. Es el verdadero teatro, y ha de estar colocado a una sensible altura del plano que ocupa el proscenio."

37. In the following productions of *El retablo,* Hermenegildo Lanz would continue to perfect the techniques and designs of his original marionettes. He engineered a human-scale puppet prototype whose body and head were attached to the manipulator and whose arms were controlled by rods (Martínez, "Orígenes" 38).

38. Igor Stravinsky had already experimented with this fragmentation between the body and the voice of the interpreter in *Histoire du soldat* (The soldier's tale, 1918), and it continued to be used in other avant-garde artistic assemblages, such as Kurt Weill and Brecht's sung ballet, *The Seven Deadly Sins* (1933; Sheppard 34).

39. "No deben mezclarse los diferentes grupos de la orquesta; los arcos se colocarán a la izquierda del director. El cémbalo y el arpa en primer plano, pero esta última a la derecha, con la madera tras cual se colocarán las trompas y la trompeta, pero de modo que ésta no esté muy alejada de la flauta. El fagot, cerca de las trompas y de los bajos de cuerda. La percusión, al fondo."

40. Filmmaker Luis Buñuel (1900–1983) chose this artificial puppet aesthetic for his actors when he directed *El retablo* in Amsterdam in 1926.

41. Jean Cocteau (1889–1963), Erik Satie (1866–1925), Léonide Massine (1896–1979), Pablo Picasso (1881–1973), Francis Picabia (1879–1953), Rolf de Maré (1888–1964).

42. Enrique Lanz and Fabiola Garrido established Títeres Ectétera in 1981. The fusion of operas and musical pieces with puppet theater is present in most of their productions, such as Sergei Prokofiev's symphonic fairy tale, *Pedro y el Lobo* (Peter and the wolf, 1936; premiered in 1997); Pergolesi's opera buffa, *La serva padrona* (The servant as mistress, 1733; premiered in 1998); Francis Poulenc's *L'histoire de Babar, le petit éléphant* (The story of Babar, the little elephant, 1940; premiered in 2001); *Soñando el carnival de los animales* (Dreaming of the carnival of the animals, premiered in 2004), based on Camille Saint-Saëns's *Carnival of the Animals* (1886); and the children's ballet *La Boîte à joujoux* (The toy box, 1913; premiered in 2009) by André Hellé and Claude Debussy.

43. On the racial overtones of the *Opera dei Pupi*, see Lisa Morse, "The Saracen of *Opera dei Pupi*: A Study of Race, Representation, and Identity."

CHAPTER 5

1. "—¡Basta!—dijo entre sí don Quijote—, aquí será predicar en desierto querer reducir a esta canalla a que por ruegos haga virtud alguna, y en esta aventura

se deben de haber encontrado dos valientes encantadores, y el uno estorba lo que el otro intenta: el uno me deparó el barco y el otro dio conmigo al través. Dios lo remedie, que todo este mundo es máquinas y trazas, contrarias unas de otras. Yo no puedo más" (*Don Quijote* 873–74).

2. Unlike the two adventures analyzed in this chapter, the enchanted boat exploit (2.39) arises without premeditation from any schemers. Don Quixote finds a small boat on the shore of the Ebro River. He thinks that by following the river's course he and Sancho will reach the equator, but the boat drifts toward the wheels of a mill. When the millers, covered in flour dust, rush to avert the disaster, the knight confuses them with malevolent beings.

3. For Frederick A. de Armas, Clavileño's flight represents the culmination of all the other deceptions undergone by Don Quixote and Sancho at the ducal palace ("Sancho" 18).

4. At this point in the novel, these tricks cannot mitigate the doubt in the Don and contribute instead to increasing his melancholy over Dulcinea's disenchantment (Ruta 230).

5. See Albert Henry's "L'ascendence littéraire de Clavileño" and Joseph E. Gillet's "Clavileño: Su fuente directa y sus orígenes primitivos" for an account of the various theories on the history of the flying wooden horse.

6. Italian philosopher Marsilio Ficino (1433–1499) edited and translated influential theurgic treatises. His *De triplici vita* (Three books on life, 1489) extensively discusses the animation of statues. For more on this topic, see my remarks in the Conclusion.

7. "De allí le ha sacado Malambruno con sus artes, y le tiene en su poder, y se sirve dél en sus viajes, que los hace por momentos por diversas partes del mundo, y hoy está aquí y mañana en Francia y otro día en Potosí; y es lo bueno que el tal caballo ni come ni duerme ni gasta herraduras, y lleva un portante por los aires sin tener alas, que el que lleva encima puede llevar una taza llena de agua en la mano sin que se le derrame gota, según camina llano y reposado" (*Don Quijote* 951–52).

8. The fictional context of this adventure shares a series of parallelisms with a performance that took place in the estate of the constable Miguel Lucas de Iranzo (c. 1453–1473). An escort of pages supposedly from distant lands came to ask the constable to defend them from a gigantic wooden serpent animated by pyrotechnical special effects (Shergold 125).

9. "Esta cabeza, señor don Quijote, ha sido hecha y fabricada por uno de los mayores encantadores y hechiceros que ha tenido el mundo, que creo era polaco de nación y dicípulo del famoso Escotillo, de quien tantas maravillas se cuentan;

el cual estuvo aquí en mi casa, y por precio de mil escudos que le di labró esta cabeza, que tiene propiedad y virtud de responder a cuantas cosas al oído le preguntaren. Guardó rumbos, pintó carácteres, observó astros, miró puntos y, finalmente, la sacó con la perfeción que veremos mañana, porque los viernes está muda, y hoy, que lo es, nos ha de hacer esperar hasta mañana. En este tiempo podrá vuestra merced prevenirse de lo que querrá preguntar, que por esperiencia sé que dice verdad en cuanto responde" (*Don Quijote* 1135).

10. Clavileño's flight has been staged on various occasions, either as its own play or as a scene in a broader adaptation of *Don Quijote*. Abraham Madroñal has identified an *entremés* (interlude) titled *La burla de Clavileño and trova de don Quijote* (The joke of Clavileño and ballad of Don Quixote, 1800) by an unknown author, entirely based on the aforementioned episode of the novel (329). Additionally, María Fernández Ferreiro points to four productions: 1) *Clavileño y los consejos de Don Quijote a Sancho* (Clavileño and the advice given by Don Quixote to Sancho), directed by Filemón Vázquez, which premiered in Salamanca in 1905 as a school performance; 2) an operetta for children, *El caballo clavileño* (Clavileño the horse), published in 1930 with lyrics by Juan Redondo y Menduiña and music by Joaquín Taboada Steger; 3) the comic opera *Clavileño*, written in 1934–1935 by Rodolfo Halffter; and 4) *La empresa de Clavileño* (The adventure of Clavileño), which premiered in El Escorial in 1947 (132–48). I will add *El vuelo de Clavileño* (Clavileño's flight), directed by Irina Kouberskaya for Teatro Tribueñe. To the best of my knowledge, I am not aware of any theatrical adaptation of the enchanted head episode as a full-length play.

11. "Paseóse don Antonio con don Quijote por todo el aposento, rodeando muchas veces la mesa, después de lo cual dijo:—Agora, señor don Quijote, que estoy enterado que no nos oye y escucha alguno y está cerrada la puerta, quiero contar a vuestra merced una de las más raras aventuras, o, por mejor decir, novedades, que imaginarse pueden, con condición que lo que a vuestra merced dijere lo ha de depositar en los últimos retretes del secreto" (*Don Quijote* 1134).

12. Although it dates to the eighteenth century, the Alameda de Osuna, built in 1784 by the dukes of Osuna and located in the vicinity of Madrid, is another example of an entertainment garden that brought together the most illustrious artists, gardeners, and set designers of the time.

13. "cuatro salvajes, vestidos todos de verde yedra" (*Don Quijote* 956). This use of natural surroundings as part of the setting was also very common in court performances that took place near ponds and in night festivities where darkness was required for intensifying the effects of the fireworks (Díez Borque, "Palacio del Buen Retiro" 168–69, 179).

14. Sancho evokes a distorted vision of the word when he narrates his experience flying on Clavileño. He sees the earth as the size of a mustard seed and man the size of hazelnuts (*Don Quixote* 725; *Don Quijote* 964).
15. See *The Gentleman, the Virtuoso, the Inquirer: Vincencio Juan de Lastanosa and the Art of Collecting in Early Modern Spain*, edited by Mar Rey-Bueno and Miguel López-Pérez.
16. See the description of the theatrical aspects of the grand-ducal cabinet of curiosities in the Uffizi collection in Florence (Lazardzig and Rößler 298).
17. Sir Francis Bacon (1561–1626) proposed that knowledge would advance if conceived of as a collective, participative endeavor (Eamon 319).
18. In other Cervantine fictions, the narrator or the characters exit the fantastic realm without giving any rational explanation, as in the denouement of "El coloquio de los perros" (The dialogue of the dogs; Castillo 101).
19. See Riskin, "The Defecating Duck, or, the Ambiguous Origins of Artificial Life."
20. Pedro Calderón de la Barca parodies the flight of Clavileño in *El astrólogo fingido* (The fake astrologer, 1632). See Carlos Mata Induráin, "Cervantes y Calderón: El episodio de Clavileño (*Quijote* 2.40–41) y la burla de Otánez en *El astrólogo fingido*."
21. Significantly, King Philip II chose the symbol of a horse leaping over a terrestrial globe to illustrate his motto "Non suffict orbis" (The world is not enough), alluding to his empire that extended over four continents.
22. Travel to space was the theme of the Christmas festivities that courtier George Ferrers (ca. 1500–1579) was appointed to organize in 1551–1552 to entertain young King Edward VI (Álvarez 11).
23. See Javier Ordoñez's article "De Rocinante a Clavileño" for his interpretation of Clavileño as a robotic horse (254).
24. The very premises of this joke are humiliating for the knight, considering that according to the laws of chivalry, the horse is an extension of its rider.
25. "Cubriéronse, y sintiendo don Quijote que estaba como había de estar, tentó la clavija, y apenas hubo puesto los dedos en ella cuando todas las dueñas y cuantos estaban presentes levantaron las voces, diciendo: ¡Dios te guíe, valeroso caballero! ¡Dios sea contigo, escudero intrépido! ¡Ya, ya vais por esos aires, rompiéndolos con más velocidad que una saeta! ¡Ya comenzáis a suspender y admirar a cuantos desde la tierra os están mirando! ¡Tente, valeroso Sancho, que te bamboleas! ¡Mira no cayas, que será peor tu caída que la del atrevido mozo que quiso regir el carro del Sol su padre!" (*Don Quijote* 961).
26. "Destierra, amigo, el miedo, que, en efecto, la cosa va como ha de ir y el viento llevamos en popa—Así es la verdad—respondió Sancho—, que por este lado

me da un viento tan recio, que parece que con mil fuelles me están soplando. Y así era ello, que unos grandes fuelles le estaban haciendo aire: tan bien trazada estaba la tal aventura por el duque y la duquesa y su mayordomo, que no le faltó requisito que la dejase de hacer perfecta. En esto, con unas estopas ligeras de encenderse y apagarse, desde lejos, pendientes de una caña, les calentaban los rostros. Sancho, que sintió el calor, dijo:—Que me maten si no estamos ya en el lugar del fuego o bien cerca, porque una gran parte de mi barba se me ha chamuscado, y estoy, señor, por descubrirme y ver en qué parte estamos" (*Don Quijote* 961–62).

27. "y queriendo dar remate a la estraña y bien fabricada aventura, por la cola de Clavileño le pegaron fuego con unas estopas, y al punto, por estar el caballo lleno de cohetes tronadores, voló por los aires con estraño ruido y dio con don Quijote y con Sancho Panza en el suelo medio chamuscados" (*Don Quijote* 963).

28. By having both protagonists blindfolded, the schemers replicate a camera obscura effect, capable of stimulating sensations through a more pro-active imagination (Ordoñez 254).

29. Derek de Solla Price has identified two extant Egyptian figures with similar characteristics: a wooden head of the jackal god of the dead, Anubis, and a large white limestone bust of the god Re-Harmakhis, which are kept at the Louvre and the Cairo Museum, respectively (10).

30. "Levantados los manteles y tomando don Antonio por la mano a don Quijote, se entró con él en un apartado aposento, en el cual no había otra cosa de adorno que una mesa, al parecer de jaspe, que sobre un pie de lo mesmo se sostenía, sobre la cual estaba puesta, al modo de las cabezas de los emperadores romanos, de los pechos arriba, una que semejaba ser de bronce" (*Don Quijote* 1134).

31. "El cual quiso Cide Hamete Benengeli declarar luego, por no tener suspenso al mundo creyendo que algún hechicero y extraordinario misterio en la tal cabeza se encerraba" (*Don Quijote* 1141).

Juan de Espina acted in a similar way to Benengeli when he was accused of necromancy by displaying his artifacts and provoking the credulity of his guests. The virtuoso resorted to scientific proof to dismantle all misunderstandings (Reula Baquero 330).

32. "Y la fábrica era de esta suerte: la tabla de la mesa era de palo, pintada y barnizada como jaspe, y el pie sobre que se sostenía era de lo mesmo, con cuatro garras de águila que dél salían para mayor firmeza del peso. La cabeza, que parecía medalla y figura de emperador romano, y de color de bronce, estaba toda hueca, y ni más ni menos la tabla de la mesa, en que se encajaba tan justamente, que ninguna señal de juntura se parecía. El pie de la tabla era ansimesmo hueco, que

respondía a la garganta y pechos de la cabeza, y todo esto venía a responder a otro aposento que debajo de la estancia de la cabeza estaba. Por todo este hueco de pie, mesa, garganta y pechos de la medalla y figura referida se encaminaba un cañón de hoja de lata muy justo, que de nadie podía ser visto. En el aposento de abajo correspondiente al de arriba se ponía el que había de responder, pegada la boca con el mesmo cañón, de modo que, a modo de cerbatana, iba la voz de arriba abajo y de abajo arriba, en palabras articuladas y claras, y de esta manera no era posible conocer el embuste. Un sobrino de don Antonio, estudiante, agudo y discreto, fue el respondiente, el cual estando avisado de su señor tío de los que habían de entrar con él en aquel día en el aposento de la cabeza, le fue fácil responder con presteza y puntualidad a la primera pregunta; a las demás respondió por conjeturas, y, como discreto, discretamente" (*Don Quijote* 1141–42).

33. Miguel de Unamuno, Luigi Pirandello, and Federico García Lorca explored the uprising of the character against its creator, as mentioned in Chapter 3, but none of them refer to mechanical beings. See Wilma Newberry's book, *The Pirandellian Mode in Spanish Literature from Cervantes to Sastre*.

34. Sancho's appropriation of the discourse around Clavileño's flight can also be interpreted as a mechanism to cope with fear by taming the horse's agency according to his own standards (Desmeule 51).

35. "Sancho, pues vos queréis que se os crea lo que habéis visto en el cielo, yo quiero que vos me creáis a mí lo que vi en la cueva de Montesinos. Y no os digo más" (*Don Quijote* 966).

36. "pero que divulgándose por la ciudad que don Antonio tenía en su casa una cabeza encantada, que a cuantos le preguntaban respondía, temiendo no llegase a los oídos de las despiertas centinelas de nuestra fe, habiendo declarado el caso a los señores inquisidores, le mandaron que lo deshiciese y no pasase más adelante, porque el vulgo ignorante no se escandalizase" (*Don Quijote* 1142).

37. For an analysis of the actual mechanisms of the talking heads used onstage as props, see Butterworth's *Magic on the English Stage* (103–06). In the specific context of early modern Spanish theater, Juan Ruiz de Alarcón's *La cueva de Salamanca* (The cave of Salamanca, 1628) features an enchanted head whose inner workings are elucidated in the stage directions (165–67).

38. "No quiero saber más" (*Don Quijote* 1141).

39. See Tom Gunning, "The Cinema of Attraction[s]: Early Film, Its Spectator, and the Avant-Garde," and William Egginton, "Reality Is Bleeding: A Brief History of Film from the Sixteenth Century."

40. "—No repares en eso, Sancho, que como estas cosas y estas volaterías van fuera de los cursos ordinarios, de mil leguas verás y oirás lo que quisieres" (*Don Quijote* 961).

41. Psycho is currently displayed at the London Museum of Science.
42. See Adolfo Ayuso Roy's article, "La voz a ti debida," on the first Spanish ventriloquists.
43. See Enric March, "Francesc Roca. Magia entre títeres, autómatas y figuras de cera."
44. We could also argue that these two attractions introduce the contemporary concept of "hard fun," based on games of make-believe that stimulate creativity, imagination, and reflection through risk-taking scenarios and problem solving. On the concept of "hard fun," see Stafford and Terpak's *Devices of Wonder: From the World in a Box to Images on a Screen* (103).

CHAPTER 6

1. See Ignacio Arellano, "Cervantes in Calderón."
2. Calderón de la Barca boasts about the connection between the two *comedias* in *El secreto a voces* (The secret spoken aloud, 1642) and in *Ni amor se libra de amor* (Not even love is free from love, 1687).
3. See Beatriz Vitar, "El mundo mágico en el Madrid de los Austrias a través de las cartas, avisos y relaciones de sucesos."
4. American anarchist Peter Lamborn Wilson, known as Hakim Bey (1945–), defines a *temporary autonomous zone* (TAZ) as a pacifist uprising driven by creativity that produces spaces of freedom and resistance without the awareness of the state. TAZs rise and disappear, only to resurface somewhere else with a different identity (Bey 95–96).
5. "Por una alacena, que estará hecha con anaqueles y vidrios en ellas, quitándose con goznes que se desencaja, salen Doña Ángela y Isabel" (*La dama* 36). For Marc Vitse, Doña Ángela's and Don Manuel's rooms are not contiguous, which implies the presence of a secret interior corridor (341). Thus, it has become a stage convention to represent both quarters directly connected by the cupboard.
6. Calderón de la Barca's mythological dramas tend to carry political undertones, and their special effects, in certain instances, were meant to activate a feeling of estrangement and a socio-critical response in the audience (C. A. Jones, "Brecht" 48).
7. In "Reason's Baroque House (Cervantes, Master Architect)," William Egginton discusses the counterproductive effect of female confinement in relation to Cervantes's "El celoso extremeño" (The jealous old man from Extremadura, 1613), with obvious similarities to *La dama*. Don W. Cruickshank sees a parallelism between Carrizales, the protagonist of "El celoso," and Doña Ángela's brothers (183).

8. "DOÑA ÁNGELA. Vuélveme a dar, Isabel, / esas tocas, ¡pena esquiva! / Vuelve a amortajarme viva, / ya que mi suerte cruel / lo quiere así" (*La dama* vv.369–73).
9. Edwin Honig, Barbara Mujica, and Juan Carlos de Miguel interpret Don Luis as unconsciously incestuous toward his sister.
10. "DOÑA ÁNGELA. No soy alba, pues la risa / me falta en contento tanto; / ni aurora, pues que mi llanto / de mi dolor no os avisa; / no soy sol, pues no divisa / mi luz la verdad que adoro; / y así lo que soy ignoro, / que sólo sé que no soy / alba, aurora o sol, pues hoy / ni alumbro, río, ni lloro" (*La dama* vv.2343–52).
11. "DON MANUEL. Como sombra se mostró, / fantástica su luz fue, / pero como cosa humana / se dejó tocar y ver. / Como mortal se temió, / receló como mujer, / como ilusión se deshizo, / como fantasma se fue" (*La dama* vv.2225–32).
12. The *vanishing lady* trick originated in the Victorian era and has a long genealogy—not without misogynistic overtones—of making women disappear in spectacular ways at the hands of a male magician. See Karen Redrobe Beckman, *Vanishing Women: Magic, Film, and Feminism*.
13. In the nineteenth century, acts of escapology were popular among male magicians because of the physical prowess they exhibited. Female magicians specialized in tricks of spiritualism staged in semi-private spaces (Mangan 162). Doña Ángela subverts this gender-oriented magic even though she is confined to her house.
14. An escape room is a contemporary role-play game set in a closed space wherein participants have to solve an enigma by following a series of clues in a limited amount of time. While it is an anachronistic concept, it rightly parallels the game Doña Ángela devises in Don Manuel's room.
15. Lope de Vega, in *La viuda valenciana* (The Valencian widow, ca. 1600), creates a whole play around the concept of the invisible mistress, in which the female protagonist takes this daring role to its ultimate consequences.
16. "tropezando en las sombras de [su] muerte" (*El galán* 220).
17. This and subsequent translations from *El galán* are mine. "JULIA. Y así te ruego que no / vayas a verme, ni pases / cubierto ni descubierto / la esfera de mis umbrales. / Deja que por unos días, / sin que allí puedan toparte / se desmienta en la sospecha, / salga tu recelo en balde. / Y, pues que yo vengo así / a persuadirte, a rogarte, / Astolfo, que no me veas, / esposo, que no me hables / menos harás tú en hacello" (*El galán* 103–04).
18. "ASTOLFO. Apenas, pues, nueva vida / mal restituido cobro, / cuando mi padre de aquel / voluntario calabozo / me saca una noche a escuras, / al mismo tiempo que oigo / en otro cuarto en mi casa / triste exequias y lloros. / Los umbrales de una puerta / pavorosamente toco, / cuando de la otra sale / un entierro sun-

tuoso. / '¿Quién es el muerto?,' pregunto / a mi padre y él dudoso / 'tú eres aquel mismo' dijo" (*El galán* 190).
19. "ORTIZ. Donde hay sótanos amantes, / galán fantasma, amor duende, / tornos, casas con dos puertas, / tabiques disimulados, / hurtarán de los tablados / tramoyas que saquen ciertas / esperanzas ya perdidas" (*En Madrid* 1285).
20. See Noelia S. Cirnigliaro, *Domus: Ficción y mundo doméstico en el Barroco español*, chapter 3 (71–92).
21. This is just the opposite of how Cervantes presents Clavileño and the enchanted head by first exposing the fantastic qualities of both artifacts and, subsequently, unraveling their real nature.
22. "RODRIGO. Y más habiendo tenido / tal recato y advertencia / que para su cuarto ha dado / por otra calle la puerta, / y la que salía a la casa, / por desmentir la sospecha / de que el cuidado la había / cerrado, o porque pudiera con facilidad abrirse / otra vez, fabricó en ella / una alacena de vidrios, / labrada de tal manera / que parece que jamás / en tal parte ha habido puerta" (*La dama* 349–62).
23. The dematerialization of space was a popular trait of baroque aesthetics. In Juan de Piña's *Casos prodigiosos y cueva encantada* (Prodigious cases and enchanted cave, 1628), the narrator describes a house, probably inspired by Juan De Espina's legendary residence, in which an entire room magically disappears.
24. "CARLOS. Un ingeniero buscó, / que, en minar la tierra diestro, / facilitase a su agravio / lo imposible de su acero / y, fiándose de mí, / por estar mi casa en puesto / más vecino a su esperanza, / más conveniente a su intento, / el hombre empezó desde ella / a designar los modelos / con que tocase una mina / a su mismo cuarto, que esto / era en él fácil, porque / era de nación flamenco, / escuela donde el valor/ pelea con el ingenio" (*El galán* 224).
25. It is worth mentioning that when Cosme falls into a ditch on street, he refers to the science of engineering as a type of black magic (Nitsch 153).
26. Edwin Honig substitutes in his translation the original mention of "Juanelo" (Juanelo Turriano) with the anecdote of Columbus's egg, which is more widely known and illustrates the same idea: "DOÑA ÁNGELA. Have you ever heard the story / of *Columbus and the egg*? / Well, the wisest men alive / had exhausted all their wits / endeavoring to set the egg / upright on a jasper table when / Columbus came along, gave the egg / a simple tap, and solved the problem / once for all. The greatest / difficulties solve themselves / once you know the simple answer" (*The Phantom Lady* 238; my emphasis). The Spanish original reads as follows: "DOÑA ÁNGELA. ¿Ahora sabes / lo *del huevo de Juanelo*? / Que los ingenios más grandes / trabajaron en hacer / que en un bufete de jaspe / se tuviese en pie, / y Juanelo / con sólo llegar, y darle / un golpecillo, le tuvo. /

Las grandes dificultades / hasta saberse lo son, / que sabido, todo es fácil" (*La dama* vv.1255–66; my emphasis).

27. "DON LUIS. ¿Ves con lo que me aseguras? / Pues con eso mismo intentas / darme muerte, pues ya dices / que no ha puesto, por defensa / de su honor, más que unos vidrios / que al primer golpe se quiebran" (*La dama* vv.363–68).

28. Fausta Antonucci also regards the cupboard as a unique stage prop among all of Calderón de la Barca's plays ("Prólogo" xli).

29. See Dann Cazés Gryj, "Construcción de la mentira sobrenatural en *La dama duende* y *El galán fantasma*."

30. See Antonio Sánchez Jiménez, "La mina que revienta en la comedia de Calderón: El caso de *Primero soy yo*."

31. In director Sophie Fiennes's *The Pervert's Guide to Cinema*, Slavoj Žižek uses psychoanalysis to read similar objects that appear in movies as *autonomous partial objects*—that is to say, objects that seem to exist as a part of human subjectivity, yet paradoxically exceed it, and appear to have control over the subject.

32. "ISABEL. ¿Ves como no hay inconveniente / para pasar hasta aquí? DOÑA ÁNGELA. Antes, Isabel parece / que todos cuanto previne / fueron muy impertinentes, / pues con ninguno topamos, / que la puerta fácilmente / se abre y se vuelve a cerrar, / sin ser posible que se eche / de ver" (*La dama* vv.780–95).

33. In artwork from the period, it is common to find the expression *fecit* (he/she made it) as a way to stress the artist's connection with his creation.

34. "DON MANUEL. Pues ¿qué es lo que pretendo? / Si es hacerme traidor si la defiendo; si la dejo, villano, / si la guardo, mal huésped; inhumano / si a su hermano la entrego; / soy mal amigo si a guardarla llego; / ingrato si la libro, a un noble trato, / y si la dejo, a un noble amor ingrato. / Pues de cualquier manera / mal puesto he de quedar, matando muera" (*La dama* vv.3023–24).

35. For Anthony Cascardi (35–36) and de Armas (*Invisible* 140–59), marriage in *La dama* implies reconciliation between Doña Ángela's fragmented self and society.

36. The influence of early modern Spanish theater is evident in *Tristana*, from Don Lope's obsession with honor to his characterization as a decrepit Don Juan.

37. "¿Eran felices uno y otro? ... Tal vez" (*Tristana* 272).

38. As with the tunnel, the cupboard has also been in disuse for a long time, and it is Isabel who discovers it by chance.

39. "JULIA. Preñada la tierra quiere, / rasgándose las entrañas / que nazcan o que revienten / prodigios, ¿No veis, no veis / cómo toda se estremece? / ¿No veis las plantas y ramos / o sacudirse o moverse?" (*El galán* 175).

40. "ábrese un escutillón y sale Astolfo lleno de tierra" (*El galán* 175).

41. In Calderón de la Barca's *El príncipe constante* (The constant prince, 1629), a play about the martyrdom of Prince Ferdinand of Portugal (1402–1443), the

protagonist also returns from death to bring a moral lesson as a true revenant.

42. "DUQUE. Pues viste a Astolfo, di que a defenderte / llegue. (*Sale Astolfo por parte que no le vea el Duque y mata la luz.*) ASTOLFO. Sí llegará de aquesta suerte. DUQUE. La luz han muerto y una voz escucho.... ASTOLFO. (Ya cielos, que sin verme estorbé su rigor, vuelvo a esconderme.) DUQUE. ¿Adónde voz, te escondes? / Si me llamas ¿por qué no me respondes?" (*El galán* 184).

43. "JULIA. Y yo, para asegurarte / tiempo que será tan poco / que aun a ti te lo parezca, / hoy con estudio ingenioso / haré cubrir esta boca / con una trampa de modo / que, con las plantas y flores / continuando los adornos / del jardín, engañar puedan / al austro, al cierzo y al noto. / Por aquí a hablarme vendrás / de noche, sabiendo sólo / un jardinero el secreto, / a quién fiarle dispongo" (*El galán* 268).

44. "PORCIA. ¿Cómo es posible que tengas / esfuerzo tan varonil / que enamorada de un muerto, / le vayas a hablar? / JULIA. En mí / no hay temor, porque hay amor. / PORCIA. Pues en mí, señora, sí: / no hay amor, porque hay temor. / Mas solo aquesto me di: / ¿Son cariñosos los muertos?" (*El galán* vv.2487–95).

45. "DUQUE. En casa de Julia fue, / donde cada noche va, / que, desde la que le vi, / ninguna falta de allí / y toda Sajonia está / llena desto" (*El galán* 203).

46. Cascardi does not see any psychological growth in the protagonist over the course of the plot (51).

47. Regarding this production, see Rebeca Rubio's doctoral dissertation, *Siglo de Oro franquista: Cinco comedias ya antes representadas* (A Francoist golden age: Five comedias never staged, 2019).

48. E. T. A. Hoffman (1776–1822) was a great admirer of Calderón de la Barca and saw the potential for the subversive fantasy in *La dama*. He made plans to collaborate with Karl Wilhelm Salice Contessa (1777–1825) on an adaptation of the play to the *buffo* genre (Tietz 207).

49. Helena Pimenta's production of Lope de Vega's *La dama boba* (Lady nitwit, 1613) in 2002 also eschewed easy comedy to delve into the personal and social tragedies of the two protagonist sisters. The director sets the play at the beginning of the Second Spanish Republic (1931–1939), a time of fleeting hope for women that will soon disappear with the Civil War (1936–1939) and Franco's dictatorship (1939–1975).

50. See this book's Introduction, "Stages of Animation," where I summarize some of the artifacts and techniques of optical illusionism.

51. The uncanny, moody, and dark atmosphere is reminiscent of the animation films of the Quay Brothers, in which puppets made of Victorian disassembled dolls play a key role in the plots and overall aesthetic.

52. Of note is the bright red cape as a statement of her rebellious personality, which the protagonist wears in those instances when she tries to defy her brothers

and escape confinement. For a review of the Pimenta adaptation, see Esther Fernández, "*La dama duende* by Calderón de la Barca."

53. Saint plays made great use of the *escotillón* for deploying special effects, especially those dealing with elements related to hell.
54. Calderón de la Barca was among the favorite authors of the German Romantic writers because of the metaphysical depth of his oeuvre.
55. Antonio de Fuentelapeña argues that *duendes* can originate as a result of the corruption of the heavy dampness and steam existing in lofts or basements. Therefore, the *duende*'s ethereal composition would justify its invisibility.
56. Harry Houdini (1874–1926), the most famous illusionist in history, had an influential social impact among the Irish immigrant community working in strenuous circumstances in the United States at the time. They interpreted his escapist shows as inspiring acts of liberation and social hope (Contreras Elvira, "La puesta" 161).
57. *La dama* became a foundational text for the eighteenth-century *comedias de magia*, and many retained the secret trapdoor as part of their plots (Doménech Rico, *La comedia* 21).

CONCLUSION

EPIGRAPH 1. "Je suppose que le corps n'est autre chose qu'une statue ou machine de terre" (805).

EPIGRAPH 2. "JUAN. Esperad, señora, / que habéis de ver cuán atento, / César, mi Príncipe, presta / a lo inanimado afectos. MARGARITA. ¿Cómo? JUAN. Para festejaros, / espíritus infundiendo / en los troncos más robustos, / y en los mármoles más yertos" (*Don Juan de Espina* vv.819–26).

1. For a study of the cultural advances and intellectual scope brought by the *novatores*, see Jesús Pérez Magallón. *Construyendo la modernidad: La cultura española en el tiempo de Los Novatores (1675–1725)*.
2. The last *comedia de magia* that features a supernatural being as a protagonist is *Duendes son alcahuetes y espíritu Foleto. Primera parte* (Goblins are go-betweens and Foleto the sprite, 1709) by Antonio de Zamora (1665–1727; Contreras Elvira, "Ciencia" 150).
3. While some magicians got married at the end of these plays, even in objectionable unions, others rejected this conventional ending and strove for their independence (Álvarez Barrientos, "Introducción" 20–21).
4. The *comedia de magia* played a crucial role in the history of European stagecraft (Doménech Rico, *La comedia* 15–16). For the more grandiose sets used in these

plays, as well as in other courtly entertainments, Italian and Spanish baroque painters and architects wrote stagecraft manuals such as *El museo pictórico, y escala óptica* (The pictorial museum and optical scale, 1797) by Acisclo Antonio Palomino de Castro y Velasco (1655–1726).

5. Kenneth Gross illustrates this human-statue interaction with a discussion on the opening scene of the movie *City Lights* (1931), directed by and starring Charlie Chaplin (1889–1977), and the sculpture *Night* (ca. 1526–1531) by Michelangelo (1475–1564). See Kenneth Gross, "Moving Statues, Talking Statues."

6. See Fernando Rodríguez de la Flor's chapter, "Pasiones Frías," on baroque dissimulation and the interpretation of the marble statue (124–25).

7. Similar to the way the servile statue behaved around magicians in dramatic fiction, some virtuosi, such as Juan de Espina, were known for having servant automata in their homes (Reula Baquero 339). José de Cañizares y Suárez dedicates two magic plays to Juan de Espina—*Don Juan de Espina en su patria* (Don Juan de Espina in his homeland, 1730) and *Don Juan de Espina en Milán* (Don Juan de Espina in Milan, 1730)—that capture the extravagant way of life of the protagonist and require sophisticated machinery to be produced onstage (Paun de García 20).

8. A comparable acting technique became popular in eighteenth-century Europe known as mimoplastic art or attitude. This style, mainly popularized by English and German actresses, uses precise gestures to imitate sculptural poses representing classical subjects. Emma, Lady Hamilton (1765–1815), Ida Brun (1792–1857), and Henriette Hendel-Schütz (1772–1849) were among the best-paid artists who specialized in this type of acting (Álvarez Barrientos, *La comedia* 159; Contreras Elvira, "Ciencia" 154).

9. See Doménech Rico, *Los Trufaldines y el Teatro de los Caños del Peral*.

10. In the Romantic period, these sculptures tended to rebel against their creators, as illustrated in Prosper Mérimée's *La Vénus d'Ille* (The Venus of Ille, 1835) and Mary Shelley's *Frankenstein; Or, The Modern Prometheus* (1831).

11. The technical and philosophical grace implied in imitating a statue became an obsession for some Romantic poets and playwrights such as Heinrich von Kleist (1777–1811) and Alexander Pushkin (1799–1837). See Kenneth Gross, "Moving Statues, Talking Statues," for what he refers to as the "paradoxical fantasy" of the living statue.

BIBLIOGRAPHY

Adillo Rufo, Sergio. "Classical Theater and Puppetry: La máquina real." *Remaking the Comedia: Spanish Classical Theater in Adaptation*, edited by Harley Erdman and Susan Paun de García. Tamesis, 2015, pp. 229–36.

Alarcón, Juan Ruiz de. *La cueva de salamanca: La prueba de las promesas*, edited by Celsa Carmen García Valdés. Madrid: Cátedra, 2013.

Allen, John J. "Melisendra's Mishap in Maese Pedro's Puppet Show." *MLN*, vol. 88, no. 2, 1973, pp. 330–35.

Álvarez, Mari-Tere. "Moon Shot: From Renaissance Imagination to Modern Reality." *Renaissance Futurities: Science, Art, Invention*, edited by Charlene Villaseñor Black and Mari-Tere Álvarez. U of California P, 2020, pp. 9–18.

Álvarez Barrientos, Joaquín. "Apariencia y realidad en la comedia de magia dieciochesca." *La comedia de magia y de santos*, edited by F. J. Blasco, E. Caldera, J. Álvarez Barrientos, and R. de la Fuente. Madrid: Ediciones Júcar, 1992, pp. 341–49.

———. "Introducción." *El anillo de Giges*, by José de Cañizares, edited by Joaquín Álvarez Barrientos. Madrid: CSIC, 1989, pp. 11–106.

———. *La comedia de magia del siglo XVIII*. Madrid: CSIC, 2011.

Amberson, Deborah. "Battling History: Narrative Wars in Roberto Rossellini's *Paisà*." *Italica*, vol. 86, no. 3, 2009, pp. 392–407.

———. "Prólogo." *La dama duende*, by Pedro Calderón de la Barca, edited by Fausta Antonucci. Barcelona: Galaxia Gutemberg, 2006, pp. xxxi–lxxiii.

Aparicio Maydeu, Javier. *Calderón y la máquina barroca: Escenografía, religión y cultura en* El José de las mujeres. Amsterdam: Rodopi, 1999.

———. "La comedia hagiográfica en el siglo XVII: Una silva de varia lección." *Calderón y la máquina barroca: Escenografía, religión y cultura en* El josé de las mujeres, edited by Javier Aparicio Maydeu. Amsterdam: Rodopi, 1999, pp. 19–113.

Aracil, Alfredo. *Juego y artificio: Autómatas y otras ficciones en la cultura del Renacimiento a la Ilustración.* Madrid: Cátedra, 1998.

Aranda, Maria. *Le* spectre *en* son miroir: *Essai sur le texte fantastique au Siècle d'or.* Madrid: Casa de Velázquez, 2011.

Arellano, Ignacio. "Cervantes en Calderón." *Anales Cervantinos*, no. 35, 1999, pp. 9–35.

———. *Convención y recepción: Estudios sobre el teatro del Siglo de Oro.* Madrid: Gredos, 1999.

Arias, Manuel, José Ignacio Hernández Redondo, and Antonio Sánchez del Barrio. *Semana Santa en Medina del Campo: Historia y obras artísticas.* Valladolid: Diputación Provincial y Junta de S. Santa de Medina del Campo, 1996, pp. 38–40.

Armas, Frederick A. de. *The Invisible Mistress: Aspects of Feminism and Fantasy in the Golden Age.* Biblioteca Siglo de Oro, 1976.

———. "'Por una hora': Tiempo bélico y amoroso en *La dama duende.*" *La dramaturgia de Calderón: Técnicas y estructuras. Homenaje a Jesús Sepúlveda*, edited by Enrica Cancelliere and Ignacio Arellano Ayuso. Madrid: Iberoamericana-Vervuert, 2006, pp. 115–32.

———. "Sancho as a Thief of Time and Art: Ovid's *Fasti* and Cervantes' *Don Quixote* 2." *Renaissance Quarterly*, vol. 61, no. 1, 2008, pp. 1–25.

Arnheim, Rudolf. *Arte y percepción visual.* Madrid: Alianza, 1979.

Aston, Margaret. "Iconoclasm in England: Official and Clandestine." *Iconoclasm vs. Art and Drama*, edited by Clifford Davidson and Ann Eljemon Nichols. Medieval Institute, 1989, pp. 47–91.

Avalle-Arce, Juan Bautista. "La cabeza encantada (*Don Quijote*, II, 62)." *Homenaje a Luis Alberto Sánchez*, edited by Robert Mead et al. Madrid: Ínsula, 1983, pp. 45–63.

Ayuso Roy, Adolfo. "La voz a ti debida. Para una historia de la ventriloquía en España (1)." *Fantoche: Arte de los títeres*, no. 12, 2018, pp. 62–89.

Bachelard, Gaston. *The Poetics of Space.* Translated by Maria Jolas. Penguin, 2014.

Baird, Bil. *The Art of the Puppet.* Macmillan, 1965.

Barreiro, Juan J., and Marcela Guijosa. *Títeres Mexicanos: Memoria y retrato de autómatas, fantoches y otros artistas ambulantes.* Roche-Syntex, 1997.

Barrionuevo, Jerónimo de. *Avisos.* Edited by Antonio Paz y Meliá. Madrid: Atlas, 1968.

Barrios, Nuria. "Lloran más los ateos que los cristianos." *El País*, 1 May 2008. elpais.com/diario/2008/05/01/ultima/1209592802_850215.html.

Base de datos de comedias mencionadas en la documentación teatral (1540–1700), edited by Teresa Ferrer Valls, et al. CATCOM, catcom.uv.es.

Bastianutti, Diego L. "La inspiración pictórica en el teatro hagiográfico de Lope de Vega." *Lope de Vega y los orígenes del teatro español: Actas del I Congreso Internacional sobre Lope de Vega*, edited by Manuel criado de Val. Madrid: EDI-6, 1981, pp. 711–18.

Beckman, Karen Redrobe. *Vanishing Women: Magic, Film, and Feminism*. Duke UP, 2003.

Beezley, William H. "Introduction." *Americas*, vol. 67, no. 3, 2011, pp. 307–14.

Bell, John. "Playing with the Eternal Uncanny: The Persistent Life of Lifeless Objects." *The Routledge Companion to Puppetry and Material Performance*, edited by Dassia N. Posner, Claudis Orenstein, and John Bell. Routledge, 2014, pp. 43–52.

Benjamin, Walter. *The Work of Art in the Age of Mechanical Reproduction*. Penguin, 2008.

Bennett, Jane. *The Enchantment of Modern Life: Attachments, Crossings, and Ethics*. Princeton UP, 2016.

Berceo, Gonzalo de. "Del Sacrificio de la Misa." *Obra Completa*, edited by Pedro M. Cátedra. Madrid: Espasa Calpe, 1992, pp. 933–1033.

Bernstein, Robin. "Dances with Things: Material Culture and the Performance of Race." *Social Text*, vol. 27, no. 4, 2009, pp. 67–94.

Bey, Hakim. *T.A.Z.: The Temporary Autonomous Zone, Ontological Anarchy, Poetic Terrorism*. The Anarchist Library, 1985. ia800208.us.archive.org/14/items/al_Hakim_Bey_T.A.Z._The_Temporary_Autonomous_Zone_Ontological_Anarchy_Poetic_Terror/Hakim_Bey__T.A.Z.__The_Temporary_Autonomous_Zone__Ontological_Anarchy__Poetic_Terrorism_a4.pdf.

Biblioteca Capitular y Colombina de Sevilla. (BCC ms. 84-7-19, ff. 244r–247v).

Bishop, Tom G. *Shakespeare and the Theater of Wonder*. Cambridge UP, 1996.

Boehn, Max von. *Puppets and Automata*. Translated by Josephine Nicoll. Dover, 1972.

Bolaños, Piedad, Mercedes de los Reyes Peña, Vicente Palacios, Juan Ruesga Navarro, and Francisco J. Cornejo Vega, "La magia de los títeres en el teatro áureo español: La Máquina Real en el Corral de Montería de Sevilla." *Anagnórisis: Revista de investigación teatral*, vol. 18, 2018, pp. 6–58.

Borlik, Todd Andrew. "More than Art: Clockwork Automata, the Extemporizing Actor, and the Brazen Head in Friar Bacon and Friar Bungay." *The Automaton in English Renaissance Literature*, edited by Wendy Beth Hyman. Routledge, 2011, pp. 129–44.

Bouchor, Maurice. *Mystères bibliques et chrétiens*. Paris: Ernest Flammarion, 1920.

———. *Mystères païens*. Paris: Ernest Flammarion, ca. 1920.

Boyle, Margaret. *Unruly Women: Performance, Penitence, and Punishment in Early Modern Spain*. U of Toronto P, 2014.

Bradbury, Nancy Mason, and Carolyn P. Collette. "Changing Times: The Mechanical Clock in Late Medieval Literature." *Chaucer Review*, vol. 43, no. 4, 2009, pp. 351–75.

Brecht, Bertolt. "Short Description of a New Technique of Acting which Produces an Alienation Effect." *The Twentieth-Century Performance Reader*, edited by Teresa Brayshaw and Noel Witts. Routledge, 2014, pp. 101–12.

Breden, Simon David. *The Creative Process of Els Joglars and Teatro de la Abadía: Beyond the Playwright*. Tamesis, 2014.

Brook, Peter. *The Empty Space: A Book about the Theatre: Deadly, Holy, Rough, Immediate*. 1968. Scribner, 1995.

Brulon Soares, Bruno. "Museums as Theme Parks: From the Informational Paradigm to the Reflexive Experience." *ICOFOM Study Series*, no. 44, 2016, pp. 17–28. journals.openedition.org/iss/649.

Buc, Philippe. "Conversion of Objects: Suger of Saint-Denis and Meinwerk of Paderborn." *Viator*, vol. 28, 1997, pp. 99–144.

Budé, Guillaume. *Lexicon Graeco-Latinum*. Geneva: Crispin, 1554.

Burke, Peter. *Popular Culture in Early Modern Europe*. Routledge, 2009.

Burningham, Bruce R. "Jongleuresque Dialogue, Radical Theatricality, and Maese Pedro's Puppet Show." *Cervantes: Bulletin of the Cervantes Society of America*, vol. 23, no. 1, 2003, pp. 164–200.

Butterworth, Philip. *Magic on the Early English Stage*. Cambridge UP, 2005.

Bynum, Caroline Walker. *Christian Materiality: An Essay on Religion in Late Medieval Europe*. MIT Press, 2011.

———. *Disssimilar Similitudes: Devotional Objects in Late Medieval Europe*. Zone Books, 2020.

———. "Notes from the Field: Materiality." *Art Bulletin*, vol. 95, no. 1, 2013, pp. 12–13, 20–37.

———. "Violent Images in Late Medieval Piety." *German Historical Institute Bulletin*, no. 30, 2002, pp. 3–35.

Calderón de la Barca, Pedro. *El galán fantasma*. Edited by Noelia Iglesias Iglesias. Madrid: Cátedra, 2015.

———. *El príncipe constante*. *Comedias*, vol. 1. Madrid: Fundación José Antonio de Castro, 2010, pp. 1057–139.

———. *El secreto a voces*. *Comedias*, vol. 6. Madrid: Fundación José Antonio de Castro, 2010, pp. 531–644.

———. *La dama duende*. Edited by Fausta Antonucci. Barcelona: Galaxia Gutemberg, 2006.

———. *La estatua de Prometeo*. *Comedias*, vol. 6. Madrid: Fundación José Antonio de Castro, 2010, pp. 441–528.

———. *La fiera, el rayo y la piedra*. *Comedias*, vol. 3. Madrid: Fundación José Antonio de Castro, 2010, pp. 1069–197.
———. *La vida es sueño*. *Comedias*, vol. 1. Madrid: Fundación José Antonio de Castro, 2010, pp. 15–109.
———. *Ni amor se libra de amor*. *Comedias*, vol. 3. Madrid: Fundación José Antonio de Castro, 2010, pp. 809–913.
———. *The Phantom Lady*. In *Six Plays*, translated by Edwin Honig. IASTA Press, 1993, pp. 206–85.
Calvin, John. *Institutes of the Christian Religion*. Translated by Ford Lewis Battles, edited by John T. McNeill, vol. 1. Westminster John Knox P, 1960. 2 vols.
Cañizares, José de. *Don Juan de Espina en su patria: Don Juan de Espina en Milán*. Edited by Susan Paun de García. Madrid: Castalia, 1997.
Cantarino, Vicente. *Civilización y cultura de España*. Prentice Hall, 2006.
Capek, Karel. *R.U.R. (Rossum's Universal Robots)*. Translated by Claudia Novack. Penguin, 2004.
Cappelletto, Chiara. "The Puppet Paradox: An Organic Prosthesis." *Res: Anthropology and Aesthetics*, nos. 59–60, 2011, pp. 325–26.
Carlson, Marvin. *Places of Performance: The Semiotics of Theatre Architecture*. Cornell UP, 1989.
Caro Baroja, Julio. *Algunos mitos españoles y otros ensayos*. Madrid: Editora Nacional, 1944.
———. *Teatro popular y magia*. Madrid: Revista de Occidente, 1974.
Cascardi, Anthony J. *The Limits of Illusion: A Critical Study of Calderón*. Cambridge UP, 1984.
Castañeda, James A. Introduction to *El esclavo del demonio de Mira de Amescua*. Madrid: Cátedra, 1980, pp. 13–54.
Castaño García, Joan. "Los símbolos de la Festa o Misterio de Elche." *Facies Domini*, vol. 2, 2010, pp. 191–209.
Castillo, David R. *Baroque Horrors: Roots of the Fantastic in the Age of Curiosities*. U of Michigan P, 2010.
Castro y Velasco, Acisclo Antonio Palomino de. *El museo pictórico, y escala óptica (Tomos I y II)*. Madrid: Imprenta de Sancha, 1797.
Cave, Stephen, and Kanta Dihal. "The Automaton Chronicles." *Nature*, vol. 559, 2018, pp. 473–74.
Cazés Gryj, Dann. "Construcción de la mentira sobrenatural en *La dama duende* y *El galán fantasma*." *Anuario Calderoniano*, vol. 6, 2013, pp. 61–73.
Cea Gutiérrez, Antonio. "Del rito al teatro: Restos de representaciones litúrgicas en la provincia de Salamanca." *Actas de las Jornadas sobre Teatro Popular en*

España, coordinated by Joaquín Álvarez Barrientos and Antonio Cea Gutiérrez. Madrid: CSIC, 1987, pp. 25–51.

Cenier, Richard. "Bocetos para un espacio escénico." Production dossier for *Misterio del Cristo de los Gascones*. www.naodamores.com/marcos/Dosier%20 Cristo/dosier%20cristo%20bocetos.html.

Cervantes Saavedra, Miguel de. *Don Quijote de la Mancha*. Edited by Francisco Rico. Barcelona: Crítica, 1998.

———. *Don Quixote*. Translated by Edith Grossman. Harper Collins, 2003.

———. "El retablo de las maravillas." *Entremeses*, edited by Adrián J. Sáez. Madrid: Cátedra, 2020, pp. 206–25.

———. *Exemplary Novels*. Translated by Edith Grossman, edited by Roberto González Echevarría. Yale UP, 2016. Kindle edition.

———. *Novelas ejemplares*. Edited by Harry Sieber. Madrid: Cátedra, 1980.

———. *Ocho comedias y ocho entremeses nuevos nunca representados* (Facsímil de la primera edición). Madrid: Real Academia Española, 1984.

———. "The Marvellous Pageant." *The Interludes of Cervantes*, edited and translated by S. Griswold Morley. Princeton UP, 1948, pp. 141–63.

Cirnigliaro, Noelia S. *Domus: Ficción y mundo doméstico en el barroco español*. Tamesis, 2015.

Cobarrubias Orozco, Sebastián de. *Tesoro de la lengua castellana o española*. Edited by Ignacio Arellano and R. Zafra. Madrid: Iberoamericana-Vervuert, 2006.

Cohen, Matthew Isaac. "Puppetry and the Destruction of the Object." *Performance Research*, vol. 12, no. 4, 2007, pp. 123–30.

Coman, Jonah. "No Strings Attached: Emotional Interaction with Animated Sculptures of Crucified Christ." *North Street Review*, 29 March 2017.

Conti, Brooke. "The Mechanical Saint: Early Modern Devotion and the Language of Automation." *The Automaton in the English Renaissance Literature*, edited by Wendy Beth Hyman. Ashgate, 2011, pp. 95–107.

Contreras Elvira, Ana María. "Ciencia y magia en el teatro español del Siglo XVIII." *ADE Teatro*, no. 132, 2010, pp. 145–55.

———. "La puesta en escena de la serie de comedias de magia *Cuando hay falta de hechiceros lo quieren ser los gallegos* y *Asombro de Salamanca* (1741–1775), de Nicolás González Martínez." PhD dissertation, Departamento de Filología Española, Universidad complutense de Madrid, 2016. eprints.ucm.es/39548/1/T37877.pdf.

Cornejo Vega, Francisco J. "Apuntes para la historia, la máquina real." *Fantoche: Arte de los títeres*, no. 0, 2006, pp. 13–31.

———. "Primeros tiempos de la máquina real de los títeres: Los actores maquinistas (hacia 1630–1750)." *Fantoche: Arte de los títeres*, no. 10, 2016, pp. 18–39.

———. "Un Siglo de Oro titiritero: Los títeres en el corral de comedias." *XVII y XXVIII Jornadas de Teatro del Siglo de Oro*. Almería: Instituto de Estudios Almerienses, 2012, pp. 11–36.

Council of Trent. *The Canons and Decrees of the Sacred and Ecumenical Council of Trent*. Edited and translated by J. Waterworth. Dolman, 1848. history.hanover.edu/texts/trent/trentall.html.

Cruickshank, Don W. *Calderón de la Barca*. Madrid: Gredos, 2011.

Cruz, Sor Juana Inés de la. *Primero Sueño y otros escritos*. Edited by Elena del Río Parra. Mexico, D.F: Fondo de cultura económica, 2006, pp. 39–73.

Daston, Lorraine, and Katherine Park. *Wonders and the Order of Nature, 1150–1750*. Zone Books, 1998.

Dailey, Alice. "Stigma and Stigmata: Medieval Hagiography and Michael Landy's *Saints Alive*." *World and Image*, vol. 32, no. 3, 2016, pp. 275–93.

Debord, Guy. *Society of the Spectacle*. Zone Books, 1994.

Del Pino, Rafael. "El retablo que el cine no ha visto: Desventuras cinematográficas de Falla y Maese Pedro." *La opinión de Granada*, 25 September 2004, p. 34.

Deleuze, Gilles. *The Fold: Leibniz and the Baroque*. Translated by Tom Conley. Minnesota UP, 1993.

Dent, Peter. "Agency, Beauty and the Late Medieval Sculptural Encounter." *The Agency of Things in Medieval and Early Modern Art: Materials, Power and Manipulation*, edited by Grażyna Jurkowlaniec, Ika Matyjaszkiewicz, and Zuzanna Sarnecka. Routledge, 2018, pp. 73–87.

"Descendimiento." YouTube video, 6:24, from performance of a mass on Good Friday at Peraleda de la Mata (Cáceres), posted by "palcholcho," 24 April 2009. www.youtube.com/watch?v=ZKvhgEMQCMI.

Descartes, Réné. *Oeuvres et Lettres*. Paris: Gallimard, 1953.

Desmeules, George. "Literatura fantástica y espectro del humor." *El relato fantástico: Historia y sistema*, edited by Antonio Risco, Ignacio Soldevila Durante, and Arcadio López-Casanova. Salamanca: Ediciones Colegio de España, 1998, pp. 43–66.

Díaz, Esmeralda. "Entrevista a Esmeralda Díaz, escenógrafa de *La dama duende*." *La dama duende de Calderón de la Barca*, edited by Mar Zubieta. Madrid: Compañía Nacional de Teatro Clásico, 2017, pp. 58–61.

Díaz-Plaja, Guillermo. *En torno a Cervantes*. Pamplona: Ediciones Universidad de Navarra, 1977.

Díaz Santiago, María Victoria. "The Necromancer Friar Bacon in the Magic World of Greene's Comedy *Friar Bacon and Friar Bungay*." *Sederi*, no. 18, 2008, pp. 5–26.

Diccionario de la lengua española. Real Academia Española, 2021. dle.rae.es.

Díez Borque, José María. "Palacio del Buen Retiro: Teatro, fiesta y otros espectáculos para el Rey." *La década de oro en la comedia española, 1630–1640: Actas de las XIX Jornadas de Teatro Clásico, Almagro, 9, 10, 11 de julio de 1996*, edited by Felipe B. Pedraza Jiménez. Castilla-La-Mancha: Universidad de Castilla-La-Mancha, 1997, pp. 167–89.

———. *Sociedad y teatro en la España de Lope de Vega*. Barcelona: Antoni Bosch, 1978.

Díez González, Soledad. "La leyenda del Cristo de los Gascones de Segovia y su trascendencia histórica." *Revista de Folklore*, no. 45, 1984, pp. 92–95.

Ditchfield, Simon. "Thinking with Saints: Sanctity and Society in the Early Modern World." *Critical Inquiry*, vol. 35, no. 3, 2009, pp. 552–84.

Doménech Rico, Fernando. *La comedia de magia*. Madrid: Fundamentos, 2008.

———. *Los Trufaldines y el Teatro de los Caños del Peral (La Commedia dell'arte en la España de Felipe V)*. Madrid: Fundamentos, 2007.

Domínguez Moreno, José María. "La función del descendimeinto en la Diócesis de Coria (Cáceres)." *Revista de Folklore*, vol. 77, no. 7, 1987, pp. 147–53.

Donahue-Wallace, Kelly. *Art and Architecture in Viceregal Latin America, 1521–1821*. U of New Mexico P, 2008.

During, Simon. *Modern Enchantments: The Cultural Power of Secular Magic*. Harvard UP, 2004.

Eamon, William. "From Secrets of Nature to Public Knowledge: The Origins of the Concept of Openness in Science." *Minerva*, vol. 23, no. 3, 1985, pp. 321–47.

———. *Science and the Secrets of Nature: Books of Secrets in Medieval and Early Modern Culture*. Princeton UP, 1994.

Eco, Umberto. "Travels in Hyperreality." *Travels in Hyperreality: Essays*, translated by William Weaver. Harcourt Brace Jovanovich, 1986, pp. 1–58.

Egginton, William. "The Baroque as a Problem of Thought." *PMLA*, vol. 24, no. 1, 2009, pp. 143–49.

———. "An Epistemology of the Stage: Theatricality and Subjectivity in Early Modern Spain." *New Literary History*, vol. 27, no. 3, 1996, pp. 391–413.

———. *How the World Became a Stage: Presence, Theatricality, and the Question of Modernity*. State U of New York P, 2003.

———. "Reason's Baroque House (Cervantes, Master Architect)." *Reason and Its Others: Italy, Spain, and the New World*, edited by David R. Castillo and Massimo Lollini. Vanderbilt UP, 2006, pp. 186–203.

———. "Reality Is Bleeding: A Brief History of Film from the Sixteenth Century." *Configurations*, vol. 9, no. 2, 2001, pp. 207–29.

Eisenstein, Sergei M. *The Film Sense*. Translated and edited by Jay Leyda. Harcourt Brace Jovanovich, 1975.

El esclavo del demonio. Written by Antonio Mira de Amescua, directed by Ángel Ojea, performed by Maribel Bayona, Raúl Esquinas, Sergio Martínez, Raquel Racionero, and Adrián Torreo (*La máquina real*). Corral de Comedias de Almagro, Spain, 17 July 2010.

El hotel eléctrico. Directed by Segundo de Chomón, performances by Segundo de Chomón and Julienne Mathieu. Pathé Frères, 1908.

El misterio del Cristo de los Gascones. Written and directed by Ana Zamora, performance by Nao D'amores Company. Teatro Abadía, Madrid, 29 March 2007.

Elliott, John R. *Playing God: Medieval Mysteries on the Modern Stage*. Toronto UP, 1989.

Eruli, Brunella. "Sotto Voce." *Puck: La marionnette et les autres arts*, no. 16: *L'opéra des marionettes*, 2009, pp. 9–14.

Falla, Manuel de. *El retablo de Maese Pedro por Manuel de Falla: Adaptación musical y escénica de un episodio del El ingenioso cavallero Don Quixote de la Mancha de Miguel de Cervantes Saavedra*. J. & W. Chester, 1923.

Fiennes, Sophie, director. *The Pervert's Guide to Cinema*. Written by Slavoj Žižek. Mischief Films, 2006.

Fernández, Esther. "*La dama duende* by Calderón de la Barca." Directed by Helena Pimenta, *Comedia Performance*, vol. 15, no. 1, 2018, pp. 92–95.

———. "La máquina real en el siglo XXI: Entrevista con Jesús Caballero." *Gestos*, vol. 54, 2012, pp. 174–82.

———. "*Lo fingido verdadero* de Lope de Vega." Directed by Claudio Hochman, *Comedia Performance*, vol. 10, no. 1, 2013, pp. 227–31.

———. "Recovering the Intangible Art of Baroque Puppetry: Interview with Jesús Caballero." *Puppetry International*, no. 45: *Our Intangible Cultural Heritage*, Spring/Summer 2019, pp. 29–31, 39.

Fernández Ferreiro, María. *La influencia del* Quijote *en el teatro español contemporáneo: Adaptaciones y recreaciones quijotescas (1900–2010)*. Alcalá de Henares: Universidad de Alcalá, 2017.

Fernández González, Ruth. "Sistemas de articulación en Cristos del Descendimiento." Master's thesis, Universitat Politècnica de València, 2012.

Fernández Paradas, Antonio Rafael. "¿Y ahora qué? El siglo XXI y la postimaginería." *Escultura Barroca Española: Nuevas lecturas desde los Siglos de Oro a la sociedad del conocimiento*, vol. 1: *Entre el Barroco y el siglo XXI*, edited by Antonio Rafael Fernández Paradas. Málaga: Exlibric, 2016, pp. 321–31.

Fernández-Turienzo, Francisco. "La visión cervantina del *Quijote*." *Anales Cervantinos*, no. 20, 1982, pp. 3–27.

Ferrer de Valdecebro, Andrés. *El templo de la Fama, con instrucciones políticas y morales*. Madrid: Imprenta Imperial viuda de Joseph Fernández Buendía, 1680.

Ferreras, Jacqueline. *Los diálogos humanísticos del siglo XVI en lengua castellana.* Murcia: Universidad de Murcia, 2003.

Ficino, Marsilio. *De triplici vita. Liber de uita: In tres libros diuisus.* Florence: Impressit ex archetypo Antonius Mischominus, 1489.

Foxe, John. *The Unabridged Acts and Monuments Online or TAMO.* Sheffield: Digital Humanities Institute, 2011. www.dhi.ac.uk/foxe/.

Freedberg, David. *El poder de las imágenes: Estudios sobre la historia y la teoría de la respuesta.* Madrid: Cátedra, 2011.

Freud, Sigmund. "The 'Uncanny.'" 1919. web.mit.edu/allanmc/www/freud1.pdf.

Fuch, Elinor. *The Death of Character: Perspectives on Theater after Modernism.* Indiana UP, 1996.

Fuente Ballesteros, Elena de la. "La comedia de Magia (I): Magos y brujas." *Revista de Folklore*, no. 165, 1994, pp. 91–98. www.biblioteca.org.ar/libros/154464.pdf.

Fuentelapeña, Antonio de. *El ente dilucidado: Discurso único novísimo que muestra que ay en naturaleza animales irracionales invisibles y quáles sean.* Madrid: Imprenta Real, 1676.

Garasa, Leocadio Delfin. *Santos en escena: Estudio sobre el teatro hagiográfico de Lope de Vega.* Bahía Blanca: Cuadernos del Sur, 1960.

Garber, Marjorie. "Out of Joint." *The Body in Parts: Fantasies of Corporeality in Early Modern Europe*, edited by David Hillman and Carla Mazzio. Routledge, 1977, pp. 23–51.

García Cárcel, Ricardo. *La cultura del Siglo de Oro: Pensamiento, arte y literatura.* Madrid: Historia 16, 1996.

García Garzón, Juan I. "En nuestro teatro no hacemos arqueología." *ABC Cultural*, 9 July 2016, pp. 24–25.

García-Reidy, Alejandro. "The Technological Environment of the Early Modern Spanish Stage." *Science on Stage in Early Modern Spain*, edited by Enrique García Santo-Tomás. Toronto UP, 2019, pp. 58–78.

García Santo-Tomás, Enrique. *The Refracted Muse: Literature and Optics in Early Modern Spain.* Translated by Vincent Barletta. U of Chicago P, 2017.

———. "Visiting the Virtuoso in Early Modern Spain: The Case of Juan de Espina." *Journal of Spanish Cultural Studies*, vol. 13, no. 2, 2012, pp. 129–47.

Gasta, Chad M. "Cervantes's Theory of Relativity in *Don Quixote.*" *Cervantes*, vol. 31, no. 1, 2011, pp. 51–82.

Gautier, Théophile. *Voyage en Espagne.* Paris: Charpentier et compagnie, 1870.

———. *Wanderings in Spain.* Translated by Thomas Robert McQuoid. London: Ingram and Cooke, 1853. www.gutenberg.org/files/52763/52763-h/52763-h.htm#CHAPTER_III.

Gaylord, Mary Malcolm. "Pulling Strings with Master Peter's Puppets: Fiction and History in *Don Quixote*." *Cervantes: Bulletin of the Cervantes Society of America*, vol. 18, no. 2, 1998, pp. 117–47.

Gell, Alfred. *Art and Agency: An Anthropological Theory*. Oxford UP, 1998.

———. *Arte y Agencia: Una teoría antropológica*. Edited by Guillermo Wilde, translated by Ramsés Cabrera. Buenos Aires: Sb Editorial, 2016.

———. "The Technology of Enchantment and the Enchantment of Technology." *Anthropology, Art, and Aesthetics*, edited by Jeremy Coote and Anthony Shelton. Oxford: Clarendon, 1994, pp. 40–63.

Gillet, Joseph E. "Clavileño: Su fuente directa y sus orígenes primitivos." *Anales Cervantinos*, no. 6, 1957, pp. 251–55.

Gilmore, David D. "'Tarasca': Ritual Monster of Spain." *Proceedings of the American Philosophical Society*, vol. 152, no. 3, 2008, pp. 362–82.

Gitliz, David. "La ruta alegórica del segundo *Quijote*." *Romanische Forschungen*, vol. 84, nos. 1–2, 1972, pp. 108–17.

Góngora y Argote, Luis de. "Desde Sansueña a París." *Romances, I*, edited by Antonio Carreira. Barcelona: Quaderns Crema, 1998, pp. 454–64.

Gónzalez García, José María. *Metáforas del poder*. Madrid: Alianza, 1998.

Goñi Pérez, José Manuel. "Reflexiones en torno al concepto de lo fantástico en la segunda mitad del siglo XIX: El lector." *De lo sobrenatural a lo fantástico: Siglos XIII–XIX*, edited by Barbara Greco and Laura Pache Carballo. Madrid: Biblioteca Nueva, 2014, pp. 215–49.

Gracián, Baltasar. *El criticón*. Edited by Alonso Santos. Madrid: Cátedra, 1980.

Grau, Jacinto. *El señor de Pigmalión: El burlador que no se burla*. Madrid: Espasa Calpe, 1997.

Greene, Robert. *Friar Bacon and Friar Bungay*. Edited by Daniel Seltzer. U of Nebraska P, 1963.

Groeneveld, Leanne. "'lyke unto a lyvely thyng': The Boxley Rood of Grace and Medieval Performance." *Medieval Theatre Performance: Actors, Dancers, Automata and Their Audiences*, edited by Philip Butterworth and Katie Normington. Cambridge: D. S. Brewer, 2017, pp. 197–214.

———. "A Theatrical Miracle: The Boxley Rood of Grace as Puppet." *Early Theatre: A Journal Associated with the Records of Early English Drama*, vol. 10, no. 2, 2007, pp. 11–50.

Gross, Kenneth. "Love among Puppets." *Raritan*, vol. 17, no. 1, 1997, pp. 67–82.

———. "The Madness of Puppets." *Hopkins Review*, vol. 2, no. 2, Spring 2009, pp. 182–205.

———. "Moving Statues, Talking Statues." *Raritan*, vol. 9, no. 2, 1989, pp. 1–25.

———. *Puppet: An Essay on Uncanny Life.* U of Chicago P, 2011.
Guardini, Romano. *The Spirit of the Liturgy.* Herder and Herder, 1998.
Gunning, Tom. "Re-Newing Old Technologies: Astonishment, Second Nature, and the Uncanny in Technology from the Previous Turn-of-the Century." *Rethinking Media Change: The Aesthetics of Transition*, edited by David Thorburn and Henry Jenkins. MIT Press, 2003, pp. 39–60.
———. "The Cinema of Attraction[s]: Early Film, Its Spectator, and the Avant-Garde." *Wide Angle*, vol. 8, nos. 3–4, 1983, pp. 63–71.
Haley, George. "The Narrator in *Don Quijote*: Maese Pedro's Puppet Show." *MLN*, vol. 80, no. 2, 1965, pp. 145–65.
Hardison, O. B., Jr. *Christian Rite and Christian Drama in the Middle Ages: Essays in the Origin and Early Modern History of Modern Drama.* Johns Hopkins UP, 1965.
Haro Tecglen, Eduardo. "Sencillez y elegancia." Review of *El galán fantasma* in *El País*, 30 April 1981. elpais.com/diario/1981/04/30/cultura/357429616_850215.html.
———. "Frontera entre la risa y el honor." Review of *El dama duende* in *El País*, 1 May 2000. elpais.com/diario/2000/05/01/cultura/957132008_850215.html.
Harris, John Wesley. *Medieval Theatre in Context: An Introduction.* Routledge, 1992.
Harris, Max. "Inanimate Performers: The Animation and Interpretative Versatility of the Palmesel." *Medieval Theatre Performance: Actors, Dancers, Automata and Their Audiences*, edited by Philip Butterworth and Katie Normington. Cambridge: D. S. Brewer, 2017, pp. 179–96.
Henry, Albert. "L'ascendence littéraire de Clavileño." *Romania*, vol. 90, no. 358, 1969, pp. 242–57.
Hess, Carol A. *Manuel de Falla and Modernism in Spain, 1898–1936.* U of Chicago P, 1992.
Hilborn, Debra. "Relating to the Cross: A Puppet Perspective on the Holy Week Ceremonies of the *Regularis Concordia*." *The Routledge Companion to Puppetry and Material Performance*, edited by Dassia N. Poshner, Claudia Orenstein, and John Bell. Routledge, 2015, pp. 164–75.
Hledíkova, Ida. "Integration of Puppetry Tradition into Contemporary Theater: The Reinvigoration of the *Vertep* Puppet Nativity Play after Communism in Eastern Europe." *The Routledge Companion to Puppetry and Material Performance*, edited by Dassia N. Poshner, Claudia Orenstein, and John Bell. Routledge, 2015, pp. 218–24.
Hodder, Ian. *Entangled: An Archeology of the Relationships between Humans and Things.* Sussex: Wiley-Blackwell, 2012.

Hoffmann, E. T. A. *The Sandman*. Penguin, 2016.
Honig, Edwin. *Calderón and the Seizures of Honor*. Harvard UP, 1972.
Huerta Calvo, Javier. "*Don Quijote* en la escena contemporánea (variaciones sobre el retablo de Maese Pedro)." *El Quijote desde el siglo XXI*, edited by Nicasio Salvador Miguel and Santiago López-Ríos Moreno. Alcalá de Henares: Centro de Estudios Cervantinos, 2005, pp. 91–100.
Huizinga, Johan. *The Autumn of the Middle Ages*. Translated by Rodney J. Payton and Ulrich Mammitzsch. U of Chicago P, 1996.
Iglesias Iglesias, Noelia. "El jardín minado de *El galán fantasma* de Calderón." *Atalanta*, vol. 1, no. 2, 2013, pp. 53–76.
Iturbe Sáiz, Antonio. "Cristo de Burgos o de San Agustín en España, América y Filipinas." *Los crucificados, religiosidad, cofradías y arte: Actas del Simposium, 3/6-IX-2010*, edited by Francisco Javier Campos and Fernández de Sevilla. San Lorenzo del Escorial: Instituto Escurialense de investigaciones históricas y artísticas, 2010, pp. 683–714.
Ivanic, Suzanna. "Early Modern Religious Objects and Materialities of Belief." *The Routledge Handbook of Material Culture in Early Modern Europe*, edited by Catherine Richardson, Tara Hamling, and David Gaimster. Routledge, 2016, pp. 322–37.
Jackson, Shelley, and Pamela Jackson. *The Doll Games*. www.ineradicablestain.com/dollgames.
Jaén, Isabel, and Julien Jacques Simon, eds. *Cognitive Approaches to Early Modern Spanish Literature*. Oxford UP, 2016.
Jalón Calvo, Mauricio, and Félix Gómez Crespo. "Matemáticas y pensamiento en el siglo XVI: Sobre el impulso científico renacentista." *Actes de les II Trobades d'Història de la Ciència i de la Tècnica: (Península, 5–8 desembre 1992)*, edited by Víctor Navarro Brotons. Barcelona: Institut d'Estudis Catalans, 1993, pp. 273–82.
Jentsch Ernst. "On the Psychology of the Uncanny." *Uncanny Modernity: Cultural Theories, Modern Anxieties*, edited by Jo Collins and John Jervis. Palgrave Macmillan, 2008, pp. 216–28.
Johnson, Barbara E. *Persons and Things*. Harvard UP, 2010.
Jones, Basil. "Puppetry, Authorship, and the Ur-Narrative." *The Routledge Companion to Puppetry and Material Performance*, edited by Dassia N. Poshner, Claudia Oreinstein, and John Bell. Routledge, 2015, pp. 61–68.
Jones, Cyril Albert. "Brecht y el drama del Siglo de Oro en España." *Segismundo*, no. 3, 1967, pp. 39–54.
———. "Some Ways of Looking at Golden Age Comedy." *Homenaje a William L. Fichter, Estudios sobre el teatro antiguo hispánico y otros ensayos*, edited by A. D. Kossof and José Amor y Vázquez. Madrid: Castalia, 1971, pp. 329–39.

Jones, Joseph R. "Historical Materials for the Study of the Cabeza Encantada Episode in *Don Quijote* II.62." *Hispanic Review*, vol. 47, no. 1, 1979, pp. 87–103.

Kallendorf, Hilaire. "La Inquisición, ¿Por qué deshace la cabeza encantada?" *Actas del XI Coloquio Internacional de la Asociación de Cervantistas*, edited by Chul Park. Seoul: Universidad Hankuk de Estudios Extranjeros, 2005, pp. 173–83.

Kang, Minsoo. *Sublime Dreams of Living Machines: The Automaton in the European Imagination*. Cambridge UP, 2011.

Kahan, Sylvia. *Music's Modern Muse: A Life of Winnaretta Singer, Princesse de Polignac*. U of Rochester P, 2003.

Kimmel, Seth. "Automatons and the Early Modern Drama of Skepticism." *Science on Stage in Early Modern Spain*, edited by Enrique García Santo-Tomás. Toronto UP, 2018, pp. 210–30.

King, Elizabeth. "Clockwork Prayer: A Sixteenth-Century Mechanical Monk." *Blackbird: An Online Journal of Literature and the Arts*, vol. 1, no. 1, 2002, pp. 1–28.

———. "Perpetual Devotion: A Sixteenth-Century Machine that Prays." *Genesis Redux: Essays in the History and Philosophy of Artificial Life*, edited by Jessica Riskin. U of Chicago P, 2007, pp. 263–92.

King, Errol L. "2013 Siglo de Oro Drama Festival, Chamizal." *Bulletin of the Comediantes*, vol. 67, no. 1, 2013, pp. 172–73.

Kircher, Athanasius. *Ars Magna Lucis et Umbrae*. Rome: Scheus, 1646.

———. *Musurgia Universalis*. Rome: Lodovico Grignani, 1650.

Klapisch-Zuber, Christiane. *Women, Family, and Ritual in Renaissance Italy*. U of Chicago P, 1985.

Knoespel, Kenneth. "Gazing on Technology: Theatrum Mechanorum and the Assimilation of Renaissance Machinery." *Literature and Technology*, edited by Mark L. Greenberg and Lance Schachterle. Lehigh UP, 1992, pp. 99–124.

Kopania, Kamil. *Animated Sculptures of the Crucified Christ in the Religious Culture of the Latin Middle Ages*. Warsaw: Wydawnictwo Neriton, 2010.

La dama boba. Written by Lope de Vega, directed by Helena Pimenta, performed by Compañía Nacional de Teatro Clásico. Teatro de la Comedia, Madrid, 16 Jan. 2002.

LaGrandeur, Kevin. "The Talking Brass Head as a Symbol of Dangerous Knowledge in *Friar Bacon* and in *Alphonsus, King of Aragon*." *English Studies*, vol. 80, no. 5, 1999, pp. 408–22.

Lama, Víctor de. "Un antecedente de Celestina a finales del siglo XIII: El teatro de sombras de Ibn Dāniyāl." *Actas del Congreso Internacional "La literatura en la época de Sancho IV" (21–24 de febrero de 1994)*, edited by Carlos Alvar and

José Manuel Lucía Megías. Alcalá de Henares: Universidad de Alcalá de Henares, 1996, pp. 399–413.

Landy, Michael. *Break Down*. 24 Oct. 2001, C&A Building, Oxford Street, London.

———. *Saints Alive*. 23 May–24 Nov. 2013, The National Gallery, London.

Landy, Thomas M. "Seville's streets flooded with 60 processions throughout Holy Week." *Catholics & Cultures*. www.catholicsandcultures.org/spain-seville-streets-flooded-60-processions-throughout-holy-week.

Lanz, Enrique. "Filiations et emboîtement du *Retable*: Propos recuellis par Yanisbel Victoria Martínez." *Puck: La marionnette et les autres arts*, no. 16: *L'opéra des marionettes*, 2009, pp. 89–96.

Lazardzig, Jan, and Hole Rößler. "Joseph Furttenbach and the Transfer of Mechanical Knowledge: New Perspectives on Early Modern Theatre Cultures." *Technologies of Theater: Joseph Furttenbach and the Transfer of Mechanical Knowledge in Early Modern Theatre Cultures*, edited by Jan Lazardzig and Hole Rößler. Frankfurt am Main: Vittorio Klostermann, 2016, pp. 271–312.

Lee, Christina H. "Don Antonio Moreno y el 'Discreto' negocio de los moriscos ricote y Ana Félix." *Hispania*, vol. 88, no. 1, 2005, pp. 32–40.

Légeret, Katia. "Mettre en scène le danseur et la marionette: Les conditions d'emergence en Inde d'un nouveau muse de l'art vivant." *La Marionette: Objet d'histoire, oeuvre d'art, objet de Civilization*, edited by Thierry Dufrêne and Joël Huthwohl. Lavérune: Editions l'entretemps, 2014, pp. 87–97.

León Pinelo, Antonio de. *Velos antiguos y modernos en los rostros de las mujeres: Sus conveniencias y daños, ilustación de la real pragmática de las tapadas*. Santiago de Chile: Centro de Investigaciones de Historia Americana, 1966.

Llano, Samuel. *Negotiating "Spanish Music" in Paris, 1908–1929*. Oxford UP, 2013.

Llewellyn, Nigel. "Baroque Sculpture: Materiality and the Question of Movement." *The Routledge Handbook of Material Culture in Early Modern Europe*, edited by Catherine Richardson, Tara Hamling, and David Gaimster. London: Routledge, 2016, pp. 401–22.

Lombard, Peter. *Libri Quattuor Sententiarum*. Paris: Migne, 1841.

Lope de Vega y Carpio. *La viuda valenciana*, edited by Teresa Ferrer Valls. Madrid: Castalia, 2001.

López Sancho, Lorenzo. "La gran versión calderoniana *El galán fantasma*, en el Español." *ABC*, vol. 55, 30 April 1981.

Luca de Tena, Cayetano. "Ensayo general: Notas, experiencias y fracasos de un director de escena, III." *Teatro*, vol. 3, 1953, pp. 45–48.

Luzán, Igancio de. *La poética, o reglas de la poesía en general, y de sus principales especies*. Barcelona: Labor, 1977.

Macho, Isaac. "Ana Zamora: 'Hemos hecho un Cristo muy humano, un títere del destino.'" *Artezblai: El periódico de las artes escénicas*, 6 April 2009. www.artezblai.com/artezblai/ana-zamora-hemos-hecho-un-cristo-muy-humano-un-titere-del-destino.html.

Macmillan, Sarah. "Phenomenal Pain: Embodying the Passion in the Life of Elizabeth of Spalbeek." *Postmedieval: A Journal of Medieval Cultural Studies*, vol. 8, no. 1, 2017, pp. 102–19.

Madroñal, Abraham. "Una colección inédita y desconocida (con la edición de *La cabeza encantada*)." *Anales Cervantinos*, no. 44, 2012, pp. 319–46.

Malkin, Michael R. "A Critical Perspective on Puppetry as Theater Art." *Puppetry Journal*, vol. 27, no. 1, 1975, pp. 3–8.

Mangan, Michael. *Performing Dark Arts: A Cultural History of Conjuring (Theatre and Consciousness)*. Intellect Books, 2007.

Maestro, Jesús G. "Cervantes y el teatro del *Quijote*." *Hispania*, vol. 88, no. 1, 2005, pp. 41–52.

March, Enric. "Francesc Roca: Magia entre títeres, autómatas y figuras de cera." *Fantoche: El arte de los títeres*, no. 8, 2105, pp. 20–35.

Marquerie, Alfredo. "*La dama duende* en el Español." *Informaciones*, 5 June 1942.

Martín-Flores Mario. "De la cueva de Montesinos a las aventuras de Clavileño: Un itinerario de carnavalización del discurso autoritario en el *Quijote*." *Hispánica*, vol. 38, 1994, pp. 46–60.

Martínez, Yanisbel V. "Orígenes." *Títeres: 30 años de Etcétera (1981–2011)*, edited by Yanisbel Victoria Martínez. Granada: Parque de las Ciencias de Granada, 2012, pp. 22–47.

———. "Telón adentro." *Títeres: 30 años de Etcétera (1981–2011)*, edited by Yanisbel Victoria Martínez. Granada: Parque de las Ciencias de Granada, 2012, pp. 50–131.

Massip Bonnet, Francesc. *El teatro medieval: Una voz de la divinidad, cuerpo de histrión*. Barcelona: Montesinos, 1992.

Mata Induráin, Carlos. "Cervantes y Calderón: El episodio de Clavileño (*Quijote*, II, 40–41) y la burla a Otáñez en *El astrólogo fingido*." *Volver a Cervantes: Actas del IV Congreso Internacional de la Asociación de Cervantistas, Lepanto 1/8 de Octubre de 2000*, vol. 2, edited by Antonio Pablo Bernat Vistarini. Palma: Universitat de les Illes Balears, 2001, pp. 999–1014.

Mauss, Marcel. *A General Theory of Magic*. Translated by Robert Brain. Routledge, 1950.

Mayr, Otto. *Authority, Liberty and Automatic Machinery in Early Modern Europe*. Johns Hopkins UP, 1986.

McCormick, John, Alfonso Cipollo, and Alessandro Napoli. *The Italian Puppet Theater: A History*. McFarland, 2010.

Mérimée, Prosper. *La Vénus d'Ille et autres Nouvelles*. Edited by Antonia Fonyi. Paris: Flammarion, 1982.

Menéndez y Pelayo, Marcelino. *Historia de los heterodoxos españoles*. Madrid: Librería Católica de San José, 1880–1881.

Merino Peral, Esther. *Historia de la escenografía en el siglo XVII: Creadores y tratadistas*. Sevilla: Universidad de Sevilla, 2010.

Metropolis. Directed by Fritz Lang, performances by Brigitte Helm, Alfred Abel, and Gustav Fröhlich. Erich Pommer, 1927.

Miguel, Juan Carlos de. "*La dama duende*: Un laberinto de pasiones." *Comedias y comediantes: Estudios sobre el teatro clásico español. Actas del Congreso Internacional sobre teatro y prácticas escénicas en los siglos XVI y XVII (Valencia, 9–11 de mayo, 1989)*, edited by Manuel V. Diago and Teresa Ferrer. Valencia: Universitat de Valencia, 1991, pp. 231–47.

Mira de Amescua, Antonio. *El esclavo del demonio*. Edited by James Agustín Castañeda. Madrid: Cátedra, 1980.

Mitchell, David T., and Sharon L. Snyder. *Narrative Prosthesis: Disability and the Dependencies of Discourse*. U of Michigan P, 2001.

Monroe, James T. "Prologomena to the Study of Ibn Quzman: The Poet as Jongleur." *El Romancero hoy: Historia, comparativismo, bibliografía crítica*, edited by Samuel G. Armistead, Diego Catalán, and Antonio Sánchez Romeralo. Madrid: Universidad Complutense, 1979, pp. 98–101.

Morgan, Luke. *The Monster in the Garden: The Grotesque and the Gigantic in Renaissance Landscape Design*. U of Pennsylvania P, 2016.

Morrison, Robert R. *Lope de Vega and the Comedia de Santos*. Peter Lang, 2000.

Morse, Lisa. "The Saracen of Opera dei Pupi: A Study of Race, Representation, and Identity." *The Routledge Companion to Puppetry and Material Performance*, edited by Dassia N. Poshner, Claudia Oreinstein, and John Bell. Routledge, 2015, pp. 144–53.

Moscoso, Javier. "Prácticas científicas en el Barroco histórico: El caso de la historia." *Barroco*, edited by Pedro Aullón de Haro. Madrid: Verbum, 2004, pp. 263–78.

Moshenska, Joe. *Iconoclasm as Child's Play*. Stanford UP, 2019.

Mujica, Barbara. *Calderón's Characters: An Existential Point of View*. Barcelona: Puvill, 1980.

———. "Tragic Elements in Calderón's *La dama duende*." *Kentucky Romance Quarterly*, no. 16, 1969, pp. 303–28.

Nállim, Carlos Orlando. "Clavileño: La tradición en una nueva obra de arte." *Para leer a Cervantes: Estudios de literatura española Siglo de Oro*, vol. 1, edited by Mechora Romanos, Alicia Parodi, and Juan Diego Vila. Buenos Aires: Universidad de Buenos Aires, 1999, pp. 83–98.

Navarro Ortega, Ana Dolores. "Astarté de El Carambolo: Who's That Girl?" *Mainake*, no. 36, 2016, pp. 483–94.

Ndalianis, Angela. "Architectures of the Senses: Neo-Baroque Entertainment Spectacles." *Rethinking Media Change: The Aesthetics of Transition*, edited by David Thorburn and Henry Jenkins. MIT Press, 2003, pp. 355–73.

Newberry, Wilma. *The Pirandellian Mode in Spanish Literature from Cervantes to Sastre*. State U of New York P, 1973.

Nitsch, Wolfam. "La cueva de Madrid: Magia y tramoya en *La dama duende*." *Anuario Calderoniano*, no. 10, 2017, pp. 143–59.

Nommick, Yvan. "Día de Reyes en casa de los Lorca: Muñecos en busca de Maese." *La opinión de Granada*, 2 January 2005, p. 62.

Onians, John. "'I wonder . . .': A Short History of Amazement." *Sight and Insight: Essays on Art and Culture in Honour of E. H. Gombricht at 85*, edited by John Onians. Phaidon, 1994, pp. 11–33.

Orazi, Verónica. "Mirabilia: Efectos especiales en la literatura medieval." *De lo sobrenatural a lo fantástico: Siglos XVII–XIX*. Madrid: Biblioteca Nueva, 2014, pp. 19–24.

Ordoñez, Javier. "De Rocinante a Clavileño." *La ciencia y El Quijote*, edited by José Manuel Sánchez Ron. Barcelona: Crítica, 2005, pp. 249–56.

Ortega y Gasset, José. *Meditaciones del* Quijote. 1914. Edited by Julián Marías. Madrid: Cátedra, 1995.

———. *Meditations on* Quixote. Translated by Evelyn Rugg and Diego Marín. W. W. Norton, 1961.

Ortiz de Zúñiga, Diego. *Anales eclesiásticos y seculares de la muy noble y muy leal ciudad de Sevilla, metrópoli de la Andalucia, que contienen sus más principales memorias desde el año 1246, en que emprendió conquistarla del poder de los moros el gloriosísimo Rey S. Fernando III de Castilla y León, hasta el de 1671 en que la Católica Iglesia le concedió el culto y título de Bienaventurado*, vol. 5. Madrid: Imprenta Real, 1796.

Osman, Jena. "The Puppet Theater Is the Epic Theater." *The Puppet Show*, edited by Ingrid Schaffner, Carin Kuoni, and John Bell. Institute of Contemporary Art and University of Pennsylvania, 2007, p. 19.

Otto, Rudolf. *Lo santo: Lo racional y lo irracional en la idea de Dios*. Madrid: Alianza Editorial, 2016.

Padilla, Ignacio. *El diablo y Cervantes*. Mexico City: Fondo de Cultura Económica, 2005.

Paun de García, Susan. "Introduction." *Don Juan de Espina en su partria: Don Juan de Espina en Milán* by José de Cañizares. Madrid: Castalia, 1997, pp. 11–62.

Paz Gago, José María. *La máquina maravillosa: Tecnología y arte en el Quijote*. Madrid: Sial, 2006.
Pemberton, John. "Their Own." *The Puppet Show*, edited by Ingrid Schaffner, Carin Kuoni, and John Bell. Institute of Contemporary Art and University of Pennsylvania, 2007, p. 20.
Penny, Nicholas B. "Director's Foreword." *Michael Landy: Saints Alive*, edited by Colin Wiggins, Richard Cork, Jennifer Sliwka, and Michael Landy. National Gallery London, 2013, p. 7.
Percas de Ponseti, Helena. "Authorial Strings: A Recurrent Metaphor in *Don Quijote*." *Cervantes: Bulletin of the Cervantes Society of America*, vol. 1, nos. 1–2, 1981, pp. 51–62.
———. *Cervantes y su concepto del arte: Estudio crítico de algunos aspectos y episodios del Quijote*. Madrid: Gredos, 1975.
Pérez Galdós, Benito. *Tristana*. Edited by Isabel González and Gabriel Sevilla. Madrid: Cátedra, 2008.
———. *Tristana*. Translated by Margaret Jull Costa. New York Review of Books, 2014.
Pérez Magallón, Jesús. *Construyendo la modernidad: La cultura española en el tiempo de los Novatores (1675–1725)*. Madrid: CSIC, 2002.
Pérez Sánchez, Alfonso E. "Los pintores escenógrafos en el Madrid del S. XVII." *La escenografía del teatro barroco*, edited by Aurora Egido. Salamanca: Universidad de Salamanca and Universidad Internacional Menéndez Pelayo, 1989, pp. 61–90.
Pérez-Simón, Andrés. *Baroque Lorca: An Archaist Playwright for the New Stage*. Routledge, 2020.
Persia, Jorge de. *Los últimos años de Manuel de Falla*. Madrid: Fondo de Cultura Economica/SGAE, 1993.
Petersen, Elizabeth M. Review of *El esclavo del demonio* by Mira de Amescua, directed by Ángel Ojea, performed by *La máquina real*. Corral de comedias, Almagro, 18 July 2010 (complete run: 17–18 July 2010). *Comedia Performance*, vol. 8, no. 1, 2011, pp. 261–65.
Pimenta, Helena. "Entrevista a Helena Pimenta, directora de *La dama duende*." *La dama duende de Calderón de la Barca*, edited by Mar Zubieta. Cuadernos Pedagógicos, no. 60. Madrid: Compañía Nacional de Teatro Clásico, 2017, pp. 44–51.
Piña, Juan de. *Casos prodigiosos y cueva encantada: Novela*. Edited by Emilio Cotarelo y Mori. Madrid: Librería de la Viuda de Rico, 1907.
Poole, William. "Kepler's *Somnium* and Francis Godwin's *The Man in the Moone*: Births of Science-Fiction 1593–1638." *New Worlds Reflected: Travel and Utopia in the Early Modern Period*, edited by Chloë R. Houston. Ashgate, 2010, pp. 57–69.

Popkin, Richard H. *The History of Scepticism from Erasmus to Spinoza*. U of California P, 1979.
Portuondo, María M. "Conclusion. Looking behind the Curtain: Clues of Early Modern Spanish Science." *Science on Stage in Early Modern Spain*, edited by Enrique García Santo-Tomás. Toronto UP, 2018, pp. 250–74.
Real Academia de la Lengua. *Diccionario de autoridades*. Madrid: Gredos, 1964.
Reed, Cory A. "Ludic Revelations in the Enchanted Head Episode in *Don Quijote* (II, 62)." *Cervantes: Bulletin of the Cervantes Society of America*, vol. 24, no. 1, 2004, pp. 189–216.
Reula Baquero, Pedro. *El camarín del desengaño: Juan de Espina, coleccionista y curioso del siglo XVII*. Madrid: Centro de Estudios Europa Hispánica, 2019.
Rey-Bueno, Mar, and Miguel López-Pérez, eds. *The Gentleman, the Virtuoso, the Inquirer: Vincencio Juan de Lastanosa and the Art of Collecting in Early Modern Spain*. Newcastle upon Tyne: Cambridge Scholars, 2008.
Riley, Edward C. "La profecía de la bruja (El coloquio de los perros)." *Actas del I Coloquio Internacional de la Asociación de Cervantistas*, edited by J. M. Casasayas. Barcelona: Anthropos, 1990, pp. 83–94.
Risco, Antonio. *Literatura y fantasía*. Madrid: Taurus, 1982.
Riskin, Jessica. "The Defecating Duck, or, the Ambiguous Origins of Artificial Life," *Critical Inquiry*, vol. 29, no. 4, 2003, pp. 599–633.
———. "Machines in the Garden." *Renaissance Futurities: Science, Art, Invention*, edited by Charlene Villaseñor Black and Mari-Tere Álvarez. U of California P, 2020, pp. 19–40.
———. *The Restless Clock: A History of the Centuries-Long Argument over What Makes Living Things Tick*. U of Chicago P, 2016.
Rivera Krakowska, Octavio, and David Aarón Estrada. "Títeres en Nueva España en el siglo XVI." *Dramaturgia y teatralidad en el Siglo de Oro I: La presencia jesuita*, edited by José Ramón Alcántara, Adriana Ontiveros, and Dann Cazés G. Mexico City: Universidad Iberoamericana, 2013, pp. 187–233.
Rodríguez Cuadros, Evangelina. "Calderón heterogéneo, Calderón heterodoxo." Biblioteca Virtual Miguel de Cervantes. www.cervantesvirtual.com/portales/calderon_de_la_barca/autor_calderon/.
Rodríguez de la Flor, Fernando. "La santidad 'rococó': Fiesta y hagiografía jesuítica en la preilustración andaluza." *La época de la Ilustración: Actas del III Coloquio Internacional sobre la Cultura en Andalucía, 19, 20 y 21 de Septiembre de 2002, Estepa*, edited by Pedro Ruiz Pérez and Klaus Wagner. Estepa: Ayuntamiento de Estepa, 2003, pp. 249–74.
———. *Pasiones frías: Secreto y disimulación en el barroco hispano*. Madrid: Marcial Pons, 2005.

Rodríguez Porto, Rosa M. "Knighted by the Apostle Himself: Political Fabrication and Chivalric Artifact in Compostela, 1332." *The Agency of Things in Medieval and Early Modern Art: Material, Power and Manipulation*, edited by Grażyna Jurkowlaniec and Ika Matyjaszkiewicz. Routledge, 2017, pp. 51–62.

Rubio, Rebeca. "Siglo de Oro franquista: Cinco comedias ya antes representadas." PhD dissertation, Department of Spanish and Portuguese, University of California, Davis, 2019.

Rublack, Ulinka. "Female Spirituality and the Infant Jesus in Late Medieval Dominican Convents." *Gender and History*, vol. 6, no. 1, 1994, pp. 37–57.

Ruiz de Alarcón, Juan. *La cueva de Salamanca: La prueba de las promesas*. Edited by Celsa Carmen García Valdés. Madrid: Cátedra, 2013.

Ruiz de Castro, Garci. *Comentario sobre la primera y segunda población de Segovia*. Transcription and notes by José Antonio Ruiz Hernando. Segovia: Excma. Diputación Provincial de Segovia, 1988.

Rupp, Stephen. "The Soul under Siege: Strategy and Neostocism in Calderón de la Barca's *El sitio de Bredá*." *Science on Stage in Early Modern Spain*, edited by Enrique García Santo-Tomás. Toronto UP, 2018, pp. 151–75.

Ruta, Maria Caterina. "La 'aventura' de la cabeza encantada en el contexto urbano." *Cervantes, El Quijote y Barcelona*, edited by Carme Riera y Guillermo Serés. Barcelona: Fundació Caixa Catalunya, 2007, pp. 213–30.

Sáez y Romero, Mariano. *Las calles de Segovia: Noticias, tradiciones y curiosidades*. Madrid: Antonio San Martín, 1998.

Salvo y Vela, Juan. *El mágico de Salerno*. Part 1. Madrid: Antonio Sanz, 1740.

———. *El mágico de Salerno*. Parts 2–5. Sevilla: Imprenta de la Viuda de Leefdael, n.d.

Samson, Alexander. "¿La muerte del héroe en la edad de las armas de fuego?" *Guerra y Paz en la comedia español: XXIX Jornadas de Teatro Clásico de Almagro, Almagro 4, 5, 6 de julio de 2006*, edited by Felipe B. Pedraza Jiménez, Rafael González Cañal, and Elena E. Marcello. Castilla-La Mancha: Universidad de Castilla-La Mancha, 2007, pp. 19–34.

Sánchez, Vicente. "Vejamen que se leyó en una Aacademia en casa del excelentísimo señor duque de Ciudad Real, príncipe de Esquilache, virrey y capitán general del reino de Aragón." *Lira poética*, edited by Jesús Duce García. Zaragoza: Larumbe, 2003, pp. 85–116.

Sánchez-Arjona, José. *El teatro en Sevilla en los siglos XVI y XVII: Estudios históricos*. Madrid: Estab. tip. de A. Alonso, 1887.

Sánchez del Barrio, Antonio. "La Función del Desenclavo." *Clausuras I: El patrimonio de los conventos de la provincia de Valladolid*. Valladolid: Diputación de Valladolid, 1999, pp. 112–13.

———. "La función del Desenclavo en un cuadro de 1722: Objetos mágicos y simbólicos en algunos de sus personajes." Biblioteca Virtual Miguel de Cervantes. www.cervantesvirtual.com/obra-visor/la-funcion-del-desenclavo-en-un-cuadro-de-1722-objetos-magicos-y-simbolicos-en-algunos-de-sus-personajes/html/.

Sánchez Jiménez, Antonio. "La mina que revienta en la comedia de Calderón: El caso de *Primero soy yo.*" *Anuario calderoniano*, no. 10, 2017, pp. 255–71.

Sánchez López, Juan Antonio. "Puesta en escena y escultura animada: Dramaturgia e ingenios." *Escultura barroca española: Nuevas lecturas desde los siglos de oro a la sociedad del conocimiento. Entre el Barroco y el siglo XXI*, edited by Antonio Rafael Fernández Paradas, vol. 1. Málaga: Exlibric, 2016, pp. 133–50.

Sawday, Jonathan. *Engines of the Imagination: Renaissance Culture and the Rise of the Machine*. Routledge, 2007.

Segel, Harold B. *Pinocchio's Progeny: Puppets, Marionettes, Automatons, and Robots in Modernist and Avant-Garde Drama*. Johns Hopkins UP, 1995.

Sharp, Samuel. *Letters from Italy, Describing the Customs and Manners of That Country, in the Years 1765, and 1766*. London: Henry and Cave, 1767.

Shaw, Donald L. *La generación del 98*. Translated by Carmen Hierro. Madrid: Cátedra, 1989.

Shelley, Mary Wollstonecraft. *Frankenstein, or, The Modern Prometheus*. Edited by Charles E. Robinson. Bodleian Library, 2008.

Sheppard, Anthony W. *Revealing Masks: Exotic Influences and Ritualized Performance in Modernist Music Theater*. U of California P, 2001.

Shergold, N. D. *A History of the Spanish Stage from Medieval Times until the End of the Seventeenth Century*. Oxford UP, 1967.

Shuger, Dale. "Pulling String: Puppets and Free Will on the Spanish Stage." *Bulletin of the Comediantes*, vol. 70, no. 2, 2018, pp. 13–31.

Sobchack, Vivian. *Carnal Thoughts: Embodiment and Moving Image Culture*. U of California P, 2004.

Sofer, Andrew. *The Stage Life of Props*. U of Michigan P, 2003.

Solla Price, Derek J. de. "Automata and the Origins of Mechanism and Mechanistic Philosophy." *Technology and Culture*, vol. 5, no. 1, 1964, pp. 2–23.

Stafford, Barbara Maria. *Artful Science: Enlightenment Entertainment and the Eclipse of Visual Education*. MIT Press, 1999.

Stafford, Barbara María, and Frances Terpak. *Devices of Wonder: From the World in a Box to Images on a Screen*. Getty Research Institute, 2001.

Steiner, Deborah Tarn. *Images in Mind: Statues in Archaic and Classical Greek Literature and Thought*. Princeton UP, 2001.

Stevens, Martin. "Illusion and Reality in the Medieval Drama." *College English*, vol. 32, no. 4, 1971, pp. 448–64.
Strauss, Linda. "Reflections in a Mechanical Mirror: Automata as Doubles and as Tools." *Knowledge and Society*, vol. 10, 1996, pp. 179–207.
Suarez Miramón, Ana. "La correspondencia de las esferas en el universo de Calderón." *Calderón de la Barca y su aportación a los valores de la cultura europea: 14 y 15 de noviembre de 2000; Jornadas Internacionales de Literatura Comparada*, edited by Tomás Albadalejo. Madrid: Universidad San Pablo-CEU, 2001, pp. 263–86.
Swift, Christopher. "Technology and Wonder in Thirteenth-Century Iberia and Beyond." *Performing Objects and Theatrical Things*, edited by Marlis Schweitzer and Joanne Zerdy. Palgrave Macmillan, 2014, pp. 21–35.
Taxidou, Olga. *Modernism and Performance: Jarry to Brecht*. Palgrave, 2008.
Thomas, Keith. *Religion and the Decline of Magic*. Penguin, 1971.
Thomas, Nicholas. *Entangled Objects: Exchange, Material Culture, and Colonialism in the Pacific*. Harvard UP, 1991.
Tietz, Manfred. "El breve entusiasmo por *La puente de Mantible* de Calderón de la Barca en el primer romanticismo alemán." *La comedia de caballerías: Actas de las XXVIII Jornadas de Teatro Clásico de Almagro: 12, 13, y 14 de julio de 2005*, edited by Felipe B. Pedraza Jiménez, Rafael González Cañal, and Elena Marcello. Almagro: Universidad de Castilla-La Mancha-Festival de Almagro, 2006, pp. 205–26.
Tigner, Amy L. *Literature and the Renaissance Garden from Elizabeth I to Charles II: England's Paradise*. Ashgate, 2012.
Tillis, Steve. "The Actor Occluded: Puppet Theatre and Acting Theory." *Theatre Topics*, vol. 6, 1996, pp. 109–15.
———. *Toward an Aesthetic of the Puppet: Puppetry as a Theatrical Art*. Greenwood, 1992.
Tirso de Molina, Gabriel Téllez (attributed). *El burlador de Sevilla*. Edited by Alfredo Rodríguez López-Vázquez. Madrid: Cátedra, 1990.
———. *En Madrid y en una casa. Obras completas III*, edited by Blanca de los Ríos. Madrid: Aguilar, 1946, pp. 538–55.
Torres Clemente, Elena. *Las óperas de Manuel de Falla: De* La vida breve *a* El Retablo de Maese Pedro. Madrid: Sociedad Española de Musicología, 2007.
———. "Manuel de Falla y *El retablo de Maese Pedro*: Una reinterpretación del romance español." *Revista de musicología*, vol. 28, no. 1, Actas del VI Congreso de la Sociedad Española de Musicología, 2005, pp. 839–56.
Uličný, Petr. "Christ in Motion: Portable Objects and Scenographic Environments in the Liturgy of Medieval Bohemia." *Theatralia*, vol. 14, no. 1, 2011, pp. 24–64.

Unamuno, Miguel de. *Tres novelas ejemplares y un prólogo*. Madrid: Espasa Calpe, 1920.

Valle-Inclán, Ramón del. *Retablo de la avaricia, la lujuria y la muerte*. Edited by Ricardo Doménech. Madrid: Austral, 1999.

Varey, John E. *Cosmovisión y escenografía: El teatro español en el Siglo de Oro*. Madrid: Castalia, 1987.

———. *Historia de los títeres en España (Desde sus orígenes hasta mediados del siglo XVIII)*. Madrid: Revista de Occidente, 1957.

———. "*La dama duende* de Calderón: Símbolos y escenografía." *Calderón: Actas del Congreso Internacional sobre Calderón y el Teatro Español del Siglo de Oro (Madrid, 8–13 de junio de 1981)*, vol. 1, edited by Luciano García Lorenzo. Madrid: CSIC, 1983, pp. 165–83.

———. "Titiriteros y volatines en Valencia (1585–1785)." *Revista Valenciana de Filología*, no. 3, 1953, pp. 215–76.

Vélez Sainz, Julio. "De teatro primitivo a primer teatro clásico: Lucas Fernández y Gil Vicente en las producciones de Nao D'amores." *Diálogos en las tablas: Ultimas tendencias de la puesta en escena del teatro clásico español*, edited by María Bastianes, Esther Fernández, and Purificació Mascarell. Kassel: Edition Reichenberger, 2014, pp. 219–46.

Veltruský, Jirí. "Man and Object in the Theater." *A Prague School Reader on Esthetics, Literary Structure and Style*, edited by Paul Garvin. Georgetown UP, 1964, pp. 83–91.

Verdi Webster, Susan. *Art and Ritual in Golden-Age Spain*. Princeton UP, 1998.

Vernant, Jean-Pierre. *Mortals and Immortals*. Princeton UP, 1991.

Viladesau, Richard. *The Pathos of the Cross: The Passion of Christ in Theology and the Arts—The Baroque Era*. Oxford UP, 2014.

Villaseñor Black, Charlene, and Mari-Tere Álvarez. "The Future is Now: Reflections on Art, Science, Futurity." *Renaissance Futurities: Science, Art, Invention*, edited by Charlene Villaseñor Black and Mari-Tere Álvarez. U of California P, 2020, pp. 1–8.

Vitar, Beatriz. "El mundo mágico en el Madrid de los Austrias a través de las cartas, avisos y relaciones de sucesos." *Revista de dialectología y tradiciones populares*, vol. 56, no. 1, 2002, pp. 97–128.

Vitse, Marc. "Sobre los espacios en *La dama duende*: El cuarto de don Manuel." *Rilce*, vol. 12, no. 2, 1996, pp. 337–56.

Von Kempelen, Wolfgang. *Mechanismus Der Menschlichen Sprache Nebst Beschreibung Seiner Sprechenden Maschine*. Austria: Stuttgart-Bad Cannstatt, 1970.

Walsham, Alexandra. "The Reformation and the Disenchantment of the World Reassessed." *Historical Journal*, vol. 51, no. 2, 2008, pp. 497–528.

Wardropper, Bruce W. "Calderón's Comedy and His Serious Sense of Life." *Hispanic Studies in Honor of Nicholson B. Adams*, edited by John E. Keller and Karl-Ludwig Selig. U of North Carolina P, 1996, pp. 179–93.

———. "Comedias." *Suma Cervantina*, edited by J. B. Avalle-Arce and E. C. Riley. Tamesis, 1973, pp. 147–69.

Weber, Eckhard. "Misterio, para voces y orquesta: Pedro Calderón de la Barca, libretista del teatro musical del siglo XX." *Calderón 2000: Homenaje a Kurt Reichenberger en su 80 cumpleaños*, vol 1, edited by Ignacio Arellano. Kassel: Reichenberger, 2002, pp. 905–18.

Webster, Susan Verdi. "Sacred Altars, Sacred Streets: The Sculpture of Penitential Confraternities in Early Modern Seville." *Journal of Ritual Studies*, vol. 6, no. 1, 1992, pp. 159–77.

Wetmore, Alex. "Sympathy Machines: Men of Feeling and the Automaton." *Eighteenth-Century Studies*, vol. 43, no. 1, 2009, pp. 37–54.

Wiggins, Colin. "Michael Landy in the National Gallery." *Michael Landy: Saints Alive*, edited by Colin Wiggins, Richard Cork, Jennifer Sliwka, and Michael Landy. London: National Gallery, 2013, pp. 15–35.

Wiggins, Colin, Richard Cork, Jennifer Sliwka, and Michael Landy, eds. *Michael Landy: Saints Alive*. London: National Gallery, 2013.

Wilde, Oscar. "Puppets and Actors." Letter. *Daily Telegraph*, 20 February 1892.

Wilder, Mitchell A., and Edgar Breitenbach. *Santos: The Religious Folk Art of New Mexico*. Taylor Museum of the Colorado Springs Fine Arts Center, 1943.

Woodward, Kenneth L. *Making Saints: How the Catholic Church Determines Who Becomes a Saint, Who Doesn't, and Why*. Touchstone, 1990.

Young, Karl. *The Drama of the Medieval Church*. 2 vols. Clarendon, 1933.

Young, Susan. *Shakespeare Manipulated: The Use of the Dramatic Works of Shakespeare in teatro di figura in Italy*. Associated University Presses, 1953.

Zamora, Ana. "Una travesía entre rito y teatro." *Misterio del Cristo de los Gascones* by Ana Zamora, pp. 11–18. www.naodamores.com/descargas/LibroEspectaculo.pdf.

———. *Misterio del Cristo de los Gascones*. Nao D'amores. www.naodamores.com/descargas/LibroEspectaculo.pdf.

Zamora, Antonio de. *Duendes son alcahuetes y el espíritu Foleto: La comedia de magia*. Edited by Fernando Doménech Rico. Madrid: Fundamentos-RESAD, 2008, pp, 49–178.

Zorrilla, José. "A buen juez, mejor testigo." *Leyendas y tradiciones*. Madrid: Espasa Calpe, 1920, pp. 9–26.

INDEX

"A buen juez, mejor testigo" (Zorrilla), 19
"abadesa preñada, La" (Gonzalo de Berceo), 20
ABC (newspaper), 151–52, *Fig. 6.3*
absolutism, 12–14
Adición a la tercera parte de Flos Sanctorum (1588), 69
A-Effect (*Verfremdungseffekt*), 86
aeolipile (aeolipyle; eolipile), 17
Æthelwold, 38
Águila, Gaspar del, 19
air-conditioning systems, 107
'Ajib wa-Gharib (Ibn Dāniyāl), 25–26
Alameda de Osuna, 179n12
Alfonso X the Wise, King of Castile, 20
Allen, John J., 88
Al-Mutayyam wa'l-yutayyim (Ibn Dāniyāl), 25–26
Álvarez, Mari-Tere, 8, 113
Álvarez, Rafael, 169n27
Álvarez Barrientos, Joaquín, 160
Amalarius of Metz, 34–35
Amar después de la muerte (Calderón de la Barca), 139

anima (life), 17–18
animal-shaped automata, 112–13.
   See also Clavileño (flying wooden horse)
animation and animated artifacts
   animated statues and, 157–61
   Astarté de El Carambolo as, 1–2, 16
   definition of, 163n2
   history of, 16–28
   mechanistic metaphor and, 10–16
   modernity and, 2–9
   as religious props, 14–15, 18–24, 29–31, 56, 66–67
   See also automata; *Cristos articulados* (jointed Christ figures); *desengaño*; puppetry and puppets
animism, 14, 81–82, 118
Anselm of Canterbury, Saint, 36
Arabic shadow theater, 24–26
araceli (moving platform), 22–23
Aracil, Alfredo, 111
Arcadia, 110
Arellano, Ignacio, 71
Aristotle, 40
Armas, Frederick A. de, 138, 178n3, 186n35

217

218 *Index*

Arnheim, Rudolph, 51
Ars magna lucis et umbrae (Kircher), 26
Art and Agency (Gell), 105
Asclepius (Hermes Trismegistus), 159
Astarté de El Carambolo (7th–6th centuries BCE), 1–2, 16
Astete, Gaspar, 132
astrólogo fingido, El (Calderón de la Barca), 180n20
Augustine, Saint, 159
aurora en Copacabana, La (Calderón de la Barca), 139
Auto de la Pasión (Campo), 48
automata
    as animal-shaped, 112–13
    Clavileño (flying wooden horse) as, 89, 104–11, 112–15, 117–18, 119, 122–23, 125–26, 160–61, *Fig. 5.1–2*
    in fiction, 118
    gardens and, 122
    mechanistic metaphor and, 11
    rationalized sense of wonder and, 4
    as religious props, 18–24, 66–67, *Fig. 3.1–2*
    See also oracular and talking heads
autos sacramentales (short religious plays), 166n21
Avalle-Arce, Juan Bautista, 105
Avisos (Barrionuevo), 138
Ayanz y Beaumont, Jerónimo de, 107

Bacon, Francis, 113, 180n17
balcones de Madrid, Los (Tirso de Molina), 136–37
Baltasara, La (Vélez de Guevara, Coello, and Rojas Zorrilla), 64
Barreiro, Juan J., 40
Barrionuevo, Jerónimo de, 138

Barrios, Nuria, 51
bavastells, 166n28
beatification, 61–62
Beleth, John, 35
Bell, John, 79
Benavente, Jacinto, 91
Benjamin, Walter, 118
Bennett, Jane, 19, 101–2
Bernard of Clairvaux, Saint, 36
Bernstein, Robin, 17–18
Beurrier, Pierre, 82
Bishop, Tom G., 129
Boîtes (Matton), 150
Bonaventure, Saint, 33
Bonnet, Francesc Massip, 42–43
Borlik, Todd Andrew, 121
Borromeo, Carlo, 34
Borromeo, Federico, 34
Bouchor, Maurice, 65–66, 167n14
Boyle, Robert, 11
Break Down (Landy), 172n28
Brecht, Bertolt, 48–49, 86, 177n38
Breitenback, Edgar, 71
Bridget of Sweden, Saint, 165n15
Brook, Peter, 53
Brulon Soares, Bruno, 160
Brun, Ida, 189n8
Budé, Guillaume, 117
Bufano, Remo, 99
Bunraku (Japanese puppet theatre), 51–52
Buñuel, Luis, 177n40
Burke, Peter, 82
burla de Clavileño and trova de don Quijote, La (anonymous, 1800), 179n10
burlador de Sevilla, El (Tirso de Molina), 21, 158

Burningham, Bruce, 173n2
Butterworth, Philip, 170n11
Bynum, Caroline Walker, 15, 30, 37, 40–41, 66, 164n13

Caballero, Jesús, 61, 68–77, 101, *Fig. 3.3–12*
Caballero Ariñano (ventriloquist), 124
Caballero Felip (ventriloquist), 124
caballo clavileño, El (operetta for children), 179n10
Calderón de la Barca, Pedro
　autos sacramentales by, 166n21
　Cervantes and, 127–28
　desengaño and, 127–28, 130–31, 143–44, 153
　Falla and, 92–93
　legacy of, 147–48
　military innovation and, 14
　parody of Clavileño by, 180n20
　See also *dama duende, La* (Calderón de la Barca); *galán fantasma, El* (Calderón de la Barca)
Calleja, Diego de, 64
Calvin, John, 33
Campo, Alonso del, 48
canard digérateur (digesting duck), 113
Cancionero de Palacio (Palacio songbook), 50
Cancionero de Segovia (Segovia songbook), 50
Cañizares y Suárez, José de, 161, 189n7
canonization, 61–62
Canseco, Manuel, 169n27
Cantigas de Santa María (Alfonso X the Wise), 20
Capek, Karel, 118
Cappelletto, Chiara, 40

Cappello, Bianca, 110
Carlos, Prince of Asturias, 67
Carlson, Marvin, 46
Caro Baroja, Julio, 128
Casa con dos puertas, mala es de guardar (Calderón de la Barca), 136–37
casas a malicia (malice houses), 137–38
Cascardi, Anthony, 140–41, 186n35, 187n46
Castellani, Alberto, 37
Castigos e documentos del rey don Sancho IV (anonymous, 1292), 19
Castillo, Fernando del, 69
Cavanillas Ávila, Luis, 123
Cebrián, Julio, 152, *Fig. 6.3*
Celestina (Comedia de Calisto y Melibea) (Rojas), 26
Cervantes, Miguel de
　Calderón de la Barca and, 127–28
　on puppetry, 56–57, 59, 60
　puppetry and, 84–86, 165n21
　See also *Don Quijote* (Cervantes)
Chaos of the World, The (puppet show), 63–64
Chaplin, Charlie, 189n5
Charles II, King of Spain, 131, 153–54
Charles III, King of Spain, 24
Chomón, Segundo, 118
Christ of Burgos, 18
cine, El (Villegas), 97–98
cinema, 97–98, 118, 122, 149
Circe (Calderón de la Barca), 92–93
Cirnigliaro, Noelia, 137–38
City Lights (Chaplin, 1931), 189n5
Claudel, Paul, 167n14
Clavileño (flying wooden horse), *Fig. 5.1–2*, 89, 104–11, 112–15, 117–18, 119, 122–23, 125–26, 160–61

Clavileño (comic opera), 179n10
Clavileño y los consejos de Don Quijote a Sancho (play), 179n10
Cobarrubias, Sebastián de, 59–60
Cocteau, Jean, 97
Coello, Antonio, 64
Cohen, Matthew Isaac, 41, 65
coin-operated fortune tellers, 124, *Fig. 5.6*
"coloquio de los perros, El" (Cervantes), 59, 85, 180n18
Comedia de Calisto y Melibea (*Celestina*) (Rojas), 26
Comedia de Merlín (play), 58
Comedia de san Alejo (López de Úbeda), 64
comedias de capa y espada (cloak-and-dagger plays), 136–37. See also *dama duende, La* (Calderón de la Barca); *galán fantasma, El* (Calderón de la Barca)
comedias de magia (magic plays), 131, 156–61, 188n57
comedias de santos (hagiographical plays), 59–66, 74–75, 78, 156–57
Comentario sobre la primera y segunda población de Segovia (1551), 48
Commandino, Federigo, 57
commedia dell'arte, 160
Compañía de Jesús (Society of Jesus), 61–62, 171n15. See also Kircher, Athanasius
Compañía de los Trufaldines (Trufaldines Theater Company), 160
Concerto for Two Pianos and Orchestra (Poulenc), 176n30

Concierto para clavecín, flauta, oboe, clarinete, violín y violonchelo (Falla), 100
Contessa, Karl Wilhelm Salice, 187n48
Coplas de Vita Christi (Mendoza), 48
Corbellá, Llorenç, 149
Cornejo Vega, Francisco J., 59–60
corregidor y la molinera, El (Falla), 94–95
cosmorama (*tutilimundi*), 27, *Fig. 1.5–7*
Council of Trent (1541–1563), 14, 33–34, 61–63, 168n17
Counter-Reformation, 14, 61–63, 120–21. See also Compañía de Jesús (Society of Jesus); Council of Trent (1541–1563)
Craig, Edward Gordon, 95
Cristo de los Gascones, 47–48, *Fig. 2.1, Fig. 2.11*. See also *Misterio del Cristo de los Gascones* (Zamora)
Cristos articulados (jointed Christ figures)
  artistic and spiritual functionality of, 38–44, 60–61, 78
  curiosity and, 160–61
  Doll Game, The (S. and P. Jackson) and, 54–55
  history of, 24
  miracles and, 19
  Misterio del Cristo de los Gascones (Zamora) and, 32, 45–54, 61, 75, 101, *Fig. 2.1, Fig. 2.10, Fig. 2.12–5*
  origins and evolution of, 31–38
  rationalized sense of wonder and, 4
criticón, El (Gracián), 12
crucifixi dolorosi (plague crosses; forked crosses), 18–19

Cruickshank, Don W., 183n7
cuernos de don Friolera, Los (Valle-Inclán), 91
cueva de Salamanca, La (Ruiz de Alarcón), 182n37
curiosity, 13–14, 112, 160–61, 163n7

Dailey, Alice, 168n16
dama boba, La (Vega), 187n49
dama de la fortuna, La (The fortuneteller, n.d.), *Fig. 5.6*
dama duende, La (Calderón de la Barca)
   contemporary productions of, 148–51, 153, *Fig. 6.1–2*
   disability in, 130–31
   invisibility in, 131–34, 141, 143, 156–57
   secret passageway in, 127–31, 136, 138, 139–44, 148, 150–51, 153
Daston, Lorraine, 28
De ecclesiastico officio (Amalarius of Metz), 34–35
De picturis et imaginibus sacris (Molanus), 34
De triplici vita (Ficino), 178n6
Debord, Guy, 101
Dekker, Thomas, 57–58
"Del sacrificio de la misa" (Gonzalo de Berceo), 35–36
Della christiana moderazione del teatro (Ottonelli), 170n9
Della pittura sacra (F. Borromeo), 34
Dent, Peter, 41
Depositio Sepulchri, 31, 36–37, 39, 40–44, *Fig. 2.3–9*. See also *Misterio del Cristo de los Gascones* (Zamora)
Descartes, René, 11, 161

Descent from the Cross, The (Rubens), 43
Descent of Christ from the Cross (Weyden), 43
"Desde Sansueña a París" (Góngora), 173n25
desengaño
   concept of, 3
   Calderón de la Barca and, 127–28, 130–31, 143–44, 153
   in *Don Quijote* (Cervantes), 12, 79, 90–91, 104
   mechanistic metaphor and, 12
Dethomas, Maxime, 99
devoción de la cruz, La (Calderón de la Barca), 92–93
devotional art, 14–15
diable boîteux, Le (Françaix), 176n30
Dialogo degli errori de' pittori (Gilio), 34
Díaz, Esmeralda, 150–51
Díaz del Castillo, Bernal, 57
Diccionario de autoridades (Cobarrubias), 59–60
Diego de Alcalá, Saint, 66–67
Dining Grotto (Grotto of the Samaritan), 122
disability, 130–31, 143–44
Discorso intorno alle immagini sacre e profane (Paleotti), 34
Dissolution of the Monasteries, 82
Ditchfield, Simon, 61
Doll Game, The (S. and P. Jackson), 54–55, 172n30
Don Cristóbal y la Señá Rosita (García Lorca), 89
Don Juan de Espina en Milán (Cañizares y Suárez), 189n7

222 Index

Don Juan de Espina en su patria (Cañizares y Suárez), 189n7
Don Quijote (Cervantes)
   adaptations into puppet theater of, 84
   Clavileño (flying wooden horse) in, 89, 104–11, 112–15, 117–18, 119, 122–23, 125–26, 160–61, *Fig. 5.1–2*
   context of, 79, 81–83
   desengaño in, 12, 79, 90–91, 104
   Falla and, 81, 92–101
   Master Pedro's puppet show in, 56, 80–81, 83–84, 85–92, 101–2, 103–4, 119, 121, 160–61, 165n21, *Fig. 4.1*, *Fig. 4.2*
   as montage-novel, 81
   oracular head in, 89, 104–10, 111–13, 115–18, 119–22, 125–26, 160–61
   technology of entertainment and, 127
   unmaking of illusions in, 78–81
Donne, John, 113
dos estrellas de Francia, Las (León and Calleja), 64
dos habladores, Los (Cervantes, attr.), 93–94
"Dream of the Rood, The" (anonymous, 10th c.), 38
duende (magic spirit), 133
Duendes son alcahuetes y Espíritu Foleto. Primera parte (Zamora), 188n2
Durandus of Mende, 35
During, Simon, 125, 128

Eamon, William, 105, 163n7
Eco, Umberto, 54
Edward VI, King of England, 180n22
Egginton, William, 16, 41, 70, 130, 183n7
Egyptian civilization, 107

Egyptian Hall (London), 123
Eisenstein, Sergei M., 97–98
Elevatio Crucis, 36–37, 39, 41. See also *Misterio del Cristo de los Gascones* (Zamora)
Emma, Lady Hamilton, 189n8
empresa de Clavileño, La (play), 179n10
Empty Space, The (Brook), 53
En Madrid y en una casa (Tirso de Molina), 136–37
encantos de la culpa, Los (Calderón de la Barca), 92–93
engiens d'esbattement (frolicsome engines), 110–11
England, 57–58, 82, 123
ente dilucidado, El (Fuentelapeña), 154
eolipile (aeolipile; aeolipyle), 17
Escamilla, Manuela de, 170n8
escape rooms, 134
esclavo del demonio, El (Mira de Amescua), 64, 68–77, *Fig. 3.3–12*
Espina, Juan de, 108, 111, 181n31, 189n7
estatua de Prometeo, La (Calderón de la Barca), 159
estatuas de recortado (cut-out statues), 159–60
Exitazo Tournée Roca (Big success Roca tour), *Fig. 5.5*
Explication simple, littérale et historique des cérémonies de l'Église pour l'instruction des nouveaux convertis (Vert), 35

Falla, Manuel de, 81, 92–101
Faria e Sousa, Manuel de, 170n8
Farsa italiana de la enamorada del rey (Valle-Inclán), 91
Fernández Ferreiro, María, 179n10

Fernández González, Ruth, 39
Fernández-Turienzo, Francisco, 172n1
Ferrers, George, 180n22
Ficino, Marsilio, 178n6
Fiennes, Sophie, 186n31
fiera, el rayo y la piedra, La (Calderón de la Barca), 159
Film Sense, The (Eisenstein), 97–98
fingido verdadero, Lo (Vega), 68
firearms, 14
First Iconoclasm (726–787), 32–33
First Piano Concerto (Tailleferre), 176n30
flying horses
  in *Don Quijote* (Cervantes), 89, 104–11, 112–15, 117–18, 119, 122–23, 125–26, Fig. 5.1–2
  in early modern Western fiction, 113
  theme-park attractions and, 122–23
  in universal folklore, 106
Foxe, John, 173n7
Françaix, Jean, 176n30
France, Anatole, 167n14
Francesco I de' Medici, Grand Duke of Tuscany, 110, 122
Francis of Assisi, Saint, 22
Franco, Cristóbal, 69
Freedberg, David, 169n34
French Symbolism, 65–66
Freud, Sigmund, 118, 164n12
Friar Bacon and Friar Bungay (Greene), 113, 120–21, Fig. 5.4
Fuentelapeña, Antonio de, 154
función del desenclavo, La (El mudo Neira), 43–44, Fig. 2.2
futurity, 8

gabinetes de muñecos (doll cabinets), 124, Fig. 5.5

Gagarin, Yuri, 123
galán fantasma, El (Calderón de la Barca)
  contemporary productions of, 148, 151–53, Fig. 6.3–6
  disability in, 130–31
  invisibility in, 134–36, 141, 144–45, 156–57
  military innovation in, 14
  secret passageway in, 127–31, 136, 138–40, 141, 144–47, 152–53
Garber, Marjorie, 81
García Lorca, Federico, 89, 91, 93–94, 182n33
García Santo-Tomás, Enrique, 111
gardens
  automata in, 122
  in *Don Quijote* (Cervantes), 109–11, 122
  in *El galán fantasma* (Calderón de la Barca), 144–46
  as liminal spaces, 110–11, 139
Garrido, Fabiola, 177n42
Gasta, Chad M., 123, 125
Gautier, Théophile, 18
Gell, Alfred, 105, 117
Generation of 1898, 92, 101
Genesius, Saint, 68
German Romanticism, 188n54
Ghelderode, Michel, 167n14
gigantes y cabezudos (giants and big-heads) folk tradition, 24, 99, Fig. 1.4
gigantones (giants), 24
Giles (Gil) of Santarém, Saint, 69
Gilio, Giovanni Andrea, 34
Girau, Antonio, 148
gitana de Menfis, Santa María Egipciaca, La (Pérez de Montalbán), 64

Gitliz, David, 104, 173n10
Godwin, Francis, 113, 118
Góngora, Luis de, 92
Gonzalo de Berceo, 20, 35–36
Gracián, Baltasar, 12
Grau, Jacinto, 89, 118
Greene, Robert, 113, 120–21, *Fig. 5.4*
Groeneveld, Leanne, 167n11, 173n6
Gross, Kenneth, 83, 158, 189n5
grottoes, 122, 139
Grueneberger, Art, 84
Guardini, Romano, 166n5
Guijosa, Marcela, 40
Gunning, Tom, 117

Halffer, Rodolfo, 179n10
Hamlet (Shakespeare), 58
Handspring Puppet Company, 164n8
hard fun, 183n44
Harris, John Wesley, 34
Harris, Max, 21
Hendel-Schütz, Henriette, 189n8
Hermes Trismegistus, 159
Hermetism, 159
Heron of Alexandria, 16–17
Hilborn, Debra, 38
Hilsey, John, 82
Histoire du soldat (Stravinsky), 177n38
historia verdadera de la conquista de la Nueva España, La (Díaz del Castillo), 57
Hobbes, Thomas, 11, 12–13
Hochman, Claudio, 68
Hodder, Ian, 17–18
Hoffmann, E. T. A., 118
hombre selvático (wild man), 111
homo artificialis (artificial man), 12, 160
Honig, Edwin, 185n26

Honorable Historie of Frier Bacon and Frier Bongay, The (Greene), 113, 120–21, *Fig. 5.4*
Honorius Augustodunensis, 35
"Hordenanzas y constituciones de la Santa Cofradía de la Virgen de la Soledad" (1672), 42
Hortus deliciarum codex (12th c.), 166n28
hotel eléctrico, El (Chomón, 1908), 118
Houdini, Harry, 154
Hugh of St. Victor, 35
Huygens, Christiaan, 26

Ibn Dāniyāl, Muḥammad, 25–26
Ibn Hazm, 25
Ibn Šuhayd, 25
Iconoclasm as a Child's Play (Moshenska), 54
Ignatius of Loyola, Saint, 113
imágenes de vestir (dressed images), 171n21
Innocent III, Pope, 35
Inquisition, 57
Instructiones fabricae et supellectilis ecclesiasticae (C. Borromeo), 34
Iranzo, Miguel Lucas de, 178n8
Islands of Adventure (Orlando, Florida), 122–23
Italian traditional puppets, 84
Italy
   commedia dell'arte in, 160
   opera dei pupi in, 84, 100–101, 170n12
   puppetry in, 57–58
   Renaissance gardens in, 110, 122, 139
Iturbe Sáiz, Antonio, 39–40

Jackson, Angus, 84

Jackson, Shelley and Pamela, 54–55, 172n30
Jarry, Alfred, 95
Java, 171n22
Jentsch, Ernst, 118, 164n12
Jesuits. *See* Compañía de Jesús (Society of Jesus)
Johnson, Barbara E., 29, 65
Jones, Basil, 16
Juana Inés de la Cruz, Sor, 26
Julius Caesar (Shakespeare), 57–58

Kallendorf, Hilaire, 120
Kang, Minsoo, 11
Kempe, Margery, 167n8
Kempelen, Wolfgang von, 123
Kepler, Johannes, 113, 118
King, Elizabeth, 66–67
King, Errol, 52–53
Kircher, Athanasius, 26, 115, 171n15, *Fig. 5.3*
Kitab al-akhlaq wa Siyar (Ibn Hazm), 25
Klapisch-Zuber, Christiane, 36, 54
Kleist, Heinrich von, 189n11
Kohler, Adrian, 164n8
Kopania, Kamil, 40, 42
Kouberskaya, Irina, 179n10
Krofta, Josef, 84
kuroko (Japanese puppet manipulators), 99

Lacey, Bruce, 172n29
Lamentaciones fechas para la Semana Santa (Manrique), 48
Landy, Michael, 61, 75–77, 101, *Fig. 3.13*
Landy, Thomas M., 20–21
Lang, Fritz, 118

Lanz, Enrique, 98–100, *Fig. 4.3–6*
Lanz, Hermenegildo, 93–94, 95–96
Lastanosa, Juan de, 111, 112–13
Lázaro, Alicia, 50
Leo III, Byzantine Emperor, 32–33
León Marchante, Manuel de, 64
León Pinelo, Antonio de, 132
Lerma, Duke of, 13
Letters from Italy (Sharp), 167n10
Leviathan (Hobbes), 13
Lexicon Graeco-Latinum (Budé), 117
Liber officialis (Amalarius of Metz), 34–35
Liber sacerdotalis (Castellani), 37
Libri quattuor sententiarum (Peter Lombard), 33
"licenciado Vidriera, El" (Cervantes), 59, 84–85
Lobregat, Miguel, 59
locus amoenus (pleasant place), 110, 145–46
London, 57–58
López de Úbeda, Francisco, 57, 64
López Sancho, Lorenzo, 151–52
Lorca, Isabel, 93–94
Lotti, Cosimo, 60
Lumière brothers, 149
lusus scientiae (jokes of knowledge), 13–14
Luzán, Ignacio de, 157

Machinandiarena, Miguel, 97
machine-driven toys, 13–14
Madroñal, Abraham, 179n10
magic lantern, 26–27
mágico de Salerno, Pedro Vayalarde, El (Salvo y Vela), 19
magos and *magas* (male and female wizards), 154

magrana (*mangrana*; pomegranate), 22–23, *23*
Maldonado, Juan, 113
Malespini, Celio, 110
malheurs d'Orphée, Les (Milhaud), 176n30
Malkin, Michael, 29
Man in the Moone, The (Godwin), 113
Mañés, José Luis Alonso, 151–52
Manrique, Gómez, 48
máquina real
    Caballero and, 61, 68–77, *Fig. 3.3–12*
    comedias de santos and, 59–66, 74–75, 78
    curiosity and, 160–61
    history of, 23–24
    Landy and, 61, 75–77, *Fig. 3.13*
    origins and use of term, 59–60
    rationalized sense of wonder and, 4
    retablos and puppets in, 69–72, *Fig. 3.3–12*
Máquina Real, La (artistic collective), 61, 68–77, 101, *Fig. 3.3–12*
Maré, Rolf de, 97
"Margarita la tornera" (Zorrilla), 20
marionette, origins and use of term, 29–30. See also puppetry and puppets
Marquerie, Alfredo, 148
Martín y Rodríguez, Diego, 43
Martínez Sierra, Gregorio, 93
Martín-Flores, Mario, 119
Maskelyne, John Nevil, 123
Massine, Léonide, 97
Matton, Charles, 150
mechanical clocks, 11, 12–13, 15, 171n15
Mechanismus der menschlichen sprache nebst beschreibung seiner sprechenden maschine (Kempelen), 123

mechanistic metaphor, 10–16
meditatio humanitatis Christi (meditation on Christ's humanity), 34
Meditationes vitae Christi (14th c.), 168n21
Méliès, Georges, 149
Mendoza, Íñigo de, 48
Menéndez y Pelayo, Marcelino, 74–75
Mérimée, Prosper, 189n10
Metropolis (Lang, 1927), 118
Michelangelo Buonarroti, 189n5
Midsummer Night's Dream, A (Shakespeare), 152
Milagros de Nuestra Señora (Gonzalo de Berceo), 20
Milhaud, Darius, 176n30
mimicry, 159–60
mimoplastic art, 189n8
Minucius Felix, Marcus, 29
Mira de Amescua, Antonio, 64, 68–77
miracles, 10–11, 19–20
Misteri d'Elx (Mistery play of Elche, ca. 13th c.), 22–23
misterio de los Reyes Magos, El (anonymous, 1100s), 93–94
Misterio del Cristo de los Gascones (Zamora), 32, 45–54, 61, 75, 101, *Fig. 2.1, Fig. 2.10, Fig. 2.12–15*
Mitchell, David T., 130
modern wonder, 116–17
modernity, 2–9, 106. See also science and Scientific Revolution
Molanus, Joannes, 34
Monroe, James T., 25
Morales, Ambrosio de, 10–11
Moreno, Wenceslao (Señor Wences), 124

Moscoso, Javier, 112
Moshenska, Joe, 39, 40, 54
Mudarse por mejorarse (Ruiz de Alarcón), 57
mundinovi, mundonovo (*tutilimundi*), 27, *Fig. 1.5–7*
museo pictórico, y escala óptica, El (Palomino), 14, 188–89n4
Musurgia universalis (Kircher), *Fig. 5.3*
Mystères bibliques et chrétiens (Bouchor), 65–66, 167n14

Nállim, Carlos Orlando, 119
Nao D'amores. See *Misterio del Cristo de los Gascones* (Zamora)
Naples, 57–58
nativity, 22, *Fig. 1.2*
Ndalianis, Angela, 123
necromancy, 57
Neira the Mute (El mudo Neira), 43–44, *Fig. 2.2*
Neoplatonism, 107
Newberry, Wilma, 173n26
Newton, Isaac, 11
Niebla (Unamuno), 91–92
Night (Michelangelo), 189n5
niña que riega la albahaca y el príncipe preguntón, La (García Lorca), 89, 93–94
novatores (innovators), 155–56
Novelas ejemplares (Cervantes), 56–57, 59, 84–85, 92
nueva democracia, La (newspaper), 123
numinous, 19

object, concept of, 17–18
Ocho comedias y ocho entremeses nuevos nunca representados (Cervantes), 60

Octavius (Minucius Felix), 29
Olivares, Count-Duke of, 13
Onians, John, 110
opera dei pupi (Sicilian puppets), 84, 100–101, 170n12, *Fig. 0.1*
oracular and talking heads
  Counter-Reformation and, 120–21
  in *Don Quijote* (Cervantes), 89, 104–10, 111–13, 115–18, 119–22, 125–26, 160–61
  necromancy and, 106–7
  origins and development of, 115, 123–24, *Fig. 5.3–5*
Ordoñez, Javier, 126
Origen, pérdida y restauración de la Virgen del Sagrario (Calderón de la Barca), 139
Orsini, Vincenzo, 110
Orti Oricellari (Rucellai Gardens), 110
Os Bonecos de Santo Aleixo (Saint Aleixo Puppets), 67–68
Otto, Rudolf, 19
Ottonelli, Gian Domenico, 170n9

Paco, Mariano de, 152–53
País, El (newspaper), 149
Paisà (Rossellini, 1946), 100–101
Paleotti, Gabriele, 34
Palmesel (Palm Sunday donkey), 20–21
Palomino de Castro y Velasco, Acisclo Antonio, 14, 188–89n4
Parade (ballet), 97
Park, Katherine, 28
Pasión trobada (San Pedro), 48
Pasionario toledano (Toledo Passion songbook), 50
pasos (processional floats), 20–21, 31
passive agency, 17–18

Pemberton, John, 90
Penny, Nicholas B., 76
Percas de Ponseti, Helena, 173n10
Pereira, Beatriz, 59
Pérez de Montalbán, Juan, 64
Pérez Galdós, Benito, 143–44, 186n36
Pérez Magallón, Jesús, 3
Pérez Sánchez, Alfonso E., 58
Pérez-Simón, Andrés, 176n34
Pervert's Guide to Cinema, The (Fiennes, 2006), 186n31
Peter Lombard, 33
Petersen, Elizabeth M., 171n23
Petrovich, Avvakum, 82
phantasmagoria, 26–27
Philip II, King of Spain, 13, 67, 79, 180n21
Philip III, King of Spain, 13, 79
Philip IV, King of Spain, 13, 79
Philip V, King of Spain, 156
Picabia, Francis, 97
pícara Justina, La (López de Úbeda), 57
Picasso, Pablo, 97
Pimenta, Helena, 149–51
Pirandello, Luigi, 182n33
Pius IV, Pope, 14
Planctus Mariae (Lament of Mary), 48–50, Fig. 2.12
Plato, 40
Podrecca, Vittorio, 97
poética, La (Luzán), 157
political philosophy, 12–14
Por el sótano y el torno (Tirso de Molina), 136–37
Portugal, 67–68
Portuondo, María M., 3, 115
Poulenc, Francis, 176n30

Practica di fabricar scene, e machine ne' teatri (Sabbatini), 14
practical magic, 128, 134
primera parte de la historia general de Santo Domingo y de su Orden de Predicadores, La (Castillo), 69
"Primero sueño" (Juana Inés de la Cruz), 26
príncipe constante, El (Calderón de la Barca), 186–87n41
procesión de la borriquilla (procession of the donkey), 20–21, 31
prop, concept of, 17–18
Protestant Reformation, 2, 14, 33
Psycho (whist-playing automaton), 123
Puente, Luis de, 15
pupi (Sicilian puppets), 84, 100–101, 170n12, Fig. 0.1
puppetry and puppets
  bavastells and, 166n28
  Bunraku (Japanese puppet theatre) and, 51–52
  evolution and popularity of, 57–59, 67–68
  opera dei pupi (Sicilian puppets) and, 84, 100–101, 170n12
  rationalized sense of wonder and, 4
  as religious props, 18–24, 29–31, 56. See also *Cristos articulados* (jointed Christ figures); *máquina real*
  shadow theater and, 24–26
  in works of fiction, 56–57. See also *Don Quijote* (Cervantes)
Pushkin, Alexander, 189n11

Quay Brothers, 187n51
Quem quaretis, 167n15

rational wonder, 107–8
Redondo y Menduiña, Juan, 179n10
Reed, Cory, 117
Regularis Concordia (Æthelwold), 38
Relâche (ballet), 97
Religion and the Decline of Magic (Thomas), 67
Renard (Stravinsky), 92
Representación del nacimiento de Nuestro Señor (Manrique), 48
retablillo de Don Cristóbal, El (García Lorca), 89
Retablo de la avaricia, la lujuria y la muerte (Valle-Inclán), 165n21
Retablo de las maravillas (Cervantes), 165n21
retablo de maese Pedro, El (Falla), 81, 92–101, Fig. 4.3–6
retablo mecánico (mechanical theater), 21–22, Fig. 1.1
retablos
  máquina real and, 69–70
  origins and use of term, 29–30
  See also puppetry and puppets
Río, Martín del, 107
Risalat al-tawabi' wa al-zawabi' (Ibn Šuhayd), 25
Riskin, Jessica, 111, 173n6
Ritz-Barr, Steven, 84
Rivas de Cherif, Cipriano, 93
Robert, Étienne-Gaspard (Robertson), 26–27
Robert I, count of Artois, 112
Roberts, Michael, 14
Roca, Francesc, 124
Rodríguez de la Flor, Fernando, 10, 67, 153
Rojas, Francisco de, 26

Rojas Zorrilla, Francisco de, 64
Romero, Mariano, 47–48
Rood of Grace, 82
Rossellini, Roberto, 100–101
Rubens, Peter Paul, 43
Ruf, Éric, 84
Ruiz de Alarcón, Juan, 57, 182n37
Ruiz de Castro, Garci, 48
R.U.R. (Capek), 118
Russian Orthodox Church, 82

Sabbatini, Nicola, 14
Sacro Bosco (Garden of Bomarzo), 110
Saints Alive (Landy), 61, 75–77, Fig. 3.13
saints and saintliness, 61–62. See also *comedias de santos* (hagiographical plays)
Salvo y Vela, Juan, 19
San Antonio Abad (Zárate y Castronovo), 64
San Pedro, Diego de, 48
Sánchez del Barrio, Antonio, 43–44
"Sandman, The" (Hoffmann), 118
Sands, William, 63–64
Santiago del espaldarazo (14th c.), 21
Santos, Alonso de, 149
Sanz, Francisco, 124
Satie, Erik, 92, 97
Sawday, Jonathan, 129
Saynete de los títeres (Suárez de Deza y Ávila), 57
Scherchen, Hermann, 97
science and Scientific Revolution, 2, 10–16, 81–83
Science and the Secrets of Nature (Eamon), 105
science fiction, 113
Second Symphony (Weill), 176n30

secret passageways
  in *comedias de capa y espada* (cloak-and-dagger plays), 136–37
  in *La dama duende* (Calderón de la Barca), 127–31, 133–34, 136, 138, 139–44, 148, 150–51, 153, 160–61
  in *El galán fantasma* (Calderón de la Barca), 127–31, 136, 138–40, 141, 144–47, 152–53, 160–61
  rationalized sense of wonder and, 4
secular magic, 125, 128
senda del amor, La (Benavente), 91
señor de Pigmalión, El (Grau), 89, 118
Sérénade pour douze instruments (Françaix), 176n30
Seven Deadly Sins, The (ballet chanté), 177n38
shadow theater, 24–26
Shakespeare, William, 57–58, 152
Sharp, Samuel, 167n10
Shuger, Dale, 63, 74
Sicardus of Cremona, 35
siete angustias de Nuestra Señora, Las (San Pedro), 48
siglo maquinístico (machinist century), 126
Singer, Winnaretta (Princesse Edmond de Polignac), 92
sitio de Bredá, El (Calderón de la Barca), 14
Snyder, Sharon L., 130
Sobchack, Vivian, 142
Socrate (Satie), 92
Sofer, Andrew, 17–18, 129, 164n10
Solla Price, Derek de, 181n29
sombrero de tres picos, El (Falla), 94–95
Somnium (Kepler), 113
Somnium (Maldonado), 113

space race, 123
space-colonizing fiction, 113
Spalbeek, Elizabeth, 67
spectrophilia, 146
Stafford, Barbara Maria, 59, 121
Stage Life of Props, The (Sofer), 129
stagecraft manuals and technologies, 13–14, 188–89n4
stone guest, 158
Strauss, Linda M., 124
Stravinsky, Igor, 92, 177n38
Suárez de Deza y Ávila, Vicente, 57
Suárez de Figueroa, Cristóbal, 10–11
Sylva Sylvarum (Bacon), 113
Sylvester II, Pope, 106

Tablado de marionetas para educación de príncipes (Valle-Inclán), 89
tableaux vivants (living pictures), 42
Taboada Steger, Joaquín, 179n10
Tailleferre, Germaine, 176n30
talking heads. See oracular and talking heads
Tarasca (ritual monster), 24, *Fig. 1.3*
Taxidou, Olga, 89
Tayf al-khayal (Ibn Dāniyāl), 25–26
Teatro da Cornucópia, 169n27
Teatro Dran, 169n27
Tecglen, Eduardo Haro, 149
Tecglen, Haro, 151
technologies of wonder, 105–6
technology, 106, 117
technology of enchantment, 116–17
technology of entertainment, 127
temporary autonomous zone (TAZ), 129
Tena, Cayetano Luca de, 148
Tesoro de la lengua castellana o española (Cobarrubias), 59–60

theater, 15–16. See also *máquina real*; puppetry and puppets
theme-park attractions, 122–23
theology, 11
thing, concept of, 17–18
thing theory, 17–18
Thomas, Keith, 67, 106
Thomas Aquinas, Saint, 33, 35, 107
Tillis, Steve, 164n11
Tirso de Molina, Gabriel Téllez, 21, 136–37, 158, 159
Títeres de la tía Norica (Aunt Norica's puppets, ca. 1790), 67–68, 176n33
Tordesillas, Treaty of (1494), 113
Torriani, Giovanni (Juanelo Turriano), 57, 67
Tratado del govierno de la familia y estado de las viudas y donzellas (Astete), 132
Travels in Hyperreality (Eco), 54
Treasure of El Carambolo (7th–6th centuries BCE), 1–2
Tres novelas ejemplares y un prólogo (Unamuno), 91
Tristana (Pérez Galdós), 143–44, 186n36
tunnel of terror, 122
Turriano, Juanelo (Giovanni Torriani), 57, 67
tutilimundi, 27, Fig. 1.5–7

Unamuno, Miguel de, 91–92, 182n33
uncanny, 19, 118

Valantin, Émilie, 84
Valentin et Orson (Carolingian romance epic), 106
validos, 13
Valle-Inclán, Ramón María del, 89, 91, 97, 165n21

vanishing lady, 133–34
Varey, John E., 63, 173n4
Vaucason, Jacques, 113
Vázquez, Filemón, 179n10
Vega, Lope de, 68, 92, 184n15, 187n49
Velazquez, Diego, 99
Vélez de Guevara, Luis, 64
Veltruský, Jiří, 164n11
Venice, 57–58
ventriloquism, 123–24
Vénus d'Ille, La (Mérimée), 189n10
Verfremdungseffekt (A-Effect), 86
Vernant, Jean-Pierre, 40
Vert, Claude de, 35
Victorian England, 123
vida es sueño, La (Calderón de la Barca), 130
Viladesau, Richard, 14
Villa di Pratolino, 122
Villegas, Manuel, 97–98
Visitatio Sepulchri, 36, 41
Vitoria, Francisco de, 107
Vitse, Marc, 183n5
viuda valenciana, La (Vega), 184n15
Voyage en Espagne (Gautier), 18
vuelo de Clavileño, El (play), 179n10

Wales, 82
Walsham, Alexandra, 173n5
War Horse (play), 164n8
warfare, 14
Webster, Susan Verdi, 31
Weill, Kurt, 176n30, 177n38
Weyden, Rogier van der, 43
widowhood, 132
Wiggins, Collin, 76
Wilde, Oscar, 63
Wilder, Mitchell A., 71

Wilkins, John, 11
Wilson, Peter Lamborn (Hakim Bey), 129
Wunderkammer (cabinet of curiosities), 111–12

Young, Karl, 37–38
Young, Susan, 57–58, 72

Zamora, Ana. See *Misterio del Cristo de los Gascones* (Zamora)
Zamora, Antonio de, 188n2
zapatera prodigiosa, La (García Lorca), 91
Zárate y Castronovo, Fernando de, 64
Žižek, Slavoj, 186n31
Zorrilla, José, 19, 20
Zuloaga, Ignacio, 99

www.ingramcontent.com/pod-product-compliance
Lightning Source LLC
Chambersburg PA
CBHW070756230426
43665CB00017B/2381